OPAL PALMER ADISA was born in Kingston, Jamaica. She grew up among the sugar estates. She moved to New York in 1970 and studied Communications: Education Media at Hunter College. When she returned to Jamaica in 1976 she worked at the Educational Broadcasting Corporation as an Education Officer/Director. There she wrote and directed television and radio programmes for children. She is the co-founder of Watoto Wa Kuumba, a children's theatre group that she directed from 1979–1982. She gained two MA degrees in English and Drama at San Francisco State University, and has a Ph.D. in Ethnic Studies, Literature from the University of California, Berkeley. Her poetry, stories and articles have been anthologised widely, and she is the author of *Pina, The Many-Eyed Fruit* (1985), *Bake-Face and Other Guava Stories* (1986), *Traveling Women* (1989), and *Tamarind and Mango Women* (1992).
Adisa now lives in California with her three children. She is currently the Chair of the Ethnic Studies/Cultural Diversity Program at California College of Arts and Crafts where she is an Associate Professor.

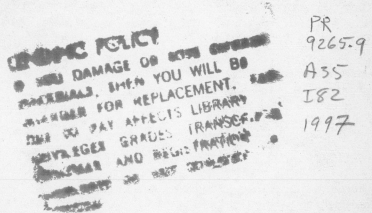

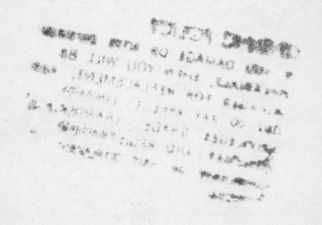

OPAL PALMER ADISA

IT BEGINS WITH TEARS

Heinemann

Special thanks to my sister, Leonie, who kept my children for several weeks during the three summers it took me to write this novel. Without her support it would not have been completed. To Karen James Cody, the first to read the manuscript and whose invaluable editorial suggestions helped me to fine-tune it; to Donna Weir who went over the manuscript with an eye for Jamaican consistency; and to Barbara Christian who made suggestions and has consistently encouraged me in my writing. Also to Amy Kossow, my agent, for her enthusiasm and belief.
Big-Up Respect
Opal

Heinemann Educational Publishers
Halley Court, Jordan Hill, Oxford OX2 8EJ
A division of Reed Educational & Professional Publishing Limited

Heinemann: A Division of Reed Publishing (USA) Inc.
361 Hanover Street, Portsmouth, NH 03801–3912, USA

Heinemann Educational Books (Nigeria) Ltd
PMB 5205, Ibadan
Heinemann Educational Botswana (Publishers) (Pty) Ltd
PO box 10103, Village Post Office, Gaborone, Botswana

FLORENCE   PRAGUE   MADRID   ATHENS
MELBOURNE   AUCKLAND   KUALA LUMPUR   TOKYO
SINGAPORE   MEXICO CITY   CHICAGO   SÃO PAULO
JOHANNESBURG   KAMPALA   NAIROBI

First published by Heinemann Publishers in 1997

Series Editors:
Chinua Achebe 1962–1990
Adewale Maja-Pearce 1990–94

British Library Cataloguing in Publication Data
A catalogue record for this book is available from the British Library.

ISBN 0 435 989464

Cover design by Touchpaper
Cover illustration by David Bridgeman
Author photograph by Paul Lawrence

Phototypeset by CentraCet Ltd
Printed and bound in Great Britain
by Cox & Wyman Ltd, Reading, Berkshire

97 98 99 10 9 8 7 6 5 4 3 2 1

To the people of rural Jamaica
and the rest of the Caribbean
who have inadvertently kept their
traditions by causing time
to stop and preventing progress from
ruining their lives, but especially
to Aunt Zilla and the people of
my mother's village.

Inhabitants of Kristoff Village

Miss Cotton and Mr Cotton, store owners and spiritual elders, high priests.

Arnella, dressmaker, priestess in training.
Velma, mother of Olive and Arnella, grandmother of Valrie, enigma.
Olive, Velma's older daughter, biological mother of Valrie, daily mother of Arnella, wife to Milford, mediator.
Valrie, Arnella's 'twin', itinerant artist, traveller.

Dahlia, high priestess, grandmother of Godfree.
Godfree, husband to Valrie, soulmate to Arnella, carpenter/sculptor.

Monica, retired whore, goddaughter of Miss Cotton, dreamer.
Beryl, daughter to Madge Gordon, sleepwalker, farmer.

Angel, African-American teacher, wife to Rupert Stewart, trainee, observer.
Rupert Stewart, recently returned Jamaican, an impossible searcher.

Grace and Desmond Burton, parents to Raymond, Althea and Peter.
Marva and Ainsworth McKenzie, parents of five sons.
Peggy and Trevor Campbell, parents of two sons.

Inhabitants of Montego Bay or MoBay

Charley, cousin to Rupert, childhood friend to Beryl, taxi-cab owner/driver, go-between.
Mazie, schoolfriend of Beryl, chef and restaurant owner, protector.
Cousin Carol, cousin to Beryl, protector.
Nathan, Godfree's partner and longtime admirer of Arnella.

Inhabitants of Eternal Valley

Devil and She-Devil, Priest and High Priestess of Eternal Valley.
Tegreg, their daughter, feminist, feisty.

Brimstone, their son, showman, adventurer.
Man-Stick, Tegreg's husband, easy-going, navigator.
Tallawah, Brimstone's fiancée, gorgeous, talented, clever.
Anansi, Tallawah's youngest son, shrewd, mischievous.

God and Sabbath Angel and their eight children, conservatives,
followers.

Other characters

Cindy and John Fairbanks, adopted parents of Angel, reside in
Manhattan.

Jasmine, Jamaican maid, surrogate mother to Angel, resides in
Brooklyn.

Prologue: Devil and She-Devil

The sun was swollen big in the sky. Heat rose from the ground like steam. The sky was clean, pale blue with fluffy clouds that danced.

Then the rain came tumbling down. The sun roared and continued to shine. The rain took shame and went away. The sun, more fierce, swept over the vegetation, parching leaves and singeing the bare feet of children at play.

Again the rain lashed out, but the sun refused to relent. The children chanted.

'Devil stop beating you wife!'

'Devil mek you must behave so bad!'

Shame. Embarrassment. Like two people fighting over a shade – one pushing it up and the other roughly lowering it to shut out the peeping eyes of neighbours – the sun and rain competed.

The old people shook their heads, sighed deeply and kissed their teeth.

'But you see we crosses!'

'De Devil is strong, yes!'

'Is wha trouble brewing eh?'

All around Kristoff Village the attention of the community was captured by the unusual weather. It wasn't the first time that the sun had shone while the rain railed down, but it never usually lasted very long, nor was it so consistent. The adults pretended they weren't caught off guard by the raining sun as they ran back and forth first spreading clothes to dry, then rushing to gather them; or digging in their fields then suddenly seeking shelter under a banana leaf or a tree. But something was not right.

The women were outraged that in these times Devil still felt he could up and beat his wife, 'In broad daylight at that!' They grumbled and mumbled, spat frequently and threatened.

'If it was me ah would pour hot oil in him ears.'

1

'Long time now me would a chop off him hand.'

'Nothing worse dan an ignorant man!'

The men were embarrassed, as if caught with their pants down during a parade. Most of them knew better than to aggravate their wives or sweethearts, who would seize the occasion to put their hands akimbo, spread their legs, raise their voices as if they were on a platform and rebuke them to no end.

'Devil is not a smart man a-tall.'

'You neva seh a more true thing, me friend. Once you start hitting a woman dere is no stopping.'

'One of oonuh go dead or have to leave. Most time man have to run cause when oman stand up, dem stand up strong.'

Back and forth, back and forth. Sun and rain, rain and sun. For days. More than a week. The people of Kristoff Village were prepared to get wet and dry from a short walk to the shop to purchase a little oil or a piece of salt-pork. It was a bewildering time, the air so clean, the sky so bright, the sun so fierce, the rain so sweet.

An incredible time.

A time of great puzzlement.

Rain ah fall, sun ah shine

Devil and She-Devil were at it again. One minute they would be talking and laughing, the next minute silence, then raised voices, and before you knew it blows would fall and all hell would break loose.

The tension was wearing on Devil's nerves, and She-Devil threatened more than a hundred times to pack her bags and go find her a harmonious place where she could be by herself. Besides, she said, 'Time to move, yes. Picknie dem grown. Me footloose and fancy free.'

Well why she must say that? Devil started to cuss in a loud voice as if he wasn't speaking to She-Devil standing right there beside him. 'Anybody tink dem gwane walk out on me betta tink again.' All the while Devil was carrying on, he would shadow-dance with his machete, the blade so silver sharp a fly pitched on it and was instantly cut in two. But She-Devil wasn't afraid of Devil's machete because she had a butcher knife and no one could wield a butcher knife more skilfully

2

than She-Devil. A leg of goat or shoulder of beef put up no resistance to She-Devil. So when Devil started shouting and cussing and fondling his machete, She-Devil got her butcher knife, went on the veranda to catch some cool air and sang at the top of her voice, 'Me is a meat grinder, grinding meat is what me do. Me is a meat grinder, bring me meat to mince for you.' That quieted Devil because he had seen She-Devil all too many times wield her butcher knife. Devil decided She-Devil was menopausal, so he stomped out the front door, his hands in his pockets, whistling, 'Hill and gully ride oh, hill and gully . . .'

That was Tuesday afternoon, and he slept out, just, he hoped, to make She-Devil worry. Devil had never ever left his side of the bed cool in the infinite years he and She-Devil had been married.

Man! Devil was feeling confident and victorious when he got home Wednesday morning to find She-Devil waiting for him on the veranda. He walked up the path as cool as air, his shoulders back, chest stuck out and a little smile playing around the side of his mouth. Devil was thinking about how he was going to walk right up to She-Devil, make as if to walk past her, then grab her from behind the waist like he used to when they were courting, and blow a warm breath in the curl where her neck and shoulder connected. They would prance about, and maybe even make love right there on the veranda since they no longer had any children around.

Devil climbed the stairs of the veranda. She-Devil was still standing to one side, leaning on the banister. Devil thought he could read worry in her eyes and he chuckled to himself, 'Good! Yuh tink is you one know daylight.' Everything was going as he hoped, but just as he was about to put his right foot in front of his left and walk past She-Devil, he felt hot water on his shirt. 'Lawd oman!' he bawled out. 'Is murder you gwane murder me?' Devil hadn't seen the kettle resting on the railing, nor had he seen She-Devil turn and reach for it. Pandemonium. There was plenty wrestling going on that morning, but no sweet words or love juices flowed. Before Devil could tear the shirt off his scaled skin, She-Devil was on him. She jumped on his back and he had a hard time dislodging her. She-Devil panted and foamed while she assaulted Devil. 'So you tink you is big man. You tink you can come and go as you please. So you sleep out last night. Well we gwane see how dis gwane work.'

All the live-long day, Devil and She-Devil were at it. One minute the day would be bright, the sun shining, and the next minute the sky would be dark and rain railed down upon the earth. Devil and She-Devil's war created quite a confusion for the people of Kristoff Village, who were of two minds. Some felt the world was coming to an end; others interpreted the dramatic changes as an omen of good things to come. Whatever the individual views, there was a fair amount of uneasiness among the residents and fear among the children.

Thursday morning, when Devil and She-Devil woke, they were both bruised and sore. She-Devil took some coconut oil and rubbed it on Devil's peeling body. Then she went outside in her garden to the cocoa tree, picked a cocoa pod, grated then boiled it and poured in four heaped tablespoons of condensed milk, stirred it in with a pinch of nutmeg and a dash of salt and served it to Devil. It was his favourite morning beverage. Next, She-Devil roasted bread-fruit with susumba and cod-fish. She sat and watched as Devil sopped up the hot cocoa with the bread-fruit, smacking his mouth as he ate the round green susumba pods seasoned with cod-fish, his lips greasy, his cheeks puffed up in delight. When Devil was done with his breakfast, he pushed back his chair and rocked back and forth on the hind legs, rubbing his stomach. Looking at She-Devil, his eyes dancing, his face round and gleaming, Devil said without reflection, 'Now you actin like oman. A good oman treat her man like him is man, and tek pleasure in him pleasure.'

She-Devil had decided when she woke that morning to let bygones be bygones. She was confident that she had made her point yesterday and she was thinking that she was getting too old for this nonsense with Devil anyway. 'Maybe is familiarity,' she thought. 'Devil and me so long together we forget we two separate people.' That was why She-Devil got up and fixed Devil his favourite breakfast. But as she was getting ready to make herself something to eat (because She-Devil never could get used to the bitter taste of susumba), she heard Devil again, as if in a dream, and realised that in all the many, many years they had been husband and wife, so long she couldn't remember a time when they weren't together, in all the however many years, not once – and she paused there on that thought – not once had Devil ever cooked her a meal.

4

She-Devil was a loner, and not into the sentiments of the days, but Tegreg, her daughter, had been telling her about this Woman's Thing. 'What's de word Tegreg used now?' She-Devil paused with one hand on her hip, her right side thrusting. 'Femi, femi-something. But whatever Tegreg called it, she had her husband, Man-Stick, helping her wid all de house work.'

Man-Stick was a lean and agile fellow, who worked hard and had a sense of humour. They liked him well enough, but Tegreg said her parents set him a bad example because whenever they came to visit Devil and Man-Stick would sit on the veranda swapping stories while She-Devil ran around, catering to their every whim. This was why, Tegreg said, she didn't come visit more often. That was where She-Devil's memory lingered, and she realised that she had not seen Tegreg, her baby, for more than a month. She hadn't even talked with her because Devil said he didn't want any telephone in the house so people could dial his number and get him just like that. Devil said he wanted people to sweat. 'Anyone want see I-man dem hafi come I yard,' and that was the end of the conversation. And She-Devil heard the logic in Devil's reasoning and didn't argue, even though she liked the idea of having a phone.

Now, however, as Devil's comment about how a woman ought to act registered, She-Devil reflected. She had risen early to prepare a breakfast to Devil's liking. And this was how he thanked her, by saying that her value was only in pleasing him. She-Devil got hot. Steaming, sweating, hot. She hauled the cast-iron pot off the stove and knocked Devil on his head. Devil flew off the chair and crashed flat on his back. He tried to get up, but fell down again. His head was weighted down with rocks, then he was struck by a tidal wave. Indeed, he was soaked, for She-Devil, momentarily fearing she might finally have killed him, dashed a pot of cold water over his face to revive him.

That did it for Devil. He was through with She-Devil. She had indeed gone crazy, and he was not going to have anything else to do with her. As soon as the big coco went down on the top of his head, Devil decided he would write to Brimstone, his second child and only son, telling him to come and get him. He was going to mail the letter himself. He wished he had a telephone; he would have called

Brimstone immediately. 'Oman is nutten but worries!' Devil grumbled, moving to the right side of the house, slamming and locking the door loudly so that She-Devil understood that he had absolutely no intention of having anything else to do with her or her irrational behaviour. Devil wasn't sure what was worse: She-Devil's monthly womanhood that visited her or the change of life that was beginning to make her unpredictable. Either way, Devil was through.

Nothing worse than silence in a house where chatter used to flow like water from a tap. Silence – that most dangerous house-guest in time of conflict – moved in with Devil and She-Devil and befriended them both. Each was determined to be the better friend of Silence. Each kept her constant company, like a dutiful yet half-resentful parent at the bedside of a fatally ill child. Silence tormented them, enjoying her short reign, glad of the friendship that normally eluded her.

Silence and Secret were companions, but very few were loyal to them, so they were always in search of recruits, and were therefore zealous when an opportunity presented itself.

◆

The people of Kristoff Village didn't know what to make of the eerie gloominess that hung over their community. The clouds were puffy and the sky was a strange purple-grey and grey-pink. The people's eyes were drawn to the sky, and sometimes, while they were searching for answers, raindrops would spill down, first from the grey-pinkish side, then from the other. The rain would begin, then stop, as though someone had opened up part of the sky, poured water out, then closed it just as quickly.

◆

Devil and She-Devil took up residence in separate parts of the house, each refusing to cross the path of the other. Silence was having the time of her life. An elder, she had impeccable manners and was very attentive to the needs of her friends. She rallied around Devil and She-Devil. Seemed like every time She-Devil turned around Silence was at her feet; several times She-Devil stepped on Silence's heels and had to call out, 'Sorry'. It was the same thing with Devil. He coughed, and Silence was there to pat his back; his head ached, and before he could sigh, Silence would sigh for him. Devil belched long and loud and had many times to say, 'Beg pardon!' to Silence. Silence was ubiquitous, able to be wherever she was needed. So, for a time, neither Devil nor She-Devil was ever without Silence, who couldn't remember ever having been so happy.

After a while, however, Silence became a bother. As the saying goes, too much of one thing is good for nothing. She-Devil decided to part company. Silence begged, but She-Devil was quietly insistent. After She-Devil firmly escorted Silence to the door, she put on her blue dress with the lace around the hem and brushed her hair, parting it straight down the middle and joining the two plaits at the back. Satisfied, she walked to where Devil was resting. She counted first to fifty; then, feeling as if she needed more time to collect her thoughts, to one hundred. Very calmly She-Devil opened the door to Devil's room, whispered 'Truce' and crept back out.

She-Devil felt good! But after that long period of silence, her breath was foul. She gargled with lemon juice with a dash of honey, then went walking through the garden. The zinnias, gerbas, red-ginger and birds-of-paradise were all in bloom. She-Devil spread wide her arms and spun around. She felt like a young woman awaiting the arrival of her beau. The air was sweet and she was alive. Devil looked from the safety of his window, watching She-Devil, wondering if he could trust her. But he knew, he was a butterfly caught in her net of charm and beauty. 'Lawd, Lawd!' Devil sighed. 'Dat dere is one fine oman. One fine oman indeed.' He could not resist She-Devil. Quickly he pulled on his clothes, gargled and went outside to twirl with his lover.

Devil and She-Devil clasped fingers, laughed into each other's eyes, whirled around and danced until they were dizzy and sweat covered their bodies, misting their clothes to their skin. Intoxicated with joy they flopped to the ground.

The earth shook, the wind rose, flowers swayed and birds chirped. The land panted.

◆

The sun shone brilliantly, a cool wind blew and after a while a sweet pungent scent perfumed the air. The people of Kristoff Village looked up at the sky. All was quiet. The grey, pink and purple areas had melted away and the sky seemed an inviting bed to the weary, the lazy and the lust-driven.

The people of Kristoff Village felt as if a weight had been lifted. Humming light, airy songs, they did their chores, walked sprightly about, filled with an openness for adventure.

'Another day to live and let live,' She-Devil sang out, stealing with Devil into the bushes, the grass their bed, the trees their roof.

I

How it began

several strands of thread
held in a hand
then woven
into a pattern
each strand
remains distinguishable
separate
from the others

Cloth

Wherever a scrap of cloth fell, she would find it, snatching it up like a stray dog gobbling at food. After she had collected several pieces, she would sit with them spread in her lap, her fingers fondling the different fabrics as she day-dreamed. The rhythm of the woven threads told her stories of all things that began before there was a time referred to as creation.

Today was going to be the day, no matter what. Arnella had got no sleep because the life inside her had played all night like playing was going out of style. She hauled her heavy body out of bed and walked naked into the dining room, opened the jalousies and stood looking out at the day coming into being. This was the time of day she liked best. All was quiet: the birds were not yet awake, and the earth itself seemed to be asleep. As she stared out at the pale blue-yellow light she fancied she saw day, like an animal, slowly coming awake, unfurling from how it slept curled like Blackie, her dog, on the front stoop. Then the morning transformed into an infant awakening. First one arm extended, then the other, now a leg, next the other, body stretched. Motion. A fluid dance. Arnella imagined a gentle wind curling around strong brown legs.

Her stomach pressed against the wood of the jalousies and she felt the child moving again. She looked down at her belly and saw the motion of life jumping about. Smiling, Arnella talked to the child. 'Ah see ah gwane have hard time keeping up wid you.' Still she had thought of no suitable name for the child, even though she had been racking her brains. She decided not to worry; a name would come once she saw the child, her daughter. She was certain it was a girl. Not for a minute had she thought about the possibility of a boy. She wasn't ready for a boy-child now; maybe later, when and if she decided to have another one. Her belief was that every woman should make herself over first; the child would be a girl.

Slowly Arnella returned to the bedroom, opened the windows, peered out at the doctor birds singing in the jimbelee tree. Suddenly,

11

startling herself and the birds, she grabbed for her dress that was lying over the bed-head and pulled it over her head. The quick motion was so unlike her normal even, almost absent-minded pace, that she frightened herself. The dress resisted her haste, she heard a rip in the seam, but she pulled it roughly over her body, as if to say, 'Me is boss.' She was suddenly irritated, at what she wasn't sure. Her shoulder blades ached and she sat massaging them, mentally running through the list of things she had to have ready. She was tired – fatigued – had slept very little for the last week. The child in her womb and the strange weather were making her crazy.

When the sun pressed in, warming her back, Arnella stirred, guessing it was close to eight, but too lazy to turn on the radio to make sure. Poised, Arnella examined her firm, strong arms that moved as deftly in the yam field as with a piece of cloth. She looked around now at the large bedroom that ran the length of her little house. She had mentally drawn a line down the middle of the room; her half, her daughter's half. At the far end, a large window looked out at sunflowers and a mango tree with gerba growing around the roots. The tree was encircled by water-washed white stones, each of which she had lovingly hauled more than a mile from the river. Sighing, Arnella surveyed the contents of her room. The yellow curtains with frilly lace along the border that were now blowing softly in the morning breeze, she had sewn. Examining them gave her a deep satisfied feeling, as did the sight of the three large wall-hangings made partly from the same piece of yellow cloth. How she had laboured over those wall-hangings, going back and forth with the different scraps of cloth before finally settling on the colourful pieces that she patched together to fashion two dogs at play, a bird sitting in a tree, and a ground lizard, similar to the turquoise serpent that had startled her near the yam patch a few weeks ago. Velma, Arnella's mother, said the wall-hangings were nice, but she couldn't remember ever seeing floral blue and red dogs, or gingham green birds or lavender leaves; but that she supposed they existed because Arnella had designed some. It didn't matter to Arnella what her mother or anyone else said; she liked her own work, and did things in her own way, at her own pace. More importantly, she felt that her daughter would like them.

12

But she wasn't sure about the rocking chair. It stood near the window, looking lonely. Arnella had painted it yellow on impulse. She still wasn't sure that she liked it. It lacked heart, somehow. But it had been a present from Godfree. And now that she had painted it and made a cushion, it felt more connected to her. A chuckle escaped her. Godfree had come a long way since that chair; his talent as a carpenter had improved remarkably. He was now a carver of wood. Arnella heard again the childhood song, 'My dear will you 'llow me to pick a rose ...' and a grin spread on her face as she remembered Godfree's bold move, his fingers pinching her breast that giddy afternoon by the river.

Her mind returned to the room. A philodendron stood in the corner, about two feet from the rocking chair. Arnella had put it there after seeing plants in a fashion book her cousin sent from America. Sister Olive said plants, like animals, didn't belong inside the house, and certainly not in the bedroom, but Arnella acted as if she didn't hear. Accustomed to Arnella's silent treatment, Olive locked her mouth. It wasn't any of her business anyway.

Arnella spread her legs wide and leaned forward. Her daughter's side of the room was complete. Two nights ago Godfree brought and put up the crib he had made: Arnella had placed it to divide the room. It was beautiful. Unlike other cribs. The size of a single bed, with drawers underneath, it had shelves and a changing table at one end, a combination bench-seat cum toy-chest at the other. On the drawers, bench-seat and toy-chest were carved fish, dogs, goats, chickens and a donkey, and except for the animals, which were in the natural varnished colour of the mahoe, the crib was painted yellow and red. Arnella had sat in the rocking chair watching Godfree set it up, and when he was done she had walked around the crib caressing it, remembering the time, upon her return from being apprenticed in Montego Bay, that Godfree had first touched her. Her memory pulled him in. His rough, gentle hands, like a plane, touched her back, massaging her spine, all the way down to her calves. His firm body pressed against her, his head now on her stomach, his tongue talking to the fetus in her womb – their child. His mouth now soliciting milk, his hands caressing her hair, and she moist and satiated, and happy when he left for home, for only then could she breathe evenly

13

again and reclaim possession of her body. That was how it always had been with them, a many-coursed meal that bordered on over-indulgence.

Hearing the chickens cackling, Arnella remembered that she hadn't fed them and the sun was fierce. She leaned over the bed and looked out the window. It was probably after nine. Still she didn't turn on the radio, and she shooed the chickens and told them to be patient and eat their own doodoo if they couldn't wait. Slowly she got off the bed and spread it. Her hand lingered on the quilt she had made. It wasn't hand-stitched but she liked it all the more. She looked, trying to discern a design, but then laughed at the idea that there should be a pattern. She hated the expected. There were geometric shapes, but no order to them. Many different fabrics were sewn together, some merely trimmed from dresses or shirts she had sewn for people: cotton, polyester, linen, taffeta.

The bed was all hers. Bought with money she pinched and saved while apprenticed to the dressmaker in Montego Bay. It was made from mahogany, made by an apprentice like herself, Nathan, who was simple-minded, except when it came to wood. He only charged for the wood because he liked her, and hoped that by making a bed for her he might have persuaded her to share it with him. She laughed at the memory. He was a few years older than she, probably twenty; she was seventeen then. It was as obvious as day that he liked her that first afternoon he came to deliver the dressmaker's chairs. At first she hadn't even noticed him, his face all shiny with sweat, until the dressmaker shouted, 'Nathan, look what you doing and keep your fly close. You think dese women send dem daughters here for you to spoil. Just put down de chairs and go back to de shop with you sweaty self.'

'Yes, mam,' he said, loud enough for Arnella to look up. His voice was like a sudden wind. She looked at him, pricking her fingers with the needle she was using to stitch button holes. Staring directly at her Nathan said, 'Me nah spoil nobody daughter, mam.'

'Boy, don't fresh wid me you hear. You sure not gwane spoil any of dese girls in here, so tek you eyes off dem and go bout you business.'

Arnella and the other three apprentices giggled at Nathan, and

14

Arnella's nose crinkled at his loud smell. She saw the perspiration marks that ran the length of his shirt, noticed that two buttons were missing and that the other three were different sizes and colours.

'So you like de chair dem? Is me alone mek dem,' Nathan said with pride. But again his voice was like a sudden gust of wind that deflated just before the last word.

The dressmaker looked at the chairs, and there was admiration in her glance. 'You made dese all by youself?' she asked. Nathan nodded his head. 'Ah tink you ready go on your own, Nathan. Dese very nice,' she ended, pushing the chairs under the table. Then, as if noticing Nathan's sweat for the first time, she asked him if he wanted a cool drink of water. He nodded vigorously. 'So get up and get this young man a tall glass of water with plenty ice,' the dressmaker now said to Arnella. As Arnella moved to the kitchen the dressmaker said to her retreating back, but loud enough for her to hear, 'You might as well get him water before him eyes dem fall right in you lap.' Then, turning to Nathan, she teased, 'But stop! Nathan, it look like you want nyam up Arnella wid you eyes.' The other girls laughed out loud and Arnella could tell that Nathan smiled broadly because a smile still lit up his entire round face when she returned with the pint glass of water.

About a week later Nathan started coming round in the evenings after he finished his trade, and the dressmaker remarked that he might make some smart woman a good husband as carpenters could make lots of money, if only he learned to wash his underarms more thoroughly and put on some deodorant. 'Is not jungle we live in any more, you know. You would tink a nice man like Nathan would rub some deodorant under his arms,' she lamented.

Arnella winced, remembering the first time Nathan awkwardly touched her. Sandpaper was smoother than his palm, she was certain. She told him he should rub coconut oil on his palms every night, and he must have taken her advice, for several months later when he tentatively placed his hand on her arm, it felt smoother. Still, she could not bear his touch. She liked him, but not enough to encourage his advances. Throughout the three years of her apprenticeship Arnella saw Nathan often, but as a friend. She got to see more of his work in other people's homes, when she went to deliver their dresses.

Also, the dressmaker had commissioned several pieces from him. Although Arnella had always assumed that Godfree would make all her furniture, after seeing Nathan's work she decided to ask him to make her a bed. She knew exactly the bed she wanted, having looked at many in books from abroad and in the furniture stores around town. But Nathan refused to look at any of the pictures she tried to show him, nor would he listen to Arnella's ideas about design. 'Ah gwane mek you a bed you gwane love,' he had insisted, and refused to hear any more about it. Arnella was doubtful, but decided that if she didn't like it she could give it to Velma.

Several months went by and Arnella prepared to leave her apprenticeship and assist another dressmaker on St James Street in Montego Bay. She had seen Nathan several times, but he had said nothing about her bed. Two more months after her move Arnella asked Nathan if he would soon be finished with her bed, but he merely said, 'Hold tight, mon. When it done, you de first to see it.' So Arnella decided never to mention the bed again. Besides, she didn't have her own place. Where would she put a bed anyway?

On a Saturday morning, almost a year to the day Arnella had asked Nathan to make the bed, he came by the dressmaking shop on St James Street. He said he had something to show her. Arnella couldn't imagine what it could be, but she saw he was wearing a clean yellow shirt that opened at the neck and illuminated his skin, and grey pants, with shoes that were clean and new-looking. Curious, and encouraged by his smile and his smart attire, Arnella agreed at last to go with him. They walked along beside each other and from time to time their hands brushed, but Arnella pulled quickly away, making a space between them.

After leading her down many streets, Nathan turned into a lane that smelled of urine and whose gutters were clogged with rubbish. Arnella pinched her nose to keep out the smell. Midway down the lane, Nathan turned and entered a yard. A brown mutt ran up and rubbed against his legs, then went back to lie under the straggly soursop tree in the smooth, dirt-swept yard. Nathan led Arnella to a large barn-like door which he opened slowly, saying as he nudged her in, 'Dis is fi me workshop.' Arnella looked around at the yard, devoid of life except for the brown mutt; she hesitated, unsure. Then, glancing at Nathan and reassured by his warm look, she entered slowly. Her eyes adjusted to the dark interior. The smell of sawdust and furniture stain tickled her nose and she sneezed. 'Guzzum!' Nathan said at her back. She felt him close behind her, and was about to accuse him. But then she saw it, directly in front of her, and knew it was her bed. Her mouth fell open but she covered it with her hands. Her eyes glittered, and she spun first to stare wide-eyed at Nathan, then back to get a closer look at the bed-head. Two diamond-shaped mirrors were embedded at each end of the frame. At the centre of the frame were carved a man, a woman and a row of children holding hands, stretching across the entire frame and seeming to disappear into the mirrors at both ends. Then, built to create a shelf effect, were a woman's breasts.

Arnella felt sweat forming at her armpits. She folded her arms across her chest and caressed her elbows. Nathan pulled the base of the bed into the shaft of light that stole through the open door. Laughter sputtered from Arnella's lips, and she bit back her excitement. The base of the bed was in the voluptuous form of a woman's bottom. It appeared as if beads were roped around the woman's waist and came to rest on her high behind. Arnella felt suddenly weak and would have lain down if there had been a mattress. Luckily there wasn't. She kneeled and sniffed at the wood, like a dog in search of a tree. Her hands lingered over the wood, the tips of her fingers tenderly circling the grains and crevices. She moved to touch the bed frame, and that was when she noticed the two built-in drawers, on which was carved the upper half of a woman's body, her head in profile, her hands raised gracefully above her head with arms and fingers curled like a dancer.

Arnella was speechless. She had never imagined anything so beautiful. She was reluctant to turn round and face Nathan because she had never suspected such depths of talent or beauty resided within him. But as this realisation came to her, she was struck by sudden apprehension. She couldn't afford this bed. Surely Nathan hadn't made something so incredible just to give it away. Arnella swallowed and faced him.

'Is how me gwane pay you for dis?'

'You like it?'

17

'How you mean if me like it? Lawd God, Nathan, it nuff pretty. It beautiful. Is a work of art!'

Nathan beamed and his hands in his pockets trembled. This was her bed. He had made it for her and she wanted it. Perhaps at last he would sleep with her. But Arnella would not lead him on any more. Nathan was an artist and deserved her honesty. She liked him a lot, but still felt no desire to have him kiss her or to be his girl. She wished she did, so she could thank him, but honesty was all the thanks she had for him.

Nathan didn't say anything when she said, 'Nathan, it no mek sense you wasting you time. Nice man like you can find a good woman fi love him.' Nathan only looked at the ground and kicked the sawdust with his feet. After a lengthy silence, with their breathing sounding out a rhythm, Nathan finally said, 'Come mek me walk you back.' Arnella walked out into the light ahead of Nathan, and waited by the gate while he padlocked his workshop. The walk back to St James Street was long. Arnella and Nathan walked like perfect strangers, and if someone had been watching them, she would have been surprised when Nathan stopped the ice-cream man riding past them on his bicycle cart and bought Arnella a chocolate fudge. When they got to the gate of the yard in which Arnella now lived and worked, Nathan took her hands in his rough, large palms, rubbed them, then walked off, his head searching the ground. Mid-way in the block, he threw over his shoulder, 'Ah will keep de bed till you ready fah it.'

In the midst of these memories, a contraction made Arnella lean forward. She stumbled off the edge of the bed and squatted, her right hand supporting her protruding stomach, the left resting slightly on the floor providing support. Lips parted, Arnella slowly drew in and blew out air until she felt relief and was able to laugh. Today was going to be the day.

She reached into a drawer and pulled out a long blue piece of cloth which she wound and wrapped around her waist, below her protruding stomach. She closed her eyes and listened to the memory.

'Aunt Velma, you see Arnella and Valrie? One a dem cut up that piece a cloth ah buy to make pillow slips. Ah bet is Arnella. Every time she see cloth, she tink is name on it.'

Aunt Velma laughed a knowing laugh. 'Ah tink when we did bury her navel-string some cloth did wrap up with it.' Again she laughed, and Arnella and Valrie, who had been hiding nearby, the piece of cloth that Olive mentioned held tight like a rope in their hands, suppressed their own devilish delight.

Arnella's full bladder called her attention.

Clay and indigo

He had told her it would be so dark she wouldn't be able to see him sitting next to her, but she had never imagined it could be this dark. Here, darkness was a thick, still life form that drew everything and everyone into it. Angel felt panic, as if she was watching someone who looked like her suddenly shoved into pitch darkness. For the first time she understood the term: pitch darkness. She respected it now, and knew instinctively that she would come to understand many new things in this, her new home. Was she foolish to have come with Rupert to the end of the earth, on a pitch-black night, not knowing anyone, not even knowing what the place looked like, except what he told her? Was she a woman in love or a foolish woman, or were both women one and the same?

Angel felt her palms sweating and shivered. She pressed her legs against the damp upholstery of the cab seat and forced herself calm. It couldn't be as dark as she was experiencing it or they certainly would have plunged off the road, as curvy and precipitous as the climb had been. She made herself relax and breathe deeply. Look ahead, she reminded herself, look ahead. For a while she steadied herself by focusing on the gleam of the car's headlights on the road; but when she glanced back she realised how quickly that light was swallowed up again by the dark night.

Something was wrong. Wrong. She had not seen any sign of life for the longest time. She couldn't remember how long they had been travelling on this bumpy road in the barely-held-together cab with their luggage and boxes tied on top and in the trunk. If she had not been immobilised by her fear of the darkness she would have sprung out of the car into the night. But no! Not into that darkness. It would devour her. Her body would probably never be found.

'We almost dere.'

Angel jumped. Rupert's voice coming towards her out of the blackness was a sudden shock. She glanced to her side but could not see him. He had become the night. She wanted to scream, run.

Why did she agree to come – no, actually beg him to bring her here? Why had she agreed, sight unseen, to make his birthplace her own home? She had been raised in Manhattan city in the constant glow of electric light. Where were the people and houses here? Where were the lights and noises? All she could hear were crickets. She half expected to hear next the growls of wild creatures, poised to leap out of the darkness.

Rupert was speaking to Charley, his cousin and the taxi-cab driver. 'De bend coming up to you right. Tek a sharp turn.'

'What a-way you remember dis road,' replied Charley. Apparently the two of them could see in this darkness well enough. How could this be? Angel peered even more intensely in front of her.

At first Angel couldn't understand what they were saying, Rupert and Charley, although she thought herself very good at interpreting Rupert's heavy accent. But in this darkness everything seemed foreign, including his once familiar baritone voice. The car turned sharply and she was pushed back into the seat.

Shortly, the car came to rest. Angel felt a cramp in her legs and feet, and tension filled her entire body. Rupert was out of the car before she could reach for him. He and Charley were talking, their voices loud like an invasion in the night. She covered her ears with her hands and sat back in the car concentrating on one thing, and one thing alone: escape from night's immense grasping hands.

She felt a slight movement of air and knew that Rupert had come around and opened the door on her side. Looking to where she heard him moving, she saw only two faint white spots almost level with her eyes. Now she felt Rupert's hands on her arms, and although her strongest impulse was to pull away in fear, she felt her own hands fastening around his wrists. He helped her out of the car, but she stumbled, hopelessly disoriented by the total absence of light. She was falling, falling into this nothingness. No! Into darkness! Fear kept her

20

from completely surrendering herself, and Rupert wrapped his arms around her while saying, 'Steady youself. Is sleep, you fall asleep? Dis is you new home.'

Was he crazy? New home! What home? All Angel saw was darkness, in front, behind and beside her. Rupert had also become a part of darkness; she was the only light. She held up her palms to her face for confirmation, but even these she could not make out. Darkness was taking her too. It was going to swallow her whole.

She thought she would faint when she realised that Rupert had steered her to a seat atop one of the boxes, then returned to the cab with Charley. She heard their two voices receding. In that instant she hated Rupert. How could he leave her there all by herself? Angry and hurt, she said to herself: 'He doesn't love me.' She folded in on herself. Courage came to her, though, when the mosquitoes began feasting on her flesh. She stomped her feet, clapped at her face and slapped at her arms. Then she got up and started to pace, gradually getting the feel of the ground beneath her feet, gradually making out the shapes of bushes and trees, gradually seeing the little match-box that was Rupert's parents' home come into focus. The house in which he was born, where he had his first meal, his first happiness, was now to be her home. She began to relax a little.

But the improvement was shortlived. She started when Charley, himself purple-black like night, emerged from the darkness, took her hand and patted it, saying with a smile (she could tell from the sudden half-moon of whiteness that shone out at the level of her forehead), 'Welcome home, sista. We glad fah de new blood.'

Angel didn't understand. What blood? Whose blood?

Once again Rupert's voice came – a loud assault, stirring the night as he bid his cousin good evening.

Evening! thought Angel. It must be midnight. What were the stories she had been told about midnight and darkness and being in strange places? She mustn't let her imagination travel on such roads. She was home. Rupert came up to her, whistling. She knew he was happy, heard it in his favourite tune, the words of which he had taught her almost thirteen months ago, in another lifetime it seemed.

21

> 'Brown skin gal
> Stay home and mind baby
> Brown skin gal
> Stay home and mind baby
> I'm going a-way
> On a sailing ship
> And if I don't come back
> Stay home and mind baby . . .'

As much as Angel hated the sexism of the lyrics, she loved it when Rupert sang this song and often, like now, she joined him. When they finished, they both burst out laughing and fell into each other's arms. Happy.

Then Rupert, holding Angel around the waist, gestured to the night. 'Now dis is real night. America no know night anymore. Light everywhere. One can't find night anymore in America. First few months me was there, me couldn't sleep. Too much light and noise.'

Angel looked out and confronted the night afresh. It was just a little deeper, denser than Rupert. She had instantly fallen in love with him, with the even purple-black sheen of his skin. It reminded her of love. Angel looked at the darkness and knew night, and fell in love with it. She realised she would have to grow new eyes, and learn other ways of seeing. Holding Rupert's hand she walked with him around the match-box house, and he pointed out trees to her that she actually could see.

But Angel's resolve vanished on the threshold of the house and she stopped, reluctant to enter. A lantern had been left by the door for them but neither of them had matches so they couldn't light it. Rupert had forgotten there was no electricity. How could he forget what used to be commonplace to him? He pushed the boxes and suitcases inside, although he knew no one would bother them. He had to get matches. The closest house to his, if his memory served him well, was Sister Beryl's.

'Come man,' Rupert said, reaching for Angel. 'We have to walk a little ways to get some light here tonight.' And they were off, Angel's feet finding their own way as she became acquainted with night.

They came to a fence and what sounded like a whole pack of dogs barked at them. Angel clutched at Rupert's arm, again on the verge of panic.

'Go weh dog!' Rupert scolded the dogs, who nevertheless kept up their fierce barking. 'Sista Beryl? Is you dat sitting pan de veranda?'

Angel peered intently over his shoulder and could just make out someone sitting yonder with a streak of light at their feet. No one moved, and no voice answered Rupert. She pressed her fingers into his shoulder blades. She was about to say let's go when his voice assaulted the night again.

'Sista Beryl. Is me, Rupert. Is not duppy trying to trick you.'

Angel heard a heaving, like someone straining to get up. The light didn't move, but she heard a rustle coming towards them. Before she could make out the form, a woman with a voice sure and precise said, 'Me know is you, but me did want mek sure. Me hear Charley cab stop by de house and know is you. But me neva expect to see you until tomorrow when me pass by fi seh me howdy. Me clean out de house and left food cover up on de table fah you. The ice probably melt by now and the ovaltine must warm, but is night now so oonu can drink it like dat.'

This was all said in one effortless stream. Angel wished she could see the face from which the voice came, but all she saw was an outline.

Now Rupert was talking. 'Thanks fah everything, Sista Beryl. Me wasn't planning to bother you tonight, but we no have no matches fi light de lantern.'

The voice laughed out goodnaturedly, and Angel heard the woman slap at her thighs with her hands. 'So you go a America and faget de basics. What a life.' Laughter again. Angel wondered when she would be introduced but she heard the voice leaving them, warning as it faded: 'Chow! Brownie and Spotty. Stop de everlasting barking. Nobody nah step pan oonuh foot.' The dogs fell quiet at this reprimand from their mistress. A stick of light left the veranda and advanced towards them. Angel held her breath; Rupert pulled her to his side. A hand moved the light up and down, then held it level with Angel's face. Then the voice said, 'So is de American wife dis dat Cousin Charley tell me bout.'

'Yes, Sista Beryl. Dis here is ma wife, Angel.'

23

No hand reached out towards Angel, and no voice said welcome. Instead the light left her body and moved off in the direction she and Rupert had come from. They walked in a single file, Angel between the two. No one spoke but the night creatures, and Angel grew easy with the night.

Sister Beryl set a fast pace and Angel found herself struggling to keep up. For some reason this woman seemed familiar, yet she was as frightening as the night. But if Angel was to live here, Sister Beryl would be her closest neighbour. She would have to learn about her new home from this woman who feared no one, and whom, she suspected, no one would cross very easily.

'Ah not stopping tonight. Ah just gwane light de lantern den walk back. Ah will bring oonuh tea in de morning.' The voice was already a distance from them, and before Angel reached the veranda, the hand placed the lit lantern in her hand. In the brief exchange of light she saw the face that belonged to the voice and felt scared and happy and angry all at once. But before she could make out any details, the voice moved behind her, declaring as it walked away, 'You fava one of we except you skin light. Sleep good.' And the voice was gone with the stick of light moving through the night.

The light that the lantern cast was not very distinct, but Angel held it up in front as she and Rupert went inside. She was both pleased and disappointed. The room was the size of an average bedroom and was in need of painting.

'Lawd, ah used to dream bout dis room. Is just like me memba it,' Rupert gushed. Angel turned to look at him, standing in the door, and as she did so a wind swept through the house. The lantern crashed at her feet and the room went dark. Kerosene splattered her legs and its vapour filled the room.

'Rupert,' she moaned, swooning into darkness.

Midday

No one else would be so bold face.

'Chow! Dem too stupid. Mek dem gwane.'

The act had been relegated to night, to privacy and secrecy, but

Monica would have none of that. She liked doing it during the day, preferably just before lunch. She threw back her head and laughed a deep belly-laugh. Passion should never be private or secret. It wasn't meant to be. Sexual acts engaged in undercover invariably came to light, usually in the form of a protruding stomach. Laughter racked her body. She used the back of her hand to wipe the tears that trailed down her face. It was too funny. This passion.

Monica had left home at fourteen because she looked and felt like a woman, and because, as her mother accused, 'You actin like you is de first girl womanhood box. Just memba you ass swing both ways.' Since then, Monica's ass had swung more than both ways, and in the faces of far too many men. Most of these she mildly disdained, others she pitied, and a few she still enjoyed. Her decision to return to Kristoff Village, her childhood home, was spurred by a desire for a more settled life. She had visited only a handful of times in the almost thirty years since her departure, including once upon her mother's death. But she was now tired of the city, the ready action and the lustful disturbance she caused no matter how casual or indifferent she behaved. While some women, no matter how much effort they invested in the colour and flair of their clothes, could arouse no attention, Monica was a woman who, even when she least intended it, created a sensation among the naked boys diving in the river and catching cray-fish, the old men sitting on empty soda crates clapping their toothless gums and swatting at flies and mosquitoes, and the strapping bucks, their muscles taut and rippling from hauling and carting boxes under the sweating sun, digging ground to produce food or building roads. Monica was like a bitch in heat, and no matter what activity a male was engaged in, he would smell her a mile away and stop work to attend to the itch in his groin, or cradle his manhood, or massage the aching muscles in his shoulders while staring off somewhere with a smile so sweet it was like a paradise plum in his mouth.

Now Monica felt she had reached the stage where she could do without a man. Well, not completely. But she preferred solitude most times. Samuel Lawrence, her married man in Spanish Town who had set her up real nice in Kristoff Village, said he would show up once a month for the weekend. Maybe twice a month if he could get away. Monica hoped once a month was all the time he could spare. Not that she didn't like him, but all he wanted was to ride her all the time, yet he could not satisfy her. She had given up trying to teach him about pace and pleasure. He was like a horse that starts strong but can barely finish the race. However, he was generous, could hold a conversation, and did like to go on walks and hold hands. Everyone has to know when to say thanks and not ask any more. Monica was not a fool. But she wished he would more often turn to his wife. Men were sure oafs, marrying someone who would be a showpiece, then having to sneak around and plot to get the fire they craved. Monica had never treasured being in the middle. She had always known she was being used, but had resigned herself to what she thought her fate. But as she matured, she was losing her appetite for other women's men. She told herself that returning to the quiet and peace of Kristoff Village would prevent her from entangling her life with that of another married man. She would give up Samuel Lawrence soon, but gradually.

If you don't want people to know your business, then keep it to yourself.

Monica intended to keep pretty much to herself in Kristoff. Not one to gossip, and not needing the companionship of other women, she was almost guaranteed some privacy. What she seemed to have forgotten was that Kristoff Village was in no way a private place. Privacy was a concept that did not exist in the minds of the inhabitants of this village. Still, she tried. Samuel Lawrence made all the arrangements. He took care of all the details, including rebuilding her parents' home and refitting it with electricity and indoor plumbing. He moved in all the furniture he'd bought for her, along with all her other belongings. Not once in the two years it took to get all this done had anyone in Kristoff Village seen Monica. But they knew the house was hers, now that her two sisters were in America, her sweet brother who had six fingers on his left hand was in Canada, and her parents were both dead. The inhabitants had pried and obtained the details about Monica's move back; they had even done some digging and found out that most of the thirty years she had been away had been dedicated to whoring, and that no bigger whore than she had ever serviced Kingston or Spanish Town. Supposedly, her legs were so wide apart and she was so large one could stand at her feet and see all the way inside her womb. Decent, God-fearing women had to watch their husbands. And though she was a big woman, in her forties, one could never tell. The women pulled in their stomachs and held their heads high. The men secretly swapped stories and speculated. Children hid beside doorways and around corners, eager to catch some of the gossip. Monica's name was on everyone's tongue. They waited for her, anxious for a show.

When the house was ready, Monica appeared at last. She had considered moving in at night, but being superstitious she decided to make her appearance in the light of day, announce her arrival to the entire community, and get it over with in one sweep. She would have preferred to arrive on Sunday, but the bus that went from one end of Kristoff Village to the junction only operated during the week, once in the morning and again in the evening. She could certainly afford a taxi, but she didn't want them to say, 'She too show-off, you see. Throwing weh good money!' So she settled on the Friday evening bus when every one would be liming and taking it easy after the working week.

Monica was the last person to dismount the bus that evening. She had selected her clothing carefully as she suspected that all the villagers would be watching her, and she wanted to give them a show. Polka-dot is not an easy pattern to settle one's eyes on. It is passable if draped over a table in a corner or hung on the wall of a child's room, but draped over a woman's body it can be unsettling. The spots call too much attention to themselves. Monica wore a tight-fitting navy-blue dress with red polka-dots that came in at her knees then flounced out around her strong calves. It was a skinny polyester fabric that appeared satin-like. She sported a round neckline, not too low to be indecent, but low enough to reveal firm and ample breasts and flawless skin, the colour of cane-juice. Her behind was tight and high, and, naturally, indecent for a woman of her age; and it swung with her every move, the hemline of her dress swishing to the beat. Her hair, pressed and shiny with oil, was swept back from her face, revealing handsome features and a haughty disposition. She had a white handkerchief in her left hand and a navy-blue purse thrown over her right arm. Her high-heel shoes were exactly the same polka-

27

dot pattern as her dress. Although she wore no hat or gloves, some later claimed she was so attired. But it was her red lips and manicured fire-red nails that sealed her fate.

'Whore!' the wives spat, their grudging admiration fuelling their anger, and pretended they didn't see her.

'Is who have time fi paint them nails?' one said sarcastically.

'Me dear! Hands fah working,' another offered.

'Well we know how she use hers.' Laughter from the wives gathered.

'And koo de lips. Red like American apple,' a toothless old woman added.

'Shameful woman.'

Imagine! In her forties with the body of a young woman. Wearing such clothes! Heels, four inches, if not higher, and stepping like she was walking on air rather than the uneven gravel road.

'Is who she think she is?'

'And she barren too. Not a picknie fi bring her water in her old age.'

'Ah tell. De Lawd work in mysterious ways. Damn wukliss whore.' All agreed she arrived like a queen, pulling everyone's eyes to her.

'Bitch. Is who gwane friend she?'

'Galang. Pride come before fall.'

'Lawd missus. Nobody nah go bruk dem neck fi see you.'

People were mulling by Miss Cotton's store, getting little supplies. The store was on a slope. Monica stopped at the bottom, and her voice, full and playful, called up to the old store owner. 'Howdy, Miss Cotton. Is me, Monica, saying howdy. Hope you keeping well?' Her voice was as clear and fresh as the sky after a shower of rain. Such poor manners, the people thought, staying at the side of the road, not climbing the stairs to greet the elder, but having Miss Cotton leave her customers and come out on the veranda to acknowledge her arrival.

'Monica, is dat you! Monica who run weh and bruk her parents' heart at fourteen? Monica! Pretty woman, Monica!' All the while Miss Cotton adjusted her glasses and scratched her head, her volume rising with each phrase.

'Is me same one, Miss Cotton. You look as good as the day ah run weh. Memba is you give me bun and cheese and aerated water to tek wid me.'

'So wait. You gwane stand down dere and have me shout out me last breath? Seems like you lose you manners in town. Just bring you womanself up here.'

Monica mounted the stairs, pausing on each, aware that all eyes were on her, and after the eighth one she came face to face with Miss Cotton, who held her by the arms before embracing her.

'Chile, is good you come home,' Miss Cotton declared loudly, turning Monica around, admiring her dress, and calling for her assistant, her granddaughter, to bring Monica her favourite drink, a cold cream-soda.

That same evening Desmond Burton's motorbike just happened to break down right in front of Monica's gate. She had barely stepped inside her house for the first time, having first spent almost an hour visiting with Miss Cotton and Master Cotton. The sensation created by her arrival was more than even she had bargained for, and finally inside the privacy of her home all she wanted to do was 'kick off de damn high-heel boots and fling meself across de bed'. So when Desmond waved to her and shouted with dance in his voice, 'Howdy Miss Monica. We glad you memba to come back home,' she did not turn around to inspect the person who greeted her so intimately, but threw 'Howdy' over her shoulder and pulled the door shut behind her.

That first night home, Monica dreamt she was washing clothes, but when she looked in the tub the water was muddy. She threw it out and filled the tub again, but again when she started to wash her delicates the water was muddy. Try as she might, the water remained muddy. Monica awoke in the middle of the night from that dream, her head feeling heavy and disoriented. Before falling back to sleep she made a promise to herself never again deliberately to take another woman's man, just because she could.

Roosters crowing. Loud. Demanding. Assured. That was the sound Monica woke to on her first morning back in Kristoff Village. She sat on the edge of the bed, stretched and rubbed the sleep from her eyes.

She looked around, taking in the room. She didn't like how Samuel, a man who never had to lift a hand in his own home, had arranged the furniture, things placed helter-skelter. Yet the house was fitted with everything, including a nineteen-inch colour television so that she could watch the programmes in colour like at the picture show. Monica really couldn't complain. Samuel had done a nice job on the house, including floor-tiles throughout. He had enlarged, practically rebuilt, the entire little cottage in which she had been raised. Now there were two large bedrooms, separated by a bathroom with an aqua tub and toilet just as she had requested, and a nice size living room that led to a dining room, off which was the kitchen. She didn't like the kitchen. It was small, with not enough cabinets. Worse, it had only one tiny window, this so far up she had to stand on a chair to reach and open it. It vexed her. She didn't like to cook, and this kitchen wasn't going to help her any. But she was going to see if there was some girl who needed a little money to do her cleaning and washing, and maybe even cooking.

Stepping outside, Monica was thrilled with what Samuel had done with the yard. He had fenced and separated it like a fancy yard in Kingston. Hers was the only yard with a concrete and grill fence; it was painted aqua and brown to match the house. Beds of flowers decorated the front yard, and fruit trees and vegetables graced the back. She also noticed a grassy area in the front, and laughed at the idea. Who ever heard of a lawn in the country? The dew tickled and soothed her feet; she sniffed at the air and filled her lungs. She had made the right decision. Walking to the back yard, she felt the sun spreading its arms. Just outside the kitchen door was a wash area that was enclosed with a nice veranda overlooking the valley. She decided then and there to write and ask Samuel Lawrence to rebuild the kitchen and extend it to the wash area. She ran inside, found pen and paper and sat and wrote the letter. But after reading it over, she decided it sounded too ungrateful. So she tore it up, and sat and thought for a long while before making a fresh start. Finally satisfied, she placed the letter in an envelope and addressed it.

Monica had to rethink her whole life, and since walking always helped her sort things out she walked around her land, aware only of the sensation of her bare feet on the soil and the sun's rays stealing through the thin blue cotton nightie that exposed her full thighs. She had not even been home a day yet, and was not expecting any caller. Yet she wasn't surprised when she heard, 'Morning Miss Monica. Ah hope you in a betta mood dan yesterday evening. Ah decided to see if ah could give you a hand.'

She turned, facing the voice that reminded her of the kind of seductive man who could immediately get her to dance intimately with him, eyes closed, head resting on his shoulder. She stared into gleaming eyes with solid brows. A man as brown as dirt and as smooth as a banana leaf, wearing a freshly starched and ironed light-blue shirt that glimmered in the sun, smiled at her.

To be caught so unaware.

Wear blue anytime. But not around me.

Monica didn't recognise this prize, but what did it matter? It was the middle of the morning, the best time. She had not turned on fire under pot. She had not opened her windows to let the sun flood her rooms. Had not hung up her navy-blue-with-red-polka-dots dress; had not moved any furniture, or unpacked a bag, except to take out the nightie which she wore; had not bathed, except to wipe a wet washcloth over her face, her underarms, between her legs. She had done nothing but return and that was enough.

He came up to her and gave her his hand. 'Desmond Burton. Ah live just where de river form an hook, opposite de big cotton tree. Me and Elton used to go a bush.'

If he was her brother's friend, then he was about thirty-eight. Monica wondered how many children he had. Not that it mattered. Standing under the bold sun in her flimsy nightclothes that revealed her body, with this man – Desmond – smiling at her, caused Monica to believe her private dream might be possible: that one man could make her smile just by his presence.

Monica realised she had already decided on Desmond despite her promises of a more settled life.

Resist temptation.

No.

Temptation sweet like sour-sop. That blue shirt.

Her vow of the night before completely forgotten, Monica said, 'No need us standing out here under de hot sun. Come inside. All ah can offer you is an orange. But ah promise you it sweet.' She laughed at her boldness, pulling her nightie close around her body, breasts free and firm. As she moved towards Desmond she felt as if the muddy basin of water in her dream was being tossed at her.

Heat produces sweat. Sweat congeals two bodies. Passion lets loose noise.

Although houses were often built at least twenty yards from the road, a loud woman was a loud woman. The villagers passing by Monica's house that morning stopped dead in their tracks. Disbelief crowded their faces. They strained their necks, listened closely. Covered their mouths in shock, scolded the children passing to mind their own business and 'go about oonuh ways, noisy'.

Monica feasted. Desmond nibbled at her ears. Squeezed her buttocks. Massaged her stomach. Kissed her neck. Sucked on her breasts and hoisted her legs on his shoulders. Monica giggled. Desmond panted. Monica moaned. Desmond roared. Monica sweated. Desmond perspired. Monica begged. Desmond pleaded. Spent, Monica turned on her side, pulled the sheet to her neck and smiled herself to sleep.

Desmond got to work after lunch, and his co-workers all asked, 'Wha sweet you so, man?' But the sugar was only for his mouth.

Returning from work, Ainsworth McKenzie knocked at Monica's door, a book in hand to welcome her. Still basking in Desmond's loving, Monica took the book and told him to come back the following day. Seven in the evening, just after Monica had her bath, ate some bread and fish, and unpacked one suitcase, Trevor Campbell stopped by with a cream-soda and a beer to see if she needed anything. She needed fresh air so she strolled with him, allowing him to show her various paths and short-cuts to get to Aunty Velma and Miss Dahlia's house, where she planned to visit the next day. Darkness enveloped them as they took the path that led to Miss Cotton's yard. Reaching for Trevor's hand, Monica felt it hot and pulsing. She thanked him for the walk and invited him to visit her again.

Miss Cotton smiled and shook her head as Monica sat in the chair set for her.

Birds will only stop flying if their wings are clipped.

A slight throb. Monica leaned sideways and massaged Miss Cotton's temples.

'Hush,' Monica said. 'Me no gwane steal anyone last piece of bread.'

The throb fluttered and moved away. Darkness was deep.

Coming home was choosing to do it during the day when the sun was hot.

Deciding on recklessness.

Left-over

Routine

Day in day out.

Working at it every day. Living but not participating. Shame blocked the path. Shame rose up when one was alone with oneself, with darkness, with night. Shame when one could not forgive oneself, and was so hungry even food was a mockery.

By three-thirty every weekday Beryl was home, sitting on her tiny veranda with the railing so high it almost obscured her view, smoking her pipe. For a very long time now she had appeared much older than she was. People called her strapping. No fat. Just muscles. Skin taut. Hair like rope. Heart a fist. Balled tight. Firm. Not to be dislodged. She was not middle-aged, but she looked it. An only child, she kept her invalid mother and herself fed and clothed. She spent three sleepless nights in the market every weekend.

Beryl cannot forget that which she remembers. She cannot find the face she seeks.

Always cold, except when she touched the soil, dug deep into its belly, planted yam-head, sweet-potato, carrot, tomato, gungu pea, turnip, sorrel, cassava, callalloo, cabbage, banana, plantain. Whatever she touched tended to yield, including animals – the three pigs, eight goats, more than a dozen chickens, two roosters, four dogs, a flock of pigeons, and five guineafowls. Beryl and her mother ate and lived well, although it was not evident from the appearance of their shack. Unlike all the homes that had been modernised (no more thatched roof made from coconut boughs, no more hut built in the circular

33

shape), Beryl's cottage had barely been altered since her father first erected it forty years ago. The rooms had not been enlarged, and there were still only two. No electricity had been wired to the house, even though it now ran past Beryl's gate, and while she had a standpipe in the back yard that separated the kitchen from the rest of the house, there was no running water. There had been several new thatched roofs, a wooden floor had been put in, and the bamboo sticks had been replaced with wood painted a cool yellow on the interior – but the cottage still looked ancient and unoccupied from outside. The boards were unpainted, and thatching alone kept the zinc roof cool in the middle of the day.

However, the ground surrounding the cottage told a different story: of order and abundance and love of beauty. Plants and flowers and herb bushes intermingled, creating a surprising, welcoming grace. Every morning Beryl emptied her mother's chamber pot in the pit-toilet off to the side of the yard, down near where the land sloped into lush ferns and grapefruit trees. Beryl abhorred change. She and her mother still cooked on a coal stove, still bathed in a drum barrel, still saw at night by lantern light, and never called anyone's name out loud after darkness.

The villagers remembered Beryl when she was pretty and young and inquisitive. Her mother had hoped she would be a teacher. She did well in school and even went to Montego Bay to attend teacher college. What happened there, only a few know. But Beryl disappeared between the ages of eighteen and twenty. When she returned to Kristoff Village, beaten, eyes sunken and vacant, skin dull, they said the cat had gone off with her tongue. Not even a howdy passed through her lips. Five years elapsed after Beryl's return before she spoke. By then, her father, who was much older than her mother, had died. He was a great farmer so Beryl took over his work, growing strong and healthy under the toil. Her skin seemed to ripen and shine with the lustre of tropical fruits ready to be picked. Many young men came around then, but after Beryl chopped Keity on the shoulder in one swift movement of the cutlass, for allegedly grabbing at her breasts, the young men left her alone.

'Is mad oman dat.'

'Is mus de devil she ah sleep wid.'

34

'She must tink she have gold between she legs.'

Men and women, the old and the young – all left her alone. She didn't go to church or visit the obeah man. She didn't go on sprees in MoBay or go to dances at the junction every two weeks. No man was known to creep into her cottage at night, and she was never seen in the company of any woman except her mother. Nothing seemed to matter to her, except her garden. Not life, nor death. Not sorrow, nor happiness. She was alive but dead.

Someone hurt her, yes.

Many nights Beryl sat on the veranda behind the high railing, her chin resting on arms slung over the crude wood. The tears that spilled from her eyes fell on her arms, stinging them. Within the last six months the frequency of her tears had increased. She felt agitated, irritable, as if she kept running into a tree, but could not break her speed or prevent her inevitable crash. She had been hearing a child calling out to her. Every night for the last month the sound had been getting closer. Even her mother, who was deaf, said she heard a child calling for Beryl. Grey hairs now framed Beryl's face. She was drowning, but longed to float.

Break the routine. Wrestle with Devil, God or people.

But Beryl had forgotten how to open her mouth and talk. She no longer remembered the pleasure of sitting with a friend and enjoying a good laugh. She no longer felt the satisfaction of telling someone her mind or knew the taste of her tears. Beryl had lied to herself too long. Some things might be indefinite. She needed someone. A caress. There. She had said it. A mirror to marvel at her reflection.

Last week when Beryl went by the junction, she stopped at the post office. A letter from Charley was there, asking her to clean and air out the house that belonged to Mabel and John Stewart who had died more than five years ago. Apparently their son, Rupert, was coming home and planned to live there. Beryl stood right in the middle of the junction reading and rereading the letter, not believing her eyes. 'Broda Rupert coming home. Fah what?' she said out loud. 'Is mad him must mad.' Then Beryl felt happy, remembering making Rupert the little brother she had never had. He was always full of stories. Like her, he was the only child of old parents.

The house wasn't in as bad a condition as Beryl had anticipated.

She remembered that once yearly Charley and his wife came and cleaned the place. The furniture was draped in sheets, and cobwebs covered the walls and ceiling. Beryl washed the walls and floor and aired out the rooms. Soon it looked presentable, even cosy, although it needed painting. Walking through the house that even had an attached kitchen, Beryl was surprised at how big and comfortable it was in comparison to her own little cottage. So much nicer than her place.

'Rupert coming home.'

Beryl then got busy with her machete, cutting away weeds, chopping back the bushes choking the house, and clearing the path from the dilapidated gate to the oval-shaped veranda. Sweat dripped from her brow as she hauled the last bundle of bush to the side, away from the house. She leaned on the gate and admired the solid, attractive house made and furnished from mahogany, with carvings on the lattice and columns.

Three nights passed. Beryl admitted to herself that she was listening out for Rupert. Anticipation was worse than disappointment. She could ponder on disappointment. It had shape and texture. Often it had a face attached to it. But anticipation was more elusive than the wind; more enigmatic than a ghost; more worrisome than a hurricane. For more than a week Beryl sat on her veranda, her ears open to any new sound. But nothing. The child was more persistent than ever. Sometimes so demanding, calling Beryl in her sleep, waking her, drenching her body in sweat. Beryl could almost make her out. She was taking form. Beryl didn't want to remember what had taken form in her body. She would not remember anything but her shame. The hope that would never be more than a used writing book with a child's scribble. Anticipation was vengeful, mocking her every waking hour.

Two days before Rupert arrived, Beryl received a telegram from Charley. Rupert would be coming with an American wife. Beryl killed, skinned and curried a goat, made mannish water, and laid the table for Rupert and his wife.

'But is wha white woman gwane do in Kristoff Village?' Beryl wondered. 'Mek her come. Mosquitoes gwane nyam her up.' She chuckled. Life sometimes changed its course. She felt like her life was being taken out of her hands. She was going to have neighbours again. Monica had moved back and already gossip was sailing through the air like suds on a Monday morning by the river, where expert hands scrubbed clothes on rocks. Beryl stopped and in her stillness listened actively to her breathing. She realised she missed going to wash clothes at the river. Missed the voices and the gossip, missed the gathering.

Modernisation. Convenience. But what to replace the community, the sharing? Everything had a cost, yes.

Reared in silence, and drilled in the virtues of obedience, Beryl had failed to grasp the importance of questioning what came to her as fact or gospel truth. But lately that is where her mind had been stuck. Her private engagement: to turn over ideas just as she turned the soil, to taste and smell the ideas, and know where best to plant what beside what. She had begun again to read the *Daily Gleaner*, walking the two-and-a-half miles to the junction every morning just to buy it. Taking it with her to the fields, spending an hour or more at noon reading it while eating her lunch. Reading all the words and turning them over, trying to understand what they meant. What were these other worlds outside Kristoff Village, even beyond the boundaries of her island home? At an earlier time, she used to wonder, used to dream about travelling. In the past she had often thought about an island, being confined, trapped by water. Run, swim or drown.

Beryl's neck ached. Her eyes were weary from reading by lantern light at night. She couldn't decide whether or not she wanted to participate in life again. Going through the motions took effort. She could not forget what she could not remember. Pain always near the surface. Denial, her mirror image. Lost, losing. The face she couldn't see. The child calling her.

Mondays when Beryl didn't work on her farm she followed the bank of the river, way out, for four miles or more, until she could hear the sea. Then she would find a spot that buried her, cast her rod and spend the day fishing. Mostly she passed the time not remembering that she was alive. For years, until now, her own silence had pleased her best. She had no desires that she made known to herself. Her mother was sometimes her mirror. They slept in the same room, on the same bed, the bed on which she was born, on which she slept until she was eleven and her father bought her a single bed, which was put in the far side of the same room. But since her father was now dead, the single bed was used to store clothes and linen; Beryl and her mother slept on the cosy, feather-mattressed, full-sized bed. Beryl's mother had insisted that nearly everything remain the same after Beryl's father died; but she did allow Beryl to pull the large four-poster bed into the middle of the small room so that neither of them had to crawl over or climb out from the corner.

Last night Beryl couldn't sleep. The presence and smell of her mother's body was disturbing. Eventually, she got up and slept in the old rocking chair on the veranda. She was discontented. Vexed. When she did fall asleep she slept until awakened by the rooster; then she burned the johnny-cakes. She swore aloud, her voice like a storm. 'Damn de devil and him blasted wife. Chow, man!' Her voice rang out, causing her mother, sitting in her customary spot by the bald-headed coconut tree awaiting her breakfast, to look in her direction and frown.

The elements

Miss Cotton was eighty and a day and as the people of Kristoff Village often said, 'She stronger dan lightning and shrewder dan God's right hand.' A few people remembered when she had been an obeah woman. That was how she got Brother Cotton.

She had been a stranger to the village with no relatives or trace of family. All she had on her side were good looks and a big behind. 'De best rump any weh!' Carlton Cotton used to boast before they were married, and although his sight was failing him at the ripe age of eighty-seven, his close friends said he still thought Miss Cotton had the best rump on any woman. Although now that Monica was back, he said, hers was making his old flesh talk in ways that only Miss Cotton's used to do. This he said laughing, his tongue curling in his five-teeth mouth, and his arms, still strong, slapping his thighs.

Miss Cotton heard him and smiled. 'Every old man need something to dream on, especially a young oman, but is only me and you in de bed at night.' He touched her hand as she passed him, heading for the shop. They smiled, still in love with each other.

Find it, then focus on it, is what Miss Cotton always said. She could see a thing before it was. She tried many times to stop what was going to be, but couldn't. Her powers didn't extend that far. She was a seer. She could see beyond the surface of things, could see inside the very depths of people and in seeing knew, but she didn't know how to stop what would hurt. All she could do was wait until the hurt began, then soothe it. Someone without name or face taught her which herbs to put against which ailment; which fire to touch which cut; which hand to mend which wound. Her head was worrying her now. Her heart was aching. She didn't want to go there any more, but she had to find the river. And what a flood there would be when it was all over.

She was orphaned, with only her looks as insurance. Even when she was a little girl, everyone said, 'Lawd, what a pretty picknie. Is must sin produce her.' Although they admired her, they didn't want her because she was too pretty. So she always had a temporary home. Pretty clothes and much attention, but no consistent love. No one scolded her, so she had to raise herself, reprimanding herself like she heard her friends' mothers brushing them up, pressing down their pride with mouthing. And she did all right. She learned to keep her legs closed and her dress down, although many boys and brazen men tried to teach her otherwise. She managed, determined; and her prettiness sometimes helped. One day she discovered that she could see what people were feeling, and she began to take people's hands, especially those of her friends, and tell them things. These friends first accused her, then feared her, then ostracised her, then came to her with their tears and petty desires: this man who didn't want or deserve them; a dress for a dance; some job they were more qualified for given to another.

Being pretty and brown helped. Teachers encouraged her, a path was made for her. Secondary school, a book-keeping course. Offers. But she could see behind it all, so smiled sweetly, took what she wanted while saying no. No. Firmly. Seeking something else besides the little room she rented in a congested yard, amid poverty and people sick on dreams. Waiting. For what? For whom? They found her. She refused to answer their questions. They hounded; she relented. Held their hands, looked into their eyes, listened to their cries, and told them everything that was plain as day. If only they would trust themselves. If only they would quiet themselves and listen. Listen. They would hear it too. They wouldn't need her. But they were too restless. They couldn't hear anything but words, so they needed her. One told two, two told many, and they spilled into the congested yard. She told them which bush to boil, what colours to wear, where to walk, who to talk to, and they believed her. They heard their own knowledge and their lives changed, improved; but still they thanked her, believed she had created the miracle that was inside themselves. Miss Cotton laughed and waited.

The waiting wasn't too long. Between four and six o'clock in the evening when everyone was busy and rushing home to shops, to bars, to somewhere, she would be out, looking. She would wrap her head in a blue cloth and throw a scarf around her neck. She rounded her shoulders, pulled her neck down, becoming an old woman, unnoticed, so allowed to observe. She could be bold to seek what she wanted. She moved invisible among them, seeking, smelling, hearing. Sometimes she stood in the middle of the street just watching their feet. Other times she stood in a corner, nestled between two buildings, and watched them from their waists up or down, depending on how she was feeling. It was while she was focusing on the waist down that she found him. His hands arrested her. Honey is what she thought, sticky and sweet. Then they were gone and because she was focusing on the waist down she couldn't see the owner of the hands. Panic. She stood rooted in that spot until the clock struck midnight; then moving like a sleep-walker she made it home, her neck stiff, her body used up. She drank warm sorrel with rum that night and many nights after spotting those dripping honey hands.

She sought in earnest after that, but the honey-coloured hands never appeared again. You won't find it if you look too hard. That's a truism, dear-heart. She knew this, but couldn't stop her search, so of course he eluded her. Then an accidental meeting. A friend from school invited her to attend a reunion party. She agreed. And the first person she saw upon her arrival was the man with the honey-coloured hands.

Calm. Calm down. Decide. Good. Now focus. The young woman

of twenty, pretty and brown, perfumed her body in honey and caught the bee, and no one ever remembered what her name was before she became Mrs Carlton Cotton.

Wood

Godfree.

'Is how you mean him can't name so? Who seh so? Is who bring him in dis world? Is who name him? Me nuh care what de paper say. Him name is Godfree. Mek me spell it fi you: GODFREE. Godfree.'

Laughter. Always laughter to dispel the seriousness, to quiet the storm, to cool the ache. He never knew mother or father, killed the former coming into the world, and drove the latter to seek his fortune in a foreign land. He never knew either so missed neither. Granny was the one he had always had – the cantankerous, loudmouth, independent, will not lie down and die, not even for God's satisfaction, Granny. Miss Dahlia, Sister Dahlia or Big-Willed Oman, Granny. Laughter that masked seriousness.

'Godfree! Boy, where you is? Come here.'

'Yes Granny.'

'Drop you pants.'

'But Granny . . .'

'Boy, ah still a head taller dan you, and dere is still strength in me hand. Now drop you pants.'

Reluctantly, but knowing the stubbornness and strength of his grandmother, the boy complied, looking around to make sure his friends weren't in the bushes watching and laughing at him. Not in the habit of wearing underpants, he stood naked before his grandmother. She stood staring at him, assessing his manhood, then walked over to him. As Granny reached for Godfree's pride, he pulled back, but her left hand on his shoulder held him firm and with her right hand she took his rod in her palm. At first she held it like something hot and delicate, then she began to feel it like one testing the ripeness of a bread-fruit, then her fingers kneaded it as if it were something dead that needed to be given life.

Finally Granny warned him. 'Miss Velma seh you chasing her girls in de bushes. Mek sure dis wood don't cause you nuh trouble. Ah don't have anymore name inna me head. Now pull up you pants and don't shame me.'

Fifteen is the age of hormones and manhood, and tears too. Godfree's tears began before he was out of sight of his grandmother, before he could find a private place. But he never shamed her, and she never had to come up with any names, not until he had one ready.

Nights, ever since he could remember, he and Granny would sit, especially when the moon was bright and the sky was full of stars, and she would say 'Guess me dis riddle or perhaps not' until the sky was white and sleep was at their fingertips. They told each other stories, and every night for as long as Godfree could remember she would say to him, 'Love and shame not de same ting. So if you love me, don't shame me.'

Many people called him Goffrey, Joffery, Godfred, but he always insisted it was Godfree. At school they said his grandmother was illiterate so wasn't sure of the spelling or the right pronunciation of his name, but after she went to the school and dressed the headmaster down, they registered him as Godfree. A new teacher might question his name but soon got it right. The Ministry of Education tried to exert its authority when he passed a scholarship for secondary school by insisting that he spelled his name Gothfrey. His granny was outraged and put pen to paper. After several letters back and forth, the Minister of Education apologised for the error.

Godfree.

The first thing he remembered tasting was wood, a bitter taste that caused his mouth to water. His granny delivered him, at home, and when she did she knew it was quite likely that her daughter, who had always been delicate and had been sick throughout the pregnancy, would die. The daughter died even before the mother finished pulling out her grandson.

Godfree was born in the longest month of the longest year of his granny's life. November. He couldn't even wait to usher in another year. He came at the end of a year that began with death.

The death of Dahlia's husband. Her only true-love. The man with whom she went to Cuba to pick tobacco; the man for whom she had eight miscarriages before giving birth to one child. After a year-long illness, after promising to hold on until their first grandchild was born, he died on her birthday, 23 May, the day before what would have been their thirty-fourth anniversary. He died, leaving her to take care of their sick, pregnant daughter who grieved because the boy she loved was simple in the head, couldn't find work, and somehow believed he could make something of himself at sea, though he was never able to make anything of himself on land.

The longest year because in July, less than two months after Godfree's grandfather died, when his granny and his sick, pregnant mother were still grieving, they got a telegram from Godfree's paternal grandmother, informing them that his father had fallen overboard and was buried at sea.

Buried at sea. There was no place for Godfree's mother to place a flower or plant a tree. No place she could mark, and say, 'This is where he lies.'

The longest year because the hurricane season was dreadful in September and the wind blew off the roof and Dahlia's one girl-child, sick and frail with grief, pregnant and the baby-father dead, got pneumonia. Dahlia also cut her foot from the zinc that blew down from the roof. And the baby who would be named Godfree was coming. It wasn't time; he was at least two months too early. Dahlia put her hands on her head and bawled. Her husband was dead, and although she didn't feel like being bothered with anything, she couldn't let her daughter have her grandchild with no relative to pat his cheeks, kiss his forehead, lift him into their lap, pull him close and hug him. Dahlia had to go on living so as to help her grandchild see the way.

The longest year and the longest month. November. Dahlia's daughter's birth-and-death month. Her daughter's bringing-forth-life month. November. No food. Not much will and too many tears. Only love kept Dahlia and Godfree going. Love that whispered his mother's, her daughter's name. Love that motivated his simple father, drowned at sea. Love his strong grandfather, her husband. Love that said Godfree and his granny and all their people were going to continue. Love.

Godfree arrived and what was Dahlia to do, but start over again? Raise a child again. Believe and love again. Love and shame. Not the

43

same things. Dahlia's suffering had freed her grandson from the tyranny of God. His grandfather was a carpenter, but now as Godfree approached his thirty-third year he was discovering that he was not only a carpenter but a sculptor who knew the taste of wood, the wood that was chiselled and saved from his grandfather's and mother's coffins, the wood his grandmother had placed into his two-day-old mouth to suck upon.

Water

The other children always teased Rupert that his parents were really his grandparents. On and off through most of his life Rupert believed that his parents were his grandparents, pretending to be his parents. Their hair was white, their backs bent, and they were very closed, as if he was intruding on their privacy. They always seemed to forget about him until seeing him reminded them of his existence. Rupert supposed he hated, or at least resented, them. He remembered feeling left out. His parents rarely spoke to him, though they were always whispering to each other. No words for him. Silence. His basic needs were always attended to. He had food and clothes, and was sent to school, although his parents never showed any interest in his lessons.

Water. Waves swirling and splashing are the images of Rupert's one happy memory, the only perfect day with his parents. A Sunday afternoon, walking for miles through tall weeds and bushes, withstanding scrapes, finally to come out on the sea. Surprised. That first time, witnessing the river's leap into the sea, and watching the sea embrace and swallow the river whole. Tasting fresh water turn salty. Watching gentle ripples fly up and swirl into foamy white laces spiralling out. Clear brown transforming to blue, green, opalescent. The wonder and surprise of it, after a hot and tedious walk. Even more wonderful, to witness two silent old persons shed their skins and raise water above their heads, and dance.

Rupert shuddered when the sun went down. The change was too drastic. He gritted his teeth when his parents gathered the food, wrapping it snugly before placing it back in the hamper.

From salt to fresh.

From waves to ripple.

From skinless and free to old and tight.

Seeing the river enter the sea was never the same again, except one other time. Although the surprise was not so great, the sight was wondrous nevertheless.

When Rupert turned thirteen, his parents sent him to Montego Bay to technical school. He could have come home daily, but they found some folks, as old as themselves, as silent, as private as they were and boarded him out. Most weekends he didn't go home, not even to help with the farm. He sensed that his parents didn't want him around. Yet it was home, the only place he knew, so he went sometimes, when wandering the city streets alone became worse than being home.

Smart enough, Rupert worked hard. He had a choice of woodwork, mechanics or electrical work. He gravitated towards electricity when he learned how easily one could be electrocuted; he was never so lucky. Yet Rupert never contemplated suicide. Killing oneself seemed absurd, frightening. He instinctively knew he didn't have the right to kill himself. He prayed his parents would do it instead, or maybe someone else would oblige him. An accident, careless or random, would suffice. In the end, he never finished school. His parents never knew, or at least he never thought they knew; and if they did, they never asked. Rupert didn't work. He did nothing, drifting, wandering, half hating himself, feeling alone and isolated, missing something. Family. Identity. Responsibility. Purpose.

Because of a tendency to stammer, he kept quiet. In an environment where brashness and loudness are equated with manhood, muteness renders one less a man. Ignored. Jeered at. Cut off. Rupert combed the beaches and plunged into the sea. He collected and sold shells. Loving their contained roar and laughter, he kept many of the deep pink-flesh shells for himself, taking them to that place that was the only home he knew, where he was always fed but never spoken to.

His parents didn't want to walk through the bushes any more, suffering scratches, to see where the river jumped into the sea. No matter how many times he tried, Rupert couldn't find the path on his own, not the way they had gone long ago that Sunday. He found several other outlets where the river dropped, opened, meandered, or floated into the sea. But it wasn't like the place where they took him when he was ten, and they all three joined hands and danced around in a circle where blue and green water melted together.

During his teenage years, Rupert craved companionship. His parents informed him that Charley was his cousin. Rupert saw him occasionally, around town, liming, whistling at women in the streets, calling to them: 'Ssst! Ssst! Pretty girl. Stop a while nuh. What's you haste?' Charley with the other would-be men leaning on buildings, massaging their groins, having fun with strangers, each other.

One day Charley went in search of Rupert and found him at the beach, streaked white with sand, his eyes red from diving too long. 'Dem signing up man to go Florida pick orange. Money to be made. Let's mek a move,' Charley said, offering Rupert his hand.

Feigned indifference. Tempting. To be one of the gang. To do something, anything different.

'Ah have a chance to go America and pick orange? Wha you tink?'

Rupert waited, uncertain of his parents' response. Initially only silence as they glanced back and forth at each other, then at Rupert.

'Is dat you wan do? You can stay here pick orange.' His father's voice was soft and even.

'Is stay you want me to stay and help you around de place?' Rupert replied, emotion in his voice.

'Ah not saying dat. Just said you can stay here pick orange just as well as in America.'

Silence, except for the sucking in of lips on the pipe and the shifting of cloth to make a stitch.

'Ah have a chance to make some money.'

'Wha you need money fah?' The unexpected sound from his mother, amused by Rupert's suggestion.

'Dese days all young people want is money.' His mother again. Then silence.

The wind rustled the leaves fronting the house. Rupert leaned first on one leg then the other.

Silence.

Breaths raspy and old.

Silence.

'Ah tink ah gwane check eh out. De change will do me good.'

'We gwane be here.'

'No place else we want to go.'

Rupert, Charley and about thirty other young men left on a Thursday morning. When they arrived in Florida, it was colder than Rupert had ever imagined; he watched, fascinated, as smoke emerged from his mouth and nostrils. Soon his fingers were numb and tiny bumps of skin covered his arms. The thin short-sleeved shirt he wore offered no protection from the cold.

As it turned out, that was a poor season for oranges in Florida, so Rupert and his gang were bussed to Georgia, then to somewhere else, and somewhere else. Half the time Rupert didn't know where he was headed or what he was supposed to pick when he got there, nor did he care.

Charley got into fights and arguments, and talked about slavery. They were not being paid what they were promised. They were bunked in shacks with gaps in the walls, often without toilets or running water. They were given food the likes of which they had never tasted, cold beans from cans, cold meat that was gelled together, bread soft like a sponge, coffee that tasted and looked like mud, water that tasted like urine. It didn't settle on Rupert, who was beyond feeling; but Charley and a few others raved, and got into the white men's faces. There was shoving and pushing and much 'bumbu-cloth' and 'rass-cloth' shouting that was not understood by the red-faced, hairy men whose skin looked like that of white rats caught in the rain; men whose eyes were empty like marbles and who acted as if they were not men: workers and order-givers, boss-man, buckra. Threats were exchanged back and forth, but they refused to send Charley and the others back to Jamaica, Grenada, Antigua, and St Lucia. Contracts, they said. Contracts.

They were housed in the middle of nowhere. No stores. No houses. Acres and acres of fruits to be picked. Home was never so far.

They planned their escape. Charley and four others got picked up and were finally sent back to Jamaica, branded trouble-makers, not likely ever to return. 'Kiss-me rass!' Charley retorted. 'Is who want return to dis? Me will die a yard. At least me know me can always find a mango fi nyam.' But Rupert decided to take his chance with others who planned to escape their servitude and find other kinds of work in some city.

Rupert's parents were dead and buried five months before he received the news. He never returned home. No need after the ashes have been thrown, the dirt has been packed tight, and the nine-night wake celebrated. No need to publicly acknowledge a loss that happened gradually, over a lifetime. No need. Flip the coin. Go on, continue. He had not given up his wandering. He didn't know he would never find what he was seeking until he knew what it was he wanted. The tears soaked Charley's letter that lay in his lap, and cooled the heat of its finality.

But the nightmares began after he received the news of his parents' death. His screams and thrashing alarmed Angel, who lived just on the other side of the wall. One day, she bravely knocked at his door.

II

Then it happened

to prevent the past from following you
walk sideways
refrain from holding salt in your mouth
and never never laugh out in the dark . . .

Push

Concentrate.

Be in the moment.

She was on all fours, breathing much too fast through her open mouth, the white sheet crumpling under her thrashing, the brown dirt spilling on the sheet. Arnella squinted up at the sky. The sun was vivacious, making stars with the trees, streaking colours and designs. It wasn't going like she had planned. Her mouth was too dry and the contractions were not easing. She crawled around on all fours looking for what she forgot. She cursed herself. She could do this alone, had to, wanted to. Determination.

Gentle. Ease yourself, gently.

She managed a squat position, and felt better, more in control. It wasn't time yet, but it was close to being time. She had to boil the water, and get the other things ready. The air around her was too hot. It hurt! Burned! Maddening! Arnella clutched at the soil and stuffed a handful in her mouth. It tasted chalky, sweet, grainy. Uncomfortable was not the word for the sensation coursing through her body; nor miserable. There was no word, just the feeling, just the sensation.

Breathe.

Squat.

If her hands could reach inside herself she would pull and pull until it was out of her.

What a wretch. She could feel all of her opening at once, all orifices widening to let escape the pain: mouth, vagina, anus. It all came spilling out. She was disgusted and collapsed on all fours, before slumping on to her side, panting.

Breathe.

51

Ring-ring

She-Devil sat by the table, her hand resting on the red cradle of the phone. She was so excited, laughter sputtered from her and she squirmed in the chair like a little girl told to sit out by her mother, forbidden to join the other children at play. She refused to call again. How many times had she called and left messages on Tegreg's answering machine? Be patient. She nibbled on her fingers, smiling at Devil whom she could see was dozing in the hammock under the mango tree.

Even before the phone completed its first ring, She-Devil had it to her ear and was anxiously saying, 'Hello! Tegreg!'

'Mommie! Ah couldn't believe de messages. You all right? Wha goin on?'

'We got a phone. Me so happy.'

'Ah can tell dat. Sounds like a major victory. Ah thought Daddy said a phone would create too much disturbance.'

'Well, dat was you fada talkin. Now dat you all gone about oonuh business ah need to reach oonuh.'

'Mommie you don't have to convince me. As me seh, it sound like a major victory. So how Daddy?'

'He dozing in he hammock.'

'Ah see some things nuh change.'

'Not true. Plenty change. You Daddy moving wid de times.'

'Ah would love to see dat.'

'Den when you and Man-Stick coming fi visit us? Ah miss you, you know.'

'Ah miss you too, Mommie. Ah was saying to Man-Stick just last night dat we due a visit. Ah tink we gwane come weekend. But don't tell Daddy. We wan surprise him.'

'Brimstone might come home too. It would be good to have all a oonuh home one time. Long time dat don't happen. Love you. Call anytime.'

She-Devil reluctantly hung up the phone. Her children were coming to visit. She had much to do. She looked out of the window, noticed that the grass needed cutting, weeds had to be pulled. And Devil was dozing! No time for fun and games any more. Her voice raised up the dirt and the hair on Red-Dog, asleep on the step; he slouched off to a safer and quieter spot under the house. Devil knew that tone in She-Devil's voice and didn't like it at all, at all. Just when he thought condensed milk was flowing like water, ants came beating his trail.

Slowly, Devil opened his eyes, hoping to delay She-Devil's request. He knew from experience that whenever she hollered like that, it meant she had a long list of things for him to do and she expected them to be done right away. Devil wasn't up to any more fighting, but he sure didn't feel like doing anything, except pulling She-Devil in the hammock with him so they could hug up real tight and snooze together. It was worth a try.

She-Devil was full of smiles like a satisfied woman. She couldn't remember the last time she felt so complete, so full, so loved. Devil was quite a man, but she didn't want their children visiting and the place looking run-down. Standing looking down at Devil, she could see from the fluttering of his lids that he wasn't asleep. He had heard her, but was faking sleep, hoping as usual to postpone or delay the inevitable work. She would have to try another tactic. Tenderly, she touched Devil on his cheeks, caressing his face; her lips were being drawn to his mouth where she planted a cooling kiss.

In that instant, Devil grabbed at She-Devil and yanked her into the hammock.

'Man, you crazy or what? You could hurt you back and mine.'

'Hush-up oman and gi you man a kiss.' Devil pressed his mouth on She-Devil's. Momentarily swept away, she found the comfort of his arms.

Cheek, their feisty parrot, interrupted them. 'Have you folks lost you minds? It's the middle of the day. Restrain yourself. People are probably watching you.'

Devil sighed and cursed himself for teaching the parrot to talk. He had never in all his many lives met anyone more proper and prudish than Cheek. He needed a name change. She-Devil laughed in the comfort of Devil's chest, but adjusted her dress. She really didn't feel like working even though the house required a good cleaning. Devil was so happy these last few days she didn't feel like nagging him about weeds and grass and sweeping. She-Devil was in love again, a dangerous but delightful state for a woman, especially a woman her age, menopausal and all. A languid sigh escaped her.

Demure. Coy. Seductive. These were the tools of a young woman too innocent to know their explosive power. But in a mature woman who has lived, these qualities were in the eyes she presented to the world, the words she didn't need to speak, the demands that she could get fulfilled before she made them. She-Devil took her art, her gifts, and made her womanliness the absolute desire of all times. Devil was eating and eating. She-Devil was smiling and smiling. They were enjoying the game, each other; they were discovering new secrets, old joys, never-before imagined pleasures and possibilities. The world was whatever they made it, and they were making it, to the disgust of Cheek, who flew off to a more secluded spot, where he could neither see nor hear them.

Listen

They slept on sheets rinsed in rose water and lemon. Angel awoke feeling clean and refreshed. All the fears of last night seemed distant. Although the windows with their wooden slats were shut, she could see the sun fighting its way through. Rupert was still snoring. She turned on her side and raised herself on her elbows to get a better look at him. He seemed boyish and vulnerable. That was what had first attracted her to him – that and his colour, the absolutely evenness of purple-black. She had never seen anyone that colour before, except in books on African culture. After glancing at the European photographer whose picture was in the back of the book, Angel remembered thinking the photographer had purposely selected out the light to emphasise the darkness. But sometime later, after Angel met and fell in love with Rupert, she had gone searching for that book and had never found it.

Rupert's colour was Africa, the same smooth, even, deep purple blackness. Naive of her to think, initially, that light could be removed from such deep sheen.

Angel placed her hand alongside Rupert's curved arm and examined their contrasting colours. People said she was yellow, but she hadn't seen a yellow that approximated her skin hue, definitely not yellow like lemon or buttercups. She racked her brain trying to think of a natural colour to attach to herself. Not maple or walnut; maybe pine, but pine was too white. What was her colour? Palomino? No. Did it matter?

Coming fully awake, Rupert smiled, and pulled Angel to him. 'Ah thought ah was dreaming. Ah was hoping you did come after all.'

'Silly,' Angel said, kissing him on the mouth even though she knew he didn't like kissing before brushing his teeth. 'Is nastiness dat!' he had once said. But Rupert didn't pull away. Whatever fears each of them might have for their future were set aside. Right then, at that moment, that beat in space and time, they were happy, in love, hopeful.

In-between

Remarkable beauty, truly, can only be detected when Monica is asleep.

Coming home to Kristoff Village meant not having to close and bolt one's windows and doors, meant not having to have ugly burglar bars to prevent one from sticking one's head out the window to see how the day was shaping up, shouting at a friend passing by, or calling out to tell the fish-man to wait a moment so you can come and see what kind of fish he has.

At nights, Monica closed the windows against the mosquitoes; but just like when she was growing up, the door was never locked. She refused to entertain the idea that someone from the village would break into another's house. Not that people didn't steal a chicken, a few eggs, a yam or a basin of sorrel; but no one would come into someone else's house and take something without asking. Unless of course no one was home and the need was urgent. But the borrower would always stop by and say, 'Sista Monica, yesterday ah took a pinch a salt, or ah cut a little piece of you corn-beef, or ah had company from town so ah borrow two of you nice tall glasses and you lemonade jar.' Then she would return the borrowed item and with much gratitude say, 'Tank you fah de loan. May blessings come to you.' Then bidding her a good day, the borrower would go about her business.

Monica was happy. Contented. Daily she complimented herself for saving her life from the ravages of the city and returning to her birthplace. She smiled in her sleep, thinking of the new life she was beginning.

Desmond set the cup of mint tea on the dresser and stood by the bed smiling down on Monica. She was handsome, he thought. Some women were pretty; but nothing could compare to a handsome woman. He drank in her smooth, even-toned skin, high cheekbones, her full inviting lips, the top lip fuller than the bottom, both stained deep brown, almost black, her nose that arched up then spread out around the base. Her neck long, but fleshy, and her hair, now that she no longer pressed it, thick and full, spread like soft grass around her face, the braids unwinding. Desmond loved the feel of untamed hair that resisted his fingers, had life and texture and strength. He placed his hand now on her head, and his fingers navigated for a place to caress her scalp. Monica turned towards him, still not awake. She's trusting for someone who has lived through so much, he thought, licking his lips. He wanted Monica; not just as a lover, someone he came to a few mornings of the week, but for his woman. It didn't matter that she was older, that she used to be a whore, even the rumours that his two best friends, Trevor Campbell and Ainsworth McKenzie, had slept with her. He wanted her, but he couldn't live with her.

Desmond was a married man, and Grace, his wife, did not deserve to be abandoned. She was a good enough mother, and although rather too quick to reach for and use the belt, made sure their three children were clean and well fed and saw to it that they did their schoolwork. She was a good woman who always considered his needs. She had a small mind though, and so feared to venture much beyond the boundaries of her yard. She found nothing more satisfying than to gossip across the fence with her friends, Peggy Campbell and Marva McKenzie, and to carry other people's business around like it was some child left in her charge. But, Desmond reflected, people didn't get divorced in Kristoff Village. One married for life. The man might stray, take up with someone else; but that was no excuse to abandon his wife and children. Desmond was responsible. His children wouldn't respect him if he were to leave their mother and take up with another woman. People would talk and he wouldn't be able to walk with his head high. He could bear the thought of people whispering behind his back that he was sleeping with Monica. Fact. Desmond was doing more than sleeping with Monica. What was he doing? Making her tea three times a week, getting to work late and buying three new light-blue shirts in less than two months. He did not understand yet that he was living the dream buried deep in his mind.

She was waking.

She turned and reached for the sheet that was crumpled at her feet. His hands moved and caressed her thighs, full and hot, before pulling the sheet to her waist.

'Ah know ah smell something good.'

'Den you mus smell youself.' They laughed into each other's eyes.

She leaned forward. Desmond pulled the pillows behind her, then went for the tea and handed it to her. While watching her sip it, he wanted to ask her if Samuel Lawrence was coming this weekend. More than the idea of her sleeping with Trevor and Ainsworth, Desmond was preoccupied with Samuel Lawrence. He had been going to bed with this man on his mind, pondering the exact nature of his and Monica's relationship. Monica was closed on the subject. Desmond wasn't sure how to broach it. But he wanted to know. He had to know, something. Monica and Samuel had a history. Samuel had rebuilt and furnished her house, yet he didn't live with her. Desmond surmised that he was probably married, but still committed to Monica. He understood that perfectly, for Monica was a woman to whom a man would naturally want to tie himself.

Jealousy was not a word Desmond knew. It was a new feeling for him. Caught him unprepared. The word was a mouthful and the sensation was like over-eating.

Rout out the opponent, his instinct advised him.

Clear the way for yourself.

Desmond sensed that Monica would not stand for him, or anyone, making decisions for her. Yet he was determined that Monica should desire him alone.

Everything about Monica was sensual, like heat rising from the ground.

Desmond was late for work, again, but still he couldn't stir. He wondered if the green Toyota, Samuel's car, would be parked in front of Monica's gate when he returned from work.

When she had finished her tea, Monica turned to Desmond and said, 'You might as well go. Waitin won't change anything.' She didn't need to say any more.

The heart was sponge, but it could also be stone.

Desmond walked to the gate and revved his motorbike.

Starting the very night after her return to the village, Monica would take a stroll around eight o'clock and end up on the little veranda in front of Miss Cotton's shop. She and Miss Cotton would sit quietly in each other's company for two or three hours, exchanging hardly a word. An occasional customer would interrupt their solitude with a, 'Night Miss Cotton, Miss Monica', and a request. But after serving the customer, Miss Cotton would return to sit with Monica until she was ready to close up shop or until Monica was sleepy and returned to her own home.

Sometimes Monica and Miss Cotton spoke. It wasn't a conversation others could follow.

'Dere was dis man ah used to sleep wid.'

Silence.

'All a we do tings widout thinking.'

A sigh, a pause. Buzzing mosquitoes.

'Every time ah look at meself in the mirror, ah see dis shadow.'

'Ah can't tell you how many evenings ah stand at dat corner watching people's feet.'

They smiled. Laughed. Nodded their heads. Sometimes reached out and held each other's hand. Often, Miss Cotton sang or hummed as if rocking a baby to sleep. Sometimes people said they came upon Monica and Miss Cotton and they couldn't tell who was whom. Sometimes it seemed Monica grew Miss Cotton's face and other times Miss Cotton hers. A few people claimed that they heard voices and saw the chairs rocking, but could see neither Monica or Miss Cotton until they called out, and Miss Cotton and Monica appeared, from thin air, rocking on the chairs.

Peggy, Grace and Marva were bosom friends, just like their husbands, Trevor, Desmond and Ainsworth.

Marva wouldn't know what happiness was even if someone was to shove it under her nose.

Grace cautioned her children, 'Walk-about gwane get you in trouble!', but they knew from the contention that always came charging loudly to their gate that one didn't have to walk about to get in trouble. For their mother sure had a knack for attracting confusion.

Peggy was tight and mean-spirited. Grudged bread out of a baby's mouth. Everyone always had more than she, and to hear her talk they didn't work for or deserve it. She was a hard worker who prided herself on having one of the nicest houses in Kristoff Village. Her family wasn't from the district, but they had land and a store in Montego Bay where she used to work, before Trevor won her heart. Folks said it was her father's money that built the four-bedroom, two-bath brick house in which she lived. Hers was the first complete brick house built in the village. Rumour also had it that she bought her furniture in Kingston. My dear. Custom made, if you please. And although Peggy rarely went out, she was always dressed, right arm covered in gold bracelets, left in silver, and her earlobes hanging low under the weight of twenty-two-carat gold loops. If you please. She 'got mouth', and people who wanted to avoid her wrath would often cross the road rather than walk in front of her yard, perched on a little hill so she could sit on her veranda, pretending to do her business, but straining her neck to mark people passing by.

Next to the preacher and the schoolmaster and Miss and Mr Cotton, Peggy and Trevor were the most prosperous people in the district. Trevor even had a car and was co-owner, with Peggy's father, of the bus that ran through the village. Peggy and Trevor Campbell were what you would call 'big people' in Kristoff Village.

Marva was big like a house. Don't know what she was trying to prove. Five tough step-stairs boys, and she was at it again. Busting at the seams and laughing: 'Me can't afford to stop till me get de girl.' She was 'country', with little formal education. She didn't complete third class, but often attempted to copy Peggy's standard speech. Except, as with most things, Marva didn't have the flair or knack that it took to pass off imitating. Behind her back people laughed at what they termed her 'speaky-spokey' voice: the way she transposed vowels and consonants, sounding ludicrous. 'Ave you hany hoatmeal, lend me some?' she might wheedle; or declare complainingly, 'Yesedeh me ead hache me so badly wata come ah me heye.' However, out of shame and embarrassment for her, people refrained from laughing right in her face. Some covered their mouths, or sucked in the laughter until they turned a corner or reached their homes where they could let it all out, throwing their heads back, leaning against a wall, pressing their thighs together to keep from urinating on themselves.

No one was able to discern why Marva was so unhappy. Maybe because her family was so poor. But whose family wasn't poor? Marva was stamped by poverty. Her hair a dull red. That dirty red from lack of protein. Her parents had fifteen of them, she was the twelfth. Food was scarce. Patience was nonexistent. Love was all used up. But laughter still found its way through a crack in the wall. There was a residue of it, the scraping on an empty pot. Marva now had much to be happy about. She was married to Ainsworth McKenzie, probably the only one in the village who went beyond high school. He went to the UWI in Kingston – University of the West Indies, if you please – and studied accounting. He had a degree, wore a white shirt and tie and worked in an air-conditioned office in Montego Bay.

Truth was, it was Kristoff Village that vexed Marva. She wanted to live in Montego Bay and go to movie shows every Friday evening. But Ainsworth was a man of simple desires. Always was as a boy. He had no intention of leaving his people's land. Besides, as a man who dealt with numbers, he knew he could not build a fine house in Montego Bay like the one he had in Kristoff Village. He certainly couldn't support five growing sons in that town either. Not to mention the corruption. The temptations. The hassle and hustle. The pace.

Marva, for all her dirty red hair, used to be a striking woman; but with five boys, and a sixth child on the way, she now looked like a bullfrog about to burst into flames. Her skin was all blotchy and discoloured, her nose swollen to twice its normal size. In fact you could barely see the face for the nose. Varicose veins had ruined whatever attractiveness men once admired in her calves and legs.

Even with five boys and a big house Marva still found time to run back and forth to gossip with Grace. She seemed a permanent fixture at Grace's gate. Throughout various times of the day they could be seen, their heads turned this way and that, chewing on someone's business. Ainsworth's parents, who lived in a small cottage behind Marva and Ainsworth's house, often saved Marva's dinner from turning to char.

Grace was afraid of lizards, afraid of rolling-calf, afraid of not being liked, afraid that some woman was about to steal her husband, afraid of ageing. In general she was afraid of most things. Her mother had tried to help her to overcome her fears. One night, when Grace was a girl of about nine, her mother locked her outside and told her that a rolling-calf was probably roaming about since it was full moon and that the croaking lizards were also watching her, so she should act bold to scare them away. Grace screamed and clutched at her mother's clothes; but her mother closed the door on her. Fifteen minutes later, when her screams could no longer be heard, Grace's mother opened the door. She nearly bit her tongue off when she saw the child lying curled up on the ground, foaming at the mouth. Grace was never locked outside again, but her fears increased, often sending her off for days, immobilised and foaming.

Grace didn't like being a mother herself. She found the task too burdensome, and her most pleasurable days were every fortnight when she took the bus alone to Savanalamar to visit her parents. Her own mother had never forgiven herself for locking her outside that night, and so still petted her and fixed her favourite foods; and Grace could feel like the fearful little girl who always sat by her mother's feet or rested gently against her arms. She waited until she visited her mother to have her thick, long hair washed and combed. Grace's mother was gentle when combing her hair, and would use the teeth of the comb to massage her scalp, parting her hair in rows and rubbing warm cocoa-butter into the skin. The sensation Grace felt was as if her scalp was opening up and drinking in the grease. It was the most wonderful feeling. Her mother had soothing hands. Then her mother plaited her hair into eight even braids.

61

Grace didn't want always to be afraid, but she couldn't always be with her mother so she had to live as best as she could with her handicap.

Grace had been with her mother the Friday when Monica moved back to Kristoff Village, but felt like she had been present on that occasion from the detailed description she got from Marva and Peggy.

Peggy was on her veranda, grating coconut because her silly cousin whom she had working for her always scraped her knuckles on the grater and she didn't want blood mixed in with the coconut milk. The bus stopped just below her gate and it was her favourite pastime to see who got off and what they brought with them, then to sing out her hello, flaring her nose or opening up her eyes if they tried to walk past without saying howdy.

Everyone in the entire village knew Monica was going to be moving back there, and they had been waiting for her return. The people weren't anxious, just curious. What other distractions were there? Peggy, however, was anxious, and even before Monica showed up she reminded people that this was a woman who hadn't even come to her father's funeral five years ago.

Shame.

Worthless.

But then again, country people's forgiveness was as abundant as the mosquitoes at night.

Rumour also had it that Monica was a big-time whore. Said she even slept with some men in the government, big-big, official men, ministers! But men, even important ones, are dogs; so that didn't signal anything.

Peggy was determined to know the moment when Monica arrived, and she did. Everyone was off the bus so Peggy was wondering why it was just idling there. Then she saw Monica. The bowl, grater and coconut flew out of her lap, and she didn't even stop to pick them up. Captivated, mouth open, she sidled all the way to the second step leading to her veranda to get a better look at Monica. She reached for her glasses; they weren't in the apron pocket where she usually kept them. She hollered to her cousin to bring her glasses so she could see better, record all the details, but the teenage girl claimed she could not find them. Even without her glasses, Peggy could see that Monica looked good. She touched her own body after Monica had walked off in the direction of Miss Cotton's shop, then she went into her bedroom, found the glasses at last on her dresser, put them on and looked at herself in the full-length mirror on the closet door. Monica was at least ten years Peggy's senior, if not more, but she looked good.

Speak the truth and shame the devil.

Peggy was deeply disturbed. She had two boys, and had been thinking about a third child lately. Monica didn't have any children. Her body hadn't gone through any wear and tear. She was barren. All she did was fuck men, other women's men. Bitch. Whore. Curse her womb and her pussy. Peggy spoke aloud in the empty room.

Peggy, who almost never went to Miss Cotton's shop, flung off her apron and walked to Miss Cotton so she could get a better view. She was certain a close-up view would reveal all the flaws. But close proximity can also highlight perfection. Peggy was speechless. Before her stood a woman with a smooth face, bright eyes and a compact figure. Such betrayal.

She had a bone to pick, but she would wait her time.

Is just suh

'How you mean nuh man nuh involve?'

'Is fool and stupid and just born you think we is?'

'So me neva know you did name Mary?'

'But even Mary did have sense find Joseph.'

'Oonuh see me war and tribulation! Oonuh see how worries come sit-down, buff, pan me head!'

Velma offered no explanation; would not announce the name of the man responsible for her condition and was not ashamed or contrite about her state. Nothing her mother and aunt said, no matter that they raised their voices, calling on the entire village to witness their tribulation; no matter that they placed their hands on their heads and bawled out loud; no matter that they threatened to throw her out like 'stale piss', send her to Bellevue in Kingston because she was obviously crazy; no matter their forceful act of taking her to an obeah woman to see who 'bad-mind' her, Velma was quietly insistent that no man was involved.

School never interested her. Very little did. She would gaze outside, at nothing. Poetry did not inspire her like the sounds and colours in the landscape. The little quibbles and fights among her peers aroused no curiosity or animation. She was in general indifferent. But like most of the children, Velma went to school to the sixth class. She could read and write her name, and read the headlines in the paper. But she had no interest. She did like butterflies and often caught them and placed them on her shoulders and her head. She liked needlework, taking coloured threads and making delicate flower designs on square pieces of cloth no larger than a handkerchief. Velma decorated all her mother's towels and even a few covers for small square cushions. She didn't talk much, only smiled or nodded her head. It wasn't that she was uncomfortable around people, she just preferred to be in her own company. She ate little, was tall and thin, but big-hipped. Her skin was like boiling molasses that glowed in the dark; her hair like heavy rope was always braided in two thick plaits that divided her head and her face. She appeared to have two separate faces that looked at each other. She was beautiful, but not desirable. She was like the wind, everywhere but invisible.

Velma tended the lime tree. She watered it daily, collected rocks and encircled it and planted Joseph-Coat plants all around the circumference. No one was allowed to pick limes from the tree without her permission, and she would throw a stone or stick after the dogs who went to relieve themselves by her tree. For five years Velma tended the lime tree, and made delicate designs on square calico cloth that she gave to her mother's visitors.

Then at fifteen she announced she was going to Montego Bay to get a job. She left one morning, early, walking six miles to the nearest bus stop, and returned that night with a bag full of biscuits. Payment for a day's work at the biscuit factory. She would receive a small brown envelope on Friday, which she brought, unopened, and placed in her mother's hand. Velma never went inside a bank. For as long as she worked and her mother and aunt were well she would give them her envelope every Friday, and they gave her money for bus fare, lunch. When eventually her mother became too old, she turned over her little brown envelope to Olive, her older daughter, who went to the bank and gave her money for bus fare and lunch. Velma never went to the bank, and she never opened her little brown envelopes herself, not once, not ever.

Velma liked walking, early in the morning before the sun was hot, or late in the evening when the sun was asleep and the heat had cooled from the ground. She couldn't remember if the first time she saw him was in the morning or in the evening, but she saw him many times and always he asked her the same thing.

'Gi me some of what you have in you bag!' It was not a command or a plea, just a fact, stated. He would be sitting on the bare ground, shirtless, his pants leg rolled up, sharpening his cutlass. He was the son of the overseer, a brown buckra man who 'gwane like him white', and who managed the sugar estate just outside Rosehall which was owned by some English people. His mother was the coolie woman who lived with and worked for the overseer. People claimed the overseer – brown buckra man – had the coolie woman and all her people slaving on the English people's sugar estate. Just like slavery times. All the East Indian workers lived in the rows of barracks at the back of the house, without a kitchen. The women were forced to cook on little coal stoves in the open, and when rain fell they had to pull those coal stoves into their little rooms on a piece of cardboard or an old crate box and blow the coal to fire, praying the wind and rain hadn't drowned the blaze. All those coolie people's backs were bent, and they were 'maga', their ribs showing right through their scant clothes. They still lived in the barracks with no electricity. The brown buckra man did install a makeshift shower with two stalls, but they still had to ease themselves in a stinking pit toilet. The children didn't though. They did just as the dogs, dug a hole or went behind some bush. Every ten years the barracks were painted a shade of green that blended into the cane fields.

This shirtless man, with rolled up pants and a cutlass, was the son of that brown buckra man and the coolie woman who took care of him. He lied to Velma that he himself was the overseer.

Velma saw him all the time. Sometimes when she had to work late he would ask her, 'You nuh fraid duppy tek you weh?' and she would smile, reach into the bag and give him two biscuits and continue to walk her way. She didn't have any time to bother with him, this brown-coolie man who did nothing but sit by the side of the road, sharpening his cutlass.

For two years, six days a week Velma walked a total of twelve miles, six miles to and six miles from work at the biscuit factory. She was five months pregnant when she told her mother. They couldn't find the father. No matter where they looked or who they asked. No one saw her with anyone. No man could be found to receive the blame. Velma smiled, and at seventeen had her first daughter, whom she called Olive, getting the name from a tin can in the biscuit factory where she worked. She worked up until a week before she had the baby, still walking the twelve miles daily. She still saw the brown-coolie man, and he still begged her for something from her bag.

She didn't work for almost two years after Olive was born. The baby took up all her time. She didn't mind, but she missed the walks, and sometimes would just walk the twelve miles with the baby hitched on her side. She always saw the brown-coolie man, especially in the evening, and he would have something for the baby, a blackie mango, a piece of cane to soothe her gum, a sweet-sop, a jackfruit, guinep, even potato pudding which he said his coolie mother made.

When Olive turned two, Velma went back to the biscuit factory. The man who used to be manager was no longer there. The new man said he had no work for her, but she went inside and began to work anyway, and that Friday she got a brown envelope which she took home to her mother. Her mother took care of Olive, and Velma went back to walking, tending to her lime tree, and making embroidered designs on square calico that she now sold to people. The brown-coolie man still sat by the road, sharpening his cutlass, took many of Velma's cloths for his mother, and often gave her fruits or pudding or some other sweet cake for her daughter; but she still didn't have any time for him, and never tarried or engaged in any lengthy conversation with him. He still wondered why she wasn't afraid of duppies, and still begged her for something from her bag, which she always gave him.

When Olive was twenty-three, having successfully completed a course in cooking at the hotel where she had been working since she was seventeen, she was surprised to learn that both she and her mother, Velma, were going to be mothers. Velma was forty when Arnella was born. She still lived with her mother, aunt and father. Miss Cotton delivered Arnella almost an hour before delivering Olive's daughter, Valrie. Arnella was a stubborn birth, even though she was the second and should have been easier. Velma was drenched in sweat by the time she pushed Arnella out. She bled more than was natural, Miss Cotton said. She was laid up in bed for almost two months and was unable to nurse Arnella; so Olive nursed her along with her own child, Valrie. That's why Arnella and Valrie were so close. But Arnella was a pretty baby, with a head full of curly black hair and eyes so navy-blue, they pulled you like a deep well with its cooling cry. The moment Velma looked at her second child, she knew she would love her too much, and they would disagree.

At the double christening, when the pastor asked for Arnella's name, Velma's mother said, 'Is god own dis one too', and everyone laughed, knowing of Velma's immaculate conception. Now Velma tended three lime trees, having buried the navel cords of both her daughters under lime trees. Velma gave limeade to everyone who visited her, and often she presented limes to the children of the village, who used them as balls.

By the time Arnella was born, and even many years before, a bus had started regularly running to the junction of Kristoff Village, so Velma only had to walk two-and-a-half miles. But sometimes she still walked the twelve miles and she still saw the brown-coolie man sharpening his cutlass. The sugar estate was closed down, but the brown man and his coolie wife still lived there. The barracks were burned down and the estate was now painted blue and yellow. The brown-coolie man still gave Velma fruits and still begged her for something from her bag. She smiled at him and went her way.

Nah-grudge

Was there a time they didn't play together, weren't each other's very best friends? Until now.

They were almost twelve when they discovered they weren't sisters. Twins everyone called them. They had the same birthday and shared the same parents, at least so they assumed. Then one day Sister Olive and Uncle Milford, her husband and head chef at the hotel where they both worked, were quarrelling. Arnella and Valrie heard Uncle Milford shout, 'Ah tired a you damn blasted family. No one know who is who. Is only two picknie me have, so me nuh know why three a call me daddy and me hafi mind three.' Arnella and Valrie was playing hopscotch in the yard and thought Uncle Milford were referring to Milton, their little brother. Certainly he didn't mean them.

But now, however, Sister Olive told Arnella that Aunt Velma was really her mother, and it was time she slept at Velma's house. Sister Olive herself was really Arnella's sister, not her mother. Arnella couldn't believe that Aunt Velma was her mother. She didn't remember ever sleeping in Aunt Velma's bed like she slept in Sister Olive's, she and Valrie squeezed in between Sister Olive and Uncle Milford. Aunt Velma was her grandmother like Valrie's, so she had always been led to believe. The new information was like a flogging and the two girls sat for a long, long time under a tree and wept and hugged each other and wept some more.

Later that day Sister Olive explained that because Arnella was born on the same day as Valrie, who was indeed her daughter, she had mothered them as if they were twins. Arnella was confused. Valrie was confused. Everyone was confused. But Arnella went along with Sister Olive, trying to figure out the beginning of it. It was all too entangled.

The new arrangement lasted less than a week; then Arnella and Valrie were back in the same bed, in the same house, calling Olive 'Sister Olive' and believing her to be their real mother, and Aunt Velma their grandmother.

From the beginning they were inseparable in play and mischief and were often flogged and sent to bed together. In a way they looked exactly like each other, and yet they did not. Whereas Arnella was deep stained mahogany, Valrie was golden cane juice; but their faces were shaped the same: a perfect oval with fine-tipped noses, full pouting mouths, their bottoms lips deep purple, the colour of star-apples. They were long-legged and hippy and their arms swung and danced and seemed wings. They were beautiful and knew it because wherever they went people would say, 'Lawd what pretty picknie! De pretty more dan de sun and de moon combine. Dem gwane bruk man's heart!' They were always given sweeties, peanuts, pinched cheeks, any little gift, acknowledgement that they created pleasure in people. But whereas Arnella's eyes were deep navy pools, Valrie's were fiery-brown that shot sparks. Together they would drain people, Arnella pulling them into a cool place with her eyes, and Valrie jarring them with sparks of light.

They went to school together. In third class they were separated for a time but created such a sensation that the headmistress was forced to put them back together. They never competed or tried to out-do each other. Always they shared, loving each other's company best. Discovering hidden places. Playing tricks on people. Laughing.

Arnella introduced Valrie to the river, and Valrie showed Arnella how to grow things. They taught each other and had fun playing pranks on Sister Olive and Aunt Velma. They were not naughty girls, nor particularly disobedient, but they were wilful.

At twelve, one day apart, they both started to menstruate, and began what would come to be known as their separating stage. Velma swore that on that day when Arnella and Valrie came to her, their eyes full of tears and fear that they were bleeding to death, their panties soaked in blood, she saw a thin layer of skin that had been connecting them dissolve.

Arnella found out that she and Olive had no father, never had. Immaculate conception, people laughed. Sister Olive, who was twenty odd years older than she, was her sister? Aunt Velma, an old woman, who told stories that sometimes made them so scared they had to sleep in Sister Olive's bed, her mother? No father?

Arnella waded in the river, waded in the river until her body was shrivelled and Valrie had to go and beg Sister Olive to come and pull her out. They hugged each other and cried, not knowing when they stopped or fell asleep, their arms still around each other, their bodies heaving. Not sisters. They would never recover from that knowledge.

They were everything together, for each other, and insisted on sharing everything, including Godfree.

'Which one a oonuh wan me fi chase you?'

'You have fi chase both a we,' they said, giggling and taking off in the direction of the mountain range.

They kissed his cheeks. They pulled down his pants and laughed at his tea-pot. They teased him. They played with him, they fell in love and slept with him, together, under the ackee tree, and they were going to remain that way forever, together. But then Aunt Velma got sick and Arnella had to move in with her, and she and Valrie didn't get to whisper their love to each other every night any more, and they soon forgot the language they had always spoken, together, just for each other.

All we have is us

'You tired. Try fi lay down a while.'

Olive helped her into the bed, opened the windows wide and pushed back the curtain so the evening breeze could sweep the room. Shortly she returned with a damp cloth and a plate of food in her hands. Placing the food by the side of the bed, she mopped Arnella's brow and blew cool breaths over her face. Then she pressed her ears to Arnella's stomach, listening for the child. Hearing the child playing, satisfied, she turned to the food.

'Don't bother give me nuh argument. Aunt Velma cook this fah you: nice, soft St Vincent yam and susumba in coconut milk. Her legs bothering her still, but she seh ah mus mek sure you eat it.' Olive mashed the yam, mixed in some susumba then raised the fork to Arnella's mouth. Arnella chewed and laughed between contractions. Olive blew cool breaths in her face and fed her.

Sister and daughter. That's what Arnella was to Olive, from the beginning. She didn't love her any less than Valrie. In fact, she never thought of them separately. Hurt for them in the same place, right under her bosom. They were almost the same person. 'Nuh care! Dat's dem! Dem head full a fancy and tales.'

Olive sat there on the side of the bed, watching night come on and glancing at Arnella dozing. It wasn't going to be much longer, she was certain. She wondered if Milford was home, and whether he had eaten the dinner that she left covered on the stove. Something was wrong with him; his stomach wasn't working right. She loved him. He was the only man who every time he touched her she left her body, even now, all these thirty years they'd been together. But she didn't want to think about Milford now.

Interference worse than tooth-ache

'You should a did leave dem alone. Is dem alone have fi deal wid each other. Who you fi tell dem how to live dem life?'

It still angered Olive, hearing Aunt Velma accuse her of meddling. But what was she to do? Milford had been at her for almost two years how it wasn't right. How it was nastiness. How she should talk to her sister and her daughter and put an end to it. What did they expect from her? Truth was she didn't care. Arnella and Valrie could talk with whomever they wanted, and if they wanted to be with same man, so what? They wouldn't be the first or last. But Milford said it was just another example of her mixed-up family, and he wasn't going to put up with the slackness any longer. If she didn't put an end to it, he was going to leave. Leave! How he mean leave? Go where? What was she supposed to do if he left? That's when she decided that Arnella was going to be apprenticed with her dressmaker. Valrie cried and said right to Olive's face that she was wicked and evil and 'bad-eye'. Arnella sucked her teeth, and looked at Olive with those eyes of hers so steady and long, the older sister felt faint. Aunt Velma didn't eat for a week, and got so sick Olive had to take time off work and nurse her for a month. But Milford was happy. Said it was the first time she did something because it should be done, whether her family liked it or not, and that it was for their good.

Godfree said he loved both Valrie and Arnella and it wasn't fair that he had to choose between them. Besides, they all got along. His grandmother told him to leave both of them alone and find another girl, unrelated to them. They were almost sixteen then, and in truth Olive's first concern was that Godfree might ruin them, impregnating them at such a young age. She had seen how both Arnella and Valrie pursued him, swinging their hips whenever he came around with the other boys. 'Lawd! Gal picknie hard fi raise,

71

sah!' So Olive forbade them to see Godfree and made separate plans for Valrie and Arnella.

For six months clouds hung over Kristoff Village and people drooped and got on each other's nerves from the absence of the sun.

It was still a difficult time for Devil and She-Devil, who were mostly at odds with each other.

Arnella and Valrie, although they saw each other daily, exchanged not a word and walked around like wilted flowers. There was no sun. Nothing that could heat one's body; nothing that would dry one's clothes, hung on the line; nothing that caused one to sweat walking the two-and-a-half miles to the junction. Nothing. Obviously, Sun was mad, vexed, and so took himself from the people of Kristoff Village. All because of Olive. How can one separate one's nose from one's face?

Everyone blamed Olive. She should have left well enough alone. She had no business interfering in the twins' business. Every dog has to make his own way. She heard it from every side, and grieved the loss of not only one daughter, but both. Valrie hardly spoke to her, never complained, never requested limeade three times daily any more, and did what Olive asked her like an obedient child, which she never had been. Arnella was even more difficult. Although she no longer lived in Olive's house she seemed always underfoot. Too many times to count, Olive tripped over her sitting in the doorway or on the step. She said nothing, but smiled, her navy-blue eyes pulling Olive into a dark wet pool that made the older sister cough and feel faint. Then Arnella decided, without consulting with anyone, to drop out of school. Valrie followed suit the very next day. No matter that Milford threatened both of them, even taking off his belt as if to flog them, they refused to budge. Olive was heartbroken. Valrie and Arnella were bright, and she and Milford had been saving every penny they could with the hope of sending Valrie to the university to become a nurse, or to get a degree like Ainsworth. Now she sat at home, mostly by her grandmother's lime trees, listening to Aunt Velma tell her stories.

Love no easy

The day turned evening. Sweat ran down Valrie's back and chest; she considered everything her grandmother had told her. They would not be separated without a fight. All their lives they had ganged up against enemies at school, people in authority and even members of the family to be together. Valrie determined to switch places with Arnella.

Milford said Arnella had to return to Velma's house and Valrie was to come home. Arnella looked at him with her navy-blue eyes, smiling, confusing his thoughts. He found that whatever he began to say didn't make sense so he kept starting over like someone who stuttered. He shouted for Olive. Olive was on the veranda, rocking. She had had enough of Arnella and Valrie and was not prepared to get involved any further. What's the use? She couldn't get them to do anything they themselves hadn't decided on. So Olive pretended not to hear Milford. He stormed on to the veranda, but when he turned to her, saw her arms folded resolutely in her lap, her eyes focused way out yonder, beyond the mountain range and the approaching night, he stormed back inside.

'You finish you dinner, Daddy?' came Arnella's voice, startling him. He was mad, but he couldn't help but smile. Every evening, if he came home after they ate, Arnella and Valrie would be waiting for him. When he sat down to eat, they sat with him, and always just before he was finished with his plate they would ask together, 'You finish wid you dinner, Daddy?' indicating that they wanted the rest of what was on his plate. They said his dinner was always sweeter. Now here was this daughter, who was not really his daughter, while his real daughter was not in his house where she should be, begging for food, like she was still a little girl. Long-legged with breasts and hips. His hand went to his balding head, and he wiped at invisible sweat. He looked at the ceiling, then at his feet, then at Arnella.

'Don't ah tell you ah not you daddy?'

'Yes, Daddy.'

'Den mek you keep calling me Daddy, mek?'

She smiled at him. What was he to do? All he had done was fall in love with Olive when she was seventeen. He never wanted to come

73

and live in this damn blasted village at the back of hell. He never wanted to mix-up, mix-up with all this family.

'Is me one me parents have,' Milford shouted out the window, gulping at the air. He was an only child of parents with a neat little house just outside Montego Bay that was fenced off and private, allowing no view from the street, secluded by trees. People didn't just come into their house anytime night or day without knocking. He found Olive, her family and most of the people in Kristoff Village too familiar. Imagine a man in his bed, sleep still in his eyes, and someone come in without knocking, sit down on the side of the bed by his wife and start talking to her, and the sun not even out yet. Imagine a man in his bathroom that he built, easing himself, reading the newspaper, with the door shut but not locked, and someone who didn't even live in his house come, open the door and start to talk with him like they were on the veranda. Imagine living in a compound with three houses a mouth-shout from each other, where family members, regularly and frequently, night and day, stick their heads through windows and talk to each other about any and everything. No privacy.

'Him peculiar, you see!'

'Wha him have fi hide?'

'Nuh all a we is family!'

They drank his favourite fruit juice, which he had covered up and left in his fridge.

'What harm?'

'You grudge we de little juice?'

'We is family, man.'

'You can drink something else.'

They took the paper he had not finished reading to wrap the intestine and scale of the fish they had just gutted. What were they supposed to do? They saw the paper folded on the veranda chair. 'Is how much reading you want to read so? Didn't you leave it there? You must be done.'

But for the love of Olive, Milford would have gone long time ago. Over the years he had done everything he could to persuade her to move.

'Tink bout de children. Dem can get betta education in MoBay; you want dem to go further dan us, don't you? Tink of de time you will save on travel. The hotel just a hop and a jump if we live in MoBay. Memba when you did sick and we couldn't find anyone fi tek you to hospital in MoBay. Suppose you did more serious. You would a dead before me could get you dere. Den wha me would a do?'

But nothing could persuade Olive. She couldn't leave her mother, her grandparents, her aunt. When they built the new house with indoor plumbing and electricity, Milford erected a fence that separated their yard from Velma's and her parents'. Velma, who was always for speaking her mind, watched him build it, and the day he was done and had painted it, feeling very proud, she made an elaborate show of coming into his yard and even closing the gate behind her. She smiled at him, and he expected to hear her praise his work, but instead she made a digging sound in her throat and called to her mother and aunt, 'Progress come to Kristoff Village. We have fence and gate like English people dem.' Then, turning to Milford, she said, 'You see any of we have fence here? Fence is to keep in goat or chicken. People no have no need fah fence. All a we living here know where our land stop, but none a we have fence. You look! Look around you! De only place you se fence is de people dem who nuh live here any more and dem family in Merica or England fence off dem place for de government people tell dem dat is de way to mark off dem place. You see any a we have fence?'

Milford felt small. He couldn't remember ever feeling so small before, not even the time teacher flogged him at school for not knowing his times table and he wet his pants. He still held the paintbrush in his hand. He felt foolish. He didn't know where to turn, and he was glad Olive wasn't home.

They never closed the gate, and the fence made no difference. They still came and went as they pleased, and in less than six months all the planks disappeared, one by one, to where he never knew, and he didn't have the heart to ask or put up another fence.

He turned his attention now to Arnella eating the remainder of his food. How could he say she wasn't his daughter? True he didn't father her, but she was always his child, just like Valrie.

What an excitement

Milford was working double shifts, so wasn't home when Valrie and Arnella were born. He was surprised because Olive wasn't due for another three weeks, and he was determined that she was going to have the baby in the hospital. He didn't want Miss Cotton, even though he trusted her, attending to Olive. People in Kristoff Village were too backward, living like their ancestors did sixty years ago. He himself was born in the hospital.

'Chow! Dem can't help it!' he mumbled, disgusted. Every time, even now, when he came to the junction he felt he was entering another, different and alien world that was way behind time.

He was tired that night and smelled of food, curried lobster and crab. He was sleepy too, and was almost on the veranda when he realised something was wrong. All the women, talking and laughing. They greeted him, 'Daddy come home, man, Daddy come home!' He knew what they meant. Olive had had the baby. He was happy and disappointed. Momentarily he panicked: was she all right? Without saying a word, he pushed past the women into his own bedroom. Olive was sitting up nursing the baby. He rushed to her and almost crushed Arnella. He looked at Olive, at the baby in her arm and the one beside her, and grinned. He had twins. He kissed all three, and it was two days before he learned that one child was not his.

Milford put his cap over his balding head, touched Olive on her shoulder as he walked past her still rocking on the veranda, and crossed the few yards to Velma's house. It now had electricity, but still no indoor plumbing. He heard the television going loud. She never watched it, but used it as a radio; it was a gift from some relative in America, he couldn't remember who. He approached the door and knocked, feeling stupid. Who knocked in Kristoff Village? No response. Milford cleared his throat. 'Miss Velma? You in there?' He heard a giggling and turned. Valrie and Velma were sitting on a little bench under the lime tree, so close to the ground they might as well have been sitting on the ground, giggling at him. Sometimes

Velma was so childlike. As he turned to them, she put her hand up to cover her amusement.

'Night Daddy,' came Valrie's sugary voice. He decided to ignore her.

'Night Miss Velma.'

'Night Master Milford. You doing well ah hope?'

Giggles again from both. Milford played with the tip of his cap. Velma always made him feel uncomfortable, wrong. He wanted yet didn't want to talk with her. Velma motioned to him to join her and Valrie under the lime tree. He had gained weight and his pants were too tight, especially to sit so low. After some straining he got down, and sat between Velma and Valrie where they made a space for him. Valrie leaned on his arms and began playing with his fingers. Velma sat very still, her arms folded, palms opened in her lap.

He was scared the first time he met Velma. Although he had known Olive for close to seven years, he had never met Velma, and as his parents reproached him, 'You wait till you ruin de woman daughter to meet her. We raise you betta.' He hadn't meant for Olive to get pregnant. He'd planned on marrying her. Olive was two months pregnant before she told him. He was happy, but scared. That same weekend, for the first time, he took the bus home with Olive. He hadn't expected to have to explain his actions to Velma with her parents listening on, but that was what occurred. Actually it wasn't bad at all. They listened to him and when he was done, Olive's grandfather took his hand and shook it. 'You decent somebody. Me little Olive did all right.'

Milford felt relieved, and for the first time during that first meeting smiled. Then Olive's grandmother, handing him a glass of limeade, said, her face a mask of seriousness, 'Before you marry keep both eyes open. Afta marriage shut one.' Then she patted him on the shoulder and went back to her chores.

Velma's welcome was equally to the purpose. Pointing to the spot where his house now stood, she said, 'You can marry Olive, and build oonuh a house right dere. Olive can't leave Kristoff Village. Is she one me have, she have to stay right here.' He was so relieved, he agreed without knowing the cost.

*

Milford stretched. He was tired. Tired of being on the outside. Tired of being thought odd. Tired of not knowing who his children were, and what jurisdiction he had over them, if any. It dawned on him, sitting there under the lime tree, that there was no war to be fought. Valrie was going to do what she wanted; she always did; Arnella too. So what if Valrie wanted to live with her grandmother? He could stay at his house, stick his head through his window and call her whenever he wanted, or walk the few yards and see her.

'Help me up, child,' he said to her now. She jumped to her feet, pulled him up and they embraced each other.

'Night Daddy, sleep well,' Valrie said, kissing him on the right cheek. Then she walked to his left side and kissed him on the left cheek. 'And gi Mommie dis kiss. Tell her, me don't vex wid her anymore.' He shook his head. Velma held up her hand for him to take. He patted it and gave it back to her to place in her lap.

'Night Miss Velma. We trading daughters.'

'How you mean? Arnella and Valrie always gwane be you picknie dem. Sleep good.'

Olive cleared her head, hearing Arnella moving about in the bedroom. She had been sitting on the veranda in the growing darkness sorting out her feelings, waiting for her first niece or nephew and her third grandchild, after Valrie's two sons, to be born. As she stood, Arnella emerged from the bedroom, naked.

'Whe you clothes?'

'Me too hot. Me neva know it would tek so long. Since morning, now night a come. Me nuh know what do dis picknie.'

At the same moment a gush of water spilled from between her legs.

'Whooh! Me a wet up meself.'

'You water-bag bust. Baby soon come now.' Olive moved to her sister-daughter and began to massage her lower back.

Gathering the clouds

It was Samuel Lawrence's weekend and he and Monica were on her veranda drinking rum and coke and marvelling at the beautiful full moon. Every so often Monica smiled to herself, thinking about Desmond. She liked him 'bad' but didn't feel right about moving in on another woman's husband. She had not planned on having affairs with any of the village men.

Although she had been back not three months yet, Monica had been pursued relentlessly. She was abrupt and short with several men, but sweet to Trevor, declining his offer while keeping his friendship. Ainsworth was turning her on to the magic of printed words. Monica admitted to herself that she was stuck on Desmond with his blue shirt and mischievous smile, preparing her tea in the morning and making her feel so sweet, honey didn't know what nectar was. She smiled, reflecting on their many conversations, knowing how much he wanted to ask her about Samuel Lawrence and what it cost him to refrain from questioning her. She liked him all the more for his understanding. That was why, after she heard his motorbike pass her house earlier, the engine revving, she had sent one of the passing children to call him, so he could meet Samuel Lawrence and know there was no competition. But also Monica wanted Sam to know she was interested in someone else. He could continue to come if he wanted and sleep in the guest room. She liked him and considered him a friend, but no longer felt any obligation or desire to sleep with him. Desmond had come as summoned, and the three of them had sat amicably in her kitchen, drinking rum and coconut water. Desmond and Samuel laughed and talked like old friends, but Monica could tell they were sparring. They agreed to get together and walk the banks of the river and catch cray-fish. Monica chuckled as she watched them first sizing each other up, then agreeing silently on a truce, and finally allowing themselves to discover their liking for each other.

She decided to make her own choice clear to both, so she placed her arms around Desmond's neck as he and Samuel talked and whispered playfully in his ear, 'Gwane home now. Me nah go mek none eat you sugar.' He was taken aback, but obviously pleased. Samuel nodded to him, they shook hands, and Desmond left with his chest stuck out.

Monica grinned, re-living the interplay. She didn't see or hear Miss Cotton's approach.

'Greetings. Ah see oonuh enjoying de night. Well ah have to

79

interrupt. Mister Sam I need to borrow Sister Monica to assist me in de birth of a child.' Miss Cotton now turned to Monica, who had jumped from the chair. 'Grab a scarf fah you head and let's go. Arnella tek in.' Monica rushed inside, then followed behind Miss Cotton, who moved swiftly for a woman in her eighties, the light from the bottle lantern that she held fanning in the dark.

Shoe-black

Beryl had heard the owl all week. She knew any day now Arnella was going to have the baby. Last night the child who had been calling her hadn't cried. She woke listening, and realised she had been listening for the child but hadn't heard her. Her! The girl. Only a girl would cry for her mother that way, demanding, not pleading, as if she had a right. Beryl pulled her arms tight over her stomach and moaned.

She had been visiting Rupert and his American wife, Angel, more often than good manners allowed, but she couldn't keep away. Besides the child, this was how she thought of Angel, needed her guidance. Angel was like fish out of water in Kristoff Village. For a moment Beryl forgot about her personal anguish and pain and put back her head and laughed, remembering Angel's gut-curdling scream when she happened on the flying cockroaches in the out-house. Beryl was on her way home from the fields, taking the short-cut that ran along Rupert's place, when she heard this screaming. She thought someone was being murdered; but when she ran, her machete raised, she saw Angel tearing at her clothes and screaming. It took Beryl a good fifteen minutes to calm Angel, who refused to go back into the out-house from then on, preferring the bushes. She had collapsed in Beryl's arms, sobbing in fear, then confessed that nothing was as she'd imagined it, and that although she loved the village and the people were friendly and nice, the mosquito repellent she brought with her did no good. See, she showed Beryl the evidence, her arms and legs covered in sores.

She went on. Not having electricity wasn't so bad, except every time she wanted something cold she had to go to Miss Cotton's store, and it was so very, very hot. On and on Angel complained until Beryl couldn't contain her laughter any more, and after a while they both were laughing and hugging each other like long-lost friends. Beryl felt good and free, like during her happy school days that seemed so very long ago. Angel realised how silly she sounded, and Beryl discovered that she liked this child who had probably bitten off too much to chew, moving to Kristoff Village.

Beryl showed Angel the bush that grew wild not far from her house, and told her to burn it every evening and she wouldn't have any more mosquito worries. She might as well throw away her mosquito repellent from America because Jamaican mosquitoes thought it was candy.

Beryl was on her veranda, getting ready to smoke her pipe, when she heard the two short hoots. She looked in the tree for the owl but didn't see it. She knew she had time to smoke her pipe, but decided against it. She went and tied her head, put the pipe in her pocket, got her lantern and machete and took the short-cut that led to Rupert's house. She had given them a brown shaggy puppy, and as Beryl approached she heard the small brave yelping and smiled. She shook her head, noting that lanterns were burning in every room. Rupert had left early this morning for the airport to clear some of their belongings from customs. He had stopped by to inform her that he would probably be gone for a day or so, depending on how much hassle the customs people gave him, so she was to look in on Angel. She knew he hadn't returned so called now to Angel, whom she was certain had never participated in a birth. Well, if she was going to be living in Kristoff Village she might as well become acquainted with its ways.

'Daughta Angel. Miss Angel. Whoyo! Is your neighbour, Beryl.'

Angel, happy for the company, bounded out. Following the ways of Rupert and the others she addressed her neighbour, 'Night, Cousin Beryl. Come in.'

'Ah not stopping. Ah come to get you. Cova you head, let's go. Tun off de lantern dem. Just bring one fi light you path.'

Angel ran inside. She was excited; why she wasn't sure. She grabbed the multiple blue-shaded scarf that she had bought a month earlier at the craft market in Montego Bay. It was hanging over the dining room chair, ready for such occasions. Angel knew now to have a scarf handy; all the women seemed to wear them. Quickly, she blew out the lanterns, pulled the door behind her and walked with Beryl in silence.

Marva and Grace were sitting with Peggy on her veranda, gossiping, crocheting and darning clothes when they saw Beryl and Angel with lanterns heading in the direction of the river. Peggy saluted them, 'Night, Sister Beryl. Night, Miss American Lady.' She had tried to befriend Angel, especially since she was from America. Angel had not taken up her invitation to come and visit, yet here she was with night approaching walking beside Beryl, who was a loner and crazy at best.

Angel resented when people called her Miss American Lady, as all too many of the inhabitants of Kristoff Village did. And she couldn't quite say why, but she didn't like Peggy, who seemed nice enough and had even brought Rupert and her a sweet-potato pudding the first week she was there. She had invited them to visit, Angel remembered now. Yet there was something about Peggy that made Angel shy from her company. But she could not ignore her in such a small community, so she greeted the women in the same manner as Beryl, 'Good night Miss Peggy, Grace, Marva . . .' Before Angel could enquire of their health, which was customary, Beryl cut her off.

'Ah see oonuh enjoying de night air. Well have a good night. We have to be on our way.'

'Is Arnella, you all going by? She tek in yet?' Grace shouted after them as they turned the bend. Beryl kissed her teeth and said under her breath, but loud enough for Angel to hear, 'Dem worse dan fowl dat have yaws.'

Valrie's sons were asleep. She didn't know where Godfree was, but she knew he wasn't too far and he wouldn't be too long because Arnella was about to have her baby. As she stood watching her sons sleeping she felt a deep love for Arnella, and momentarily doubled over as a sympathy contraction racked her body. It was time for them to end their forced separation and be together again, a leaf divided by a stem, like they had been from birth.

She reached behind the door and pulled her scarf from the hook, draped it around her head, wrapped the ends at the nape of her neck, then brought them together at the top of her head where she made a bow. She pulled off her house dress and slipped over her head a loose-fitting blue and white cotton smock that was pear-shaped when she spun around. Valrie looked through her bedroom window and noticed that her parents' house was in darkness, except for a square filter of light coming from the living room. She knew her mother was at Arnella's, so her father must be watching TV. She turned a lamp on in the living room, then hurried down the steps. The pain was circling her body. She had to hurry. Her voice was an alarm cutting through the night silence: 'Daddy, ah gwane down by Arnella. De boys dem asleep. Godfree not home.' She didn't wait for a reply. He had heard, she knew, and would listen out.

Valrie's slippers glided over the gravel road as she jogged, the labour pains sending her forward.

Long-pants

Lately, Dahlia had been feeling poorly. Fact was her old body ached too much, and very little she could do without some pain or fatigue slowing her down. Seventy-two. She didn't feel old, but her body was; it all too often now refused to keep up with her mind's energy. More often she cursed it, another betrayal like the taking of her dear husband and sweet daughter. But at least she had her grandson, Godfree, and two great-grandsons. Godfree was a consolation to her. He never shamed her. He would have made his mother and grandfather proud. He was a good man, and he hadn't deserted her. Every other day he brought her dinner, and spent time sweeping up, helping with the fowls and dogs, working the land because he knew how much it meant to her. And lately he had been coming every evening to keep her company, going into the room that used to be his, working with his hands, carving, moulding the wood she had made him taste, so loved. He was in there right at this minute working away feverishly, intensely, shaping a form that he did not yet recognise. Dahlia knew what it was, from the beginning. The twins. That was his only failure, but it wasn't really a failure. Dahlia did try to get him to leave Arnella and Valrie alone, but he wouldn't and they wouldn't leave him, either; so she washed her hands of the whole thing, and just stood back and waited and watched. Poor Olive could have saved herself all the fuss, because 'When love step in, nothing to do but wait and watch if love leave.'

Dahlia heard Godfree in there now working away, his breathing laboured. She crawled off the bed where she had been resting, took off the old rag she used to tie her head when she slept, went to her bureau, reached in the back for the beautiful variegated blue silk scarf, and carefully tied her head. Next she went to the vanity and pulled out her white pleated dress with blue buttons and put it on. The carved cane that Godfree had made for her stood by the door. She raised the cane now and again marvelled that Godfree had carved out of memory the people who were most dear to her and him. She cradled the cane to her bosom, then brought it to her nose and sniffed the wood. She was about to go way back in memory to a time before that November thirty-three years ago – but she heard the call and reached in her cabinet for the bottle. She was about to be a great-grandmother again, and she would not miss the entrance of the life – not for all her swollen ankles or the ache in the joints of her arms.

Locking spirits

Velma and Dahlia were the last to arrive, meeting each other by the path, both walking slowly, shoulders down from the ache that irritated their spirits and slowed down their bodies. It was a full moon and the sky was so pale it barely seemed like night. Stars were everywhere, luminous, prancing. Velma spotted the owl in the bread-fruit tree right away. A sheet was spread on the ground, a lantern was at each end, the tamarind leaves were burning, keeping the mosquitoes at bay. Velma and Dahlia walked up to Miss Cotton, and the three elders joined palms in a criss-cross fashion, nodded greetings to each other, turned to the left, fanned the hems of their dress three times right to left, then separated to greet the other women present. Olive brought two stools for Velma and Dahlia; then Beryl brought them basins with warm water and soap to wash their hands.

Angel had been transfixed since she got there. Now she watched Arnella and Valrie doing what appeared to her like a sequence in Capoeira. They circled each other, then squatted, seeming to tumble, then stood up again and walked. But it wasn't like just circling, or squatting or walking, it was a dance, each was in tune with the other. Suddenly Angel realised that Valrie was mirroring Arnella. The beauty of their matched movements brought tears to her eyes. Arnella was somewhat ahead of Valrie, but still their movements were fluid, synchronised. Uncanny.

Angel looked up at the sky. She had never imagined the sky could be this clear, the moon so silver, so many stars. It was like a postcard. Now she focused on listening: crickets, lizards, mosquitoes – but they were not feasting on her tonight. She smelled burning – the bush that Beryl had brought. The bread-fruit tree, under which Arnella had insisted on giving birth, was pregnant with fruits and as Angel looked up a white leaf, curled and soft, floated down, landing on her head before falling to her feet. She bent, picked up the leaf, stuffed it in her bosom. Surprised by her action, she looked around to see if anyone noticed her, but if they had, there was no indication. When she turned again to the sheet she noticed that Arnella and Valrie were both squatting, hands on each other's shoulders, one breathing out, the other breathing in. Both of them appeared pregnant, both rocked with pain. Every so often Olive came and mopped both their brows, but otherwise everyone left them alone, standing or sitting off to the sides. Arnella was partially naked, no panty or bra, and her loose shift was open all the way down front. Her stomach was shiny and pointed, and her navel protruded. Sometimes, Angel could see the movement of the child in her stomach. Now Valrie was massaging Arnella's nipples. Angel felt herself sweating from the intensity of it, and when Arnella suddenly jumped up in pain, hopping from one leg to the next and snapping her index finger against her thumb and middle finger, Angel too began breathing hard, pacing and rubbing below her stomach. Velma and Dahlia started singing then, really humming, a slow tune that felt heavy with water. Beryl and Olive took off their slippers and joined Valrie and Arnella on the sheet, and the four seemed engaged in a private dance of breathing and stooping and healing hands. Angel found herself dancing around the sheet, rubbing first below her stomach then above, breathing in and out, while Velma and Dahlia hummed and softly clapped their hands to a one, pause, one-two-clap, then snap fingers beat. Monica and Miss Cotton stood to one side, their arms folded; but their bodies swayed to a tune Angel did not hear, and this is the story Velma and Dahlia told about the bread-fruit tree.

One version

Used to be, long ago, during slavery it happened and the women kept the story and passed it on. For a long time after the slavery business was almost done with, but not quite, the women still continued to have their babies outdoors, until they got ashamed of being thought primitive and backwards so they went to having their babies indoors, laying flat. This caused more pain, and made their babies ugly when they were born. These women, recently freed and desperate to fit in, weren't even aware that they had become primitive in these so-called new ways that their ancestors had long ago determined detrimental to women giving birth.

Anyway you can check the record books and you will see, 'Is not lie dem telling.' There was a period when most of the slave women refused to give birth. They knew what bush to drink or what to do if they were too far gone and the bush tea did not produce blood. They refused to bring their tomorrow into the fields – because that's what a child was to them, their tomorrow. But those who failed to drink the bush tea or visit the old aunt who knew great secrets had no choice. They watched their stomachs rise in front of them and waited. Well, time was, a young woman who had drunk many bush tea and had even visited the old aunty once found herself watching her stomach. Her mouth grew sour with the thought, and every time she spoke to someone they would look away or move a little distance from her, for the foulness of her breath sprayed in their faces like acid. The larger the woman's stomach rose, the more foul her breath became, until she was unbearable. But the people knew what troubled her, and what troubled her worried them too. They saw the steam rising around her nose, and the fear oozing from her pores. She stunk, seeing no way out of her life, and knowing she was to bring her tomorrow to a hopeless future.

Her time approached and one bright full-moon night she took in.

She didn't tell anyone; just hauled herself off yonder, but couldn't make it further than the bread-fruit tree. She felt wetness, and when she touched herself and brought her hand to her face she saw blood. She embraced the bread-fruit tree and laughed, pain and joy. When they found her, laughter was still written on her face, even her open eyes were merry. They had to use a knife and pry her hands from the bread-fruit tree, and there they buried her with the triplets she was carrying. That year the bread-fruit tree bore until its branches broke. It was said that every child-bearing woman who ate its sweet yellow fruit conceived a child, and their stomach and breasts were full like ripe bread-fruits, and all the women who laboured under the tree brought forth healthy sons and daughters. Not one of those many who were born the following year became slave to the fields; they were of the tomorrow who forged ahead, creating waves and sounding changes.

Possibilities

Angel heard the baby cry. She couldn't see; Monica was blocking her view. Hesitantly, she moved towards the sheet, and at the same moment Monica stepped to the side, allowing Angel a view of the child on the sheet, smeared and bloody. Arnella was squatting and so too was Miss Cotton. Valrie was behind Arnella massaging her shoulders. Monica handed Miss Cotton the scissors and she cut the cord while Monica wrapped the child and passed it to Olive, who blew on its face then passed it to Velma and Dahlia. Too much for Angel to take in. Where should she focus? On Arnella, who still was breathing heavily, or on what Velma and Dahlia were doing to the baby?

'Is gal pickney!'

'Look how she fava me daughta!'

'Me first grand gal baby.'

'What a way she pretty! Watch her no. Skin smooth and deep brown like de soil after rain.'

Miss Cotton and Monica gathered the after-birth and handed it to Beryl for proper planting; Olive and Valrie sponged down Arnella, rubbed her joints with bay-rum and placed a clean yellow nightdress on her. She was ready for her daughter, who instantly snuggled to her and began sucking. The women clapped and passed their comments.

'Look how she greedy.'

'Is a true indication dat she gwane be in everything.'

Then, taking her tiny hands and forcing her fingers open, Miss Cotton declared, 'Is beauty and brain dis one, but she gwane walk about; she gwane do nuff travelling.'

'Dat all right wid me, as long as she tek me along,' Arnella said, smiling down at the child.

Beryl, who had just returned from planting the after-birth with a yam head on which she poured honey for a good life, stood looking at Arnella cradling the child. Tears filled her eyes and silently rolled down her cheeks on to her dress, but no one suspected that her tears were not for Arnella's baby, but her own, forever lost to her.

Olive insisted that Arnella and the baby go inside, and once everyone was packed in the living room she served hot cocoa, fried bread-fruit, and corn-beef seasoned with tomatoes and onions. Arnella didn't have a name for the baby so Dahlia called her Baby-Girl, and pledged her support to help raise the child and correct her rude behaviour. Monica offered to help school her; Angel said she would teach her to read; Valrie said her house would always be Baby-Girl's other home; Velma said she would tell her the stories; Miss Cotton promised to teach her how to run a business and keep her private life her own affair; Beryl offered to teach her how to turn over the soil to grow food and Olive said she would indulge her without fear of making her unfit for anyone else. It was about that time that Milford and Godfree, each carrying a boy child, arrived. Arnella and Baby-Girl were dozing, but still Milford insisted on his right as a grandfather of his first granddaughter, and Godfree as father of his first daughter and his sons' first sister – all had a right not only to see the baby, but to hold and smell her and welcome her into this life. So they invaded Arnella's room, took the child from her arms, rocked and sniffed at her, kissed her forehead, curled her tight-fisted finger around their index fingers, blew their life-breath into her face before resting her, still asleep, in her mother's arms. Milford was all smiles. He reached into his back pocket, took the pint flask of over-proof white rum, went to the front door, poured some on the steps, went to the back door and poured some on the steps, then came inside where Olive had a glass ready for him and Velma had lime juice in a bottle. Milford poured a generous helping of rum, added lime juice and water, took one long gulp, then walked back home and went to bed, a happy and contented man.

Dahlia insisted on spending the night at Arnella's with Velma and Valrie, and nothing Godfree said could persuade her otherwise. Olive didn't even try with Velma or Valrie, just agreeing to bring them extra pillows and sheets so they could be comfortable. Angel didn't want to leave, but Beryl said she was ready and all of them, Monica, Miss Cotton and Angel could all walk together. As Angel got her lantern she saw Beryl's tear-stained face and wanted to reach out and take her in her arms. Monica's face was light and peaceful, Miss Cotton's serene, but Angel was feeling her own emptiness. She and Rupert were married over a year now. Perhaps it was time to start a family.

They walked spread out across the road: Monica and Miss Cotton, arms pulled through each other's elbows like the schoolgirls Angel had seen, and she and Beryl close but not touching.

The talk was all about the Baby-Girl and Arnella and Valrie back close together, twins, sisters and friends.

III

Vengeance like a storm

never look someone
in the eye
after you've laughed
at them
never forget
to say thanks
to throw salt at your back
or spit in the sky
be thankful
remember
you'll never know
when you might need
to collect

Run, but you can't hide

The memories walked over her. She could not sleep. She sat up in bed, paced the room, moved to the living room, looked out at the night. The watch on her wrist, which she wore to bed from habit, said it was three thirty.

Until she was eleven Angel believed she was white, and although there had always been whispers, for the most part everyone accepted her as white. And why shouldn't they? After all her father and mother were white, all the families in her condominium complex were white except for the maids, all the children at her school were white, as were the teachers. Then without warning her father died. Heart attack. She and her mother mourned and grieved, then they got over him. Her mother much sooner, being flattered by men, most of whom looked at Angel strangely, and asked, 'Is she . . .' But they never completed their thought. 'What am I?' she began to wonder, afraid herself to probe beyond the question.

One man was bold, didn't care about her feelings. 'That's your child! She's coloured! She's a nigger!' Sent to her room. No explanation. 'Coloured! Nigger! Please, anything but a nigger.' Tears, wanting to die, to be killed, to jump off the nineteenth floor on to Park Avenue. 'Not white! How can that be?'

Her mother went out that night with the man, and didn't come in until an hour before breakfast. Angel heard when she returned, but said nothing. They had breakfast together but were silent, avoiding each other's eyes. When Jasmine, the maid from Jamaica, came she asked her, 'Jasmine, do I look different?'

'Different? How, Miss Angel?'

'Different, like different from my mom, from everyone else?'

'No, Miss Angel. You're pretty like your mom.'

So she wasn't different. She wasn't coloured. Certainly not a nigger. But her mom began to avoid her, and whenever a certain person was visiting she was either sent to her room and told to stay there or sent to a friend.

Then a new teacher at her preparatory school during social science asked her, 'Can you tell the class what it's like to be mixed?' She turned like the rest of the seventeen students to see to whom the teacher referred. There was no one. Everyone looked around. Then the teacher said, 'Well, Angel, can you tell us?' All eyes were on her now. 'Mixed? With what?' She felt the tears swelling up and she swallowed, hoping to drink them down, but still they came. She felt all eyes turned on her so she pushed back her chair and ran sobbing from the room. 'I'm not mixed. I'm not different. I'm just like you.' Her mom came and Angel was happy to discover that both their eyes were red. She never returned to that school, but she found out from her best friend, who also lived in her condo complex, that the teacher was fired. She felt vindicated, but that was the beginning of her discovery of how different she was.

She began therapy. Her mom said it was so that they could deal with the loss of her dad, but much later Angel realised it was to deal with being different. Before that summer was over she would learn that she was adopted, was coloured (well, mixed), that her mother's new fiancé didn't like her because she was a 'nigger', and that the reason people had always looked and made much of her all these years was because she was coloured and they were so surprised to see her in their setting acting like one of them.

Angel's mom no longer took her on shopping sprees, to lunch or other places. More and more she was left at home with a sitter, or sent to a friend when certain company came by. There were no more walks holding hands, no more concerts. But when left alone she pretended she was not different, not adopted, not coloured – and that her father was still alive.

These are the memories that assailed her in the small hours. Her hand reached for the box of tissues and she blew her nose. She hadn't been aware that she was crying, but the pile of tissues on the floor at her feet served as evidence. Even now it hurt to re-live the pain of the little girl that she had been.

Angel opened the door and stepped out into the morning air. The sun would be up soon. She paced around the little veranda, then walked off on to the damp earth that stuck to her bare feet. For a moment all was still. She made herself stop breathing as she listened.

Someone was calling her. She was about to answer, then she remembered Rupert's warning about not answering until you were sure it wasn't a ghost – a duppy, he said. She laughed at his silly superstition, yet she refrained from answering. Who knew? This was a different environment. She gulped for air, and felt as if she had been held under water, but still she heard the voice. It was a woman's voice, she was certain, and although the woman wasn't saying her name, she knew the woman meant her.

Angel felt goose-bumps on her arms; she thought she saw someone, yet when she spun round no one was there. Was she going crazy, coming to Kristoff Village where time was just a word and feelings were moving forces? She walked back to the veranda, ran her feet up and down the side of the step to scrape off the dirt. She wanted some tea, but didn't feel like fighting with the coal stove; so she settled for an orange instead, using a knife to peel the skin like Rupert had shown her, and sat on the veranda in her skimpy teddy-bear nightie savouring the sweet fruit.

There had been no discussion, she remembered. Her bags were packed, uniforms were bought, and she was taken to a boarding school. It was better for her. Christmas, she was sent to a ski resort, and when she returned to school she got the postcard which announced her mother's marriage. Somehow she managed the news. She also survived the girls, who all called her names and made her know she was different, not one of them. She tried hard, but still was not one of them. So she turned to her books and excelled.

The next summer, as she watched the only home she had ever known being packed into boxes and tried to keep out of the way of the movers while talking to her mother, Angel learned that turning twelve had made her an adult and an outcast. She could not join her mother in her new Long Island home because she was not welcome there. It was not put so bluntly, but that was the reality. She would continue boarding school until she graduated (her father had left money for her education), and during the holidays she could visit various resorts or camps, or she could go to Jasmine. Her mother had made arrangements, and Jasmine had fixed up a room in her own house just for Angel, a room that she could go to any time during the holidays.

That night Angel dissolved sixty aspirins in her milk and drank it in one gulp. She awoke in a hospital room, and her therapy increased from once weekly to three times. But she did not speak, refused to eat, and was still recuperating when the new school year began. She saw her mother less and less. In fact, she was told not to call her 'mother' any more; Cindy was more appropriate. Angel listened silently while Cindy whispered greetings over the telephone, told her how much she loved her, that Angel should be happy for her, and that what she, Cindy, was doing was going to be best for Angel in the long run. Angel listened silently, feeling betrayed, sensing she was being discarded.

Angel would probably still be in that hospital if Jasmine hadn't turned up one afternoon to visit her. Black women have always spoken to each other. Straight. Getting right to the heart of the matter. Angel was surprised to see her, in her yellow maid's uniform as if she had just finished working. They stared at each other for a long while, each daring the other to see who could out-stare whom. Jasmine was obviously an expert. When Angel lowered her eyes, Jasmine walked to the side of the bed, touched her tenderly on her shoulder. Then, cupping Angel's chin so their glances were locked, she said, 'Wha so bad about being coloured dat you go run from life?'

Angel hadn't thought about it in that way. Always it was that she wasn't white. It had never occurred to her that it might be perfectly fine to be coloured. But with Jasmine's hand still on her chin she allowed herself to reflect on that possibility. Who were the women she admired, and who showed her as much love as Cindy and John – or more? Jasmine, and before her at least three other women: Hortense, also from Jamaica, and Pam and Carol from Barbados and Grenada where she had gone several times on vacation. She remembered the water so clear, she saw her toes wiggling in it. She remembered feeling free, alive, loved.

'Is where you gone again?' Jasmine's voice brought her back to the moment and the question. Angel smiled and got out of bed. Mostly she listened while Jasmine talked about her four children, whom she had finally succeeded in bringing to America, and how Angel would meet them when she came home; 'home' was the word she used. Jasmine told her that her room was ready and was almost exactly like the room she had on Park Avenue except not quite as large. Also, she would have to share the bathroom with everyone, and the neighbourhood was loud and not as clean and pretty as what she was accustomed to.

The hug did it. It was warm and soothing. Angel felt her tears on Jasmine's shoulders, but Jasmine didn't seem to mind. Jasmine rocked her, which brought forth more tears. They rocked until the tears dried up. Jasmine called her baby, patted and kissed her on the forehead. 'Honey child, de ground not even; not even at all, but we all have to learn to walk on it.'

A week later Angel was discharged and Jasmine picked her up. Cindy sent money for a taxi so they rode from Manhattan to Brooklyn. Angel believed she had accepted being coloured until the cab stopped in front of what was to be her new home. It was nothing like what she had imagined. She didn't want to be coloured any more. Nothing was familiar: not the way they spoke, what they ate, and mostly not their familiarity, sharing everything, no privacy. She had been rash. She should have stayed in the hospital. There was no place she could go, not even the room that was reserved for her alone, and not hear others through the thin walls. She suffered, phoned Cindy, and had herself sent off to boarding school. She wouldn't be coloured. And she wasn't for the next four years, travelling all over Europe during school recess, getting herself invited to the homes of the few friends she made who didn't ask, 'Are you mixed?' or 'What are you? Italian? Spanish?' Sure, anything but coloured or black or nigger.

Angel graduated from Wilmick Boarding School for Girls with honours and was the school valedictorian. Consequently she was offered places at all the universities to which she applied, including Princeton, Harvard, Columbia, Stanford and Howard. The latter was an afterthought. But in the end she decided that Howard was where she would attend. Cindy could not be present at Angel's graduation, although she sent flowers and matching pearl earrings, necklace and bracelet. Angel had seen Cindy no more than five times in the previous five years, and not at all since she had finally done the impossible and become a real mother, giving birth to a boy. None the less, Cindy telephoned to say that she would not support Angel if she attended Howard. All the years of being neglected and abandoned rose in

Angel, and she heard herself scream so loud, her own ears rang, 'Who the hell are you to tell me where I may or may not go? I am a nigger and I will attend a nigger school. You are supposed to be my mother, you adopted me, but I've never been to your home because your husband doesn't want a nigger around. Well, that's what I am. I can make my own way.' Then she hurled the phone across the room, and began throwing things until there was nothing else to throw. Then she ran to the stable, selected a horse and rode far into the woods where it was so quiet she couldn't hear even herself think. She probably would have stayed there if the school hadn't sent a search party for her.

Angel and Cindy never mentioned that incident again; it became one of the many unmentioned aspects of their lives. On the day of graduation a special delivery letter arrived for Angel. Inside was an open plane ticket to any destination in Europe, and a note saying, 'Your tuition for Howard will be paid, and an apartment is being secured for you near the campus. Cindy.' No hello. No dear. No love. But it was Cindy's handwriting. Angel never contacted her after that. But for the four years she was at Howard her tuition and expenses were taken care of, and when she graduated she received flowers, simply signed Cindy, and diamond earrings that she gave to Jasmine the following Christmas. That was the end of her relationship with Cindy Fairbanks-Kirk.

The bus huffed and growled as it climbed the slight incline, on its first morning trip through Kristoff Village. The driver honked the horn in greeting as it passed the house and Angel jumped, startled from the chair in which she sat. Momentarily she wasn't sure where she was. She felt the heat pressing the clothes to her body, looked down at herself, turned to look at the house, then began laughing, unable to stop tears running down her cheeks, doubling up on the veranda. Then the daydream faded. Kristoff Village was nothing like Brooklyn had been eleven years ago. She felt comfortable, as if she belonged here in a way she never had in Brooklyn, even long after she had accepted her identity, referred to herself as black, wore her hair in a short natural style and called herself Anaya. She heard the bus turn around at the cul-de-sac, near the path where Arnella lived, right opposite the main entrance to the river, where a few women still washed their clothes, children swam, and the older boys dived. She wondered if Beryl had already gone to her field. She hadn't heard her pass by the short-cut. She hoped she hadn't left because she would go with her. She felt that Beryl needed her company as much as she, Angel, had come to depend on Beryl being around. She hastened to get dressed.

Tie a knot

Beryl's arm ached. She felt exhausted and irritable. She poured water from the jar, washed her hands and face, then dropped loudly in the bed beside her mother and was almost instantly in a deep sleep. She never heard her mother cry out, never felt her feeble hands reach for her.

The rooster cocka-doodle-doed one, twice, but still Beryl refused to get up. She was in pain.

Someone was crying? Was it the child who no longer called out to her? She was somewhere sitting under a poui tree in bloom. A few of the yellow petals fell at her feet. She looked about her and saw a few women sitting near the road, their large pots bubbling: boiling corn, dumpling, green banana and salt-fish. Suddenly hungry, she walked over to the women and held out her hand. They looked her over from head to foot, as if they were about to trace her; she waited for their curses. Then one of them smiled and offered her a corn which, though sheltered in its husk, still burned her hand. Satisfied, she thanked the woman and wandered further, where she saw a man selling coconut from his hand cart. Beryl smiled at him, picked a tiny piece of husk from his matted beard, and he repaid her kindness with a jelly coconut, so sweet, its soft jelly slid between her fingers. She continued to walk, finding herself back under the poui tree. Not knowing what else to do, she sat, waiting.

By the time Beryl stirred morning was upon her. She turned, surprised that her mother was still asleep. Then she became alarmed. She jumped out of bed, ran to her mother's side and saw her stiff, eyes glazed not seeing anything. Yet she was breathing. Beryl tried to lift her, but she was heavy like wet wood. But she was breathing. Beryl made herself slow down, went to the door and hollered to Monica, shouted to someone passing to get Miss Cotton. Monica arrived first, said it looked like a stroke, and shortly after Miss Cotton arrived, confirmed Monica's diagnosis, and said there was nothing she could do. Someone ran over to Monica's and summoned her man, Samuel Lawrence, to drive Beryl and her mother the twelve miles to the hospital. When Angel arrived, a small group of people were gathered, and Desmond and Samuel were lifting Beryl's mother into Samuel's car. Without asking, Angel jumped into the back seat. As the car sped off, she tried to reassure Beryl that everything would be all right.

However, everything was not all right. The stroke was severe. Beryl's mother was left with her entire right side paralysed and her speech restricted; she didn't speak much as it was since she had gradually lost her hearing over the years. The doctors asked Beryl why she'd waited so long to bring in her mother. She stood there looking lost and defeated. Angel came to her rescue, explaining that they lived twelve miles into the interior. The doctors shook their heads, shrugged their shoulders in acknowledgement and frustration, and one said to the other as they walked away to their duties, 'Dis damn island. No good road and no transportation. Is a miracle we still have poor people to grow our food.'

Finding a bed for Beryl's mother proved a challenge. The hospital, as usual, was overcrowded. A bed was secured by two in the afternoon, but no clean linen could be found. The nurse asked Beryl if she had brought any, and when Beryl said no, the nurse looked at her, sucked her teeth, and declared, 'So is what you expect? You no hear public hospital don't have no sheets? She gwane have to lie down on de bare mattress.' With that, the nurse spun round and swung off. Angel, outraged, ran after her, grabbed her arms and swung her back to face them. 'How dare you speak to her like that with her mother near death? Where is your humanity? You're a side of Jamaica I haven't seen yet, and I hope there aren't many more of you.' Although Angel had tried since college to sound 'black' she didn't. She was a product of her affluent upbringing, private schools, and travel to Europe. The nurse was thrown off. She had assumed Angel was related to Beryl. 'Another ignorant country bumkin' with her head tied. She hadn't stopped to note her dress, for if she had she would have realised that although simple looking, it was tailored, and the fabric was silk, and the sandals on her feet were Italian leather in the same teal colour as the dress. But the nurse, who had been working for fifteen years in the public hospital, and who had applied for transfer several times, had long stopped looking at people closely. Most of those whom she served she dismissed as backwards, superstitious country people who only came to the hospital when they were near death, after they had consumed all the bush tea and other nonsense they believed could cure whatever ailed them. The nurse was about to trace Angel, but now she realised the young woman was not Jamaican. The accent wasn't fake; she had heard enough dry-land tourist, phoney American or British accents to distinguish the real from the fake. She stared at Angel now and said, 'Excuse me mam, but ah only doing my job. Dis woman know we don't have no linens. People have to provide their own because de wukless thieving workers steal everything dat not nail down.'

Angel was contrite. Her unexpected outburst had surprised her.

The nurse stood arms akimbo, in preparation for a heated argument. Angel shook her head to clear it, and remembered Charley, who lived not far from the hospital. Working on a plan of action, she said to the nurse, 'Perhaps you can find a sheet to cover our mother until we return with proper linen.' She said it more heatedly than she had planned to, then added, to soften the words, 'We would be forever grateful.' She managed a smile. The nurse relaxed and nodded; Angel took Beryl's hand and led her outside into the heat and hustle that was the character of Montego Bay.

Once outside, Angel panicked, realising she didn't have a purse, or money, or identification. Samuel Lawrence had long gone. They stood in the heat, looking around as if waiting on someone, but no one approached them. Finally Angel decided they had to do something, even if it meant walking.

'Cousin Beryl, how far does Charley live from here?'

'Not too far, jus up de road.'

Angel didn't trust that. People's sense of far, she had discovered, varied. Not too far might be two miles or more. It was too hot to walk; besides, she was hungry. Then she remembered that she and Rupert had opened a bank account. Maybe she could get money there; it was worth a try. Beryl directed her to the bank, half a mile away. Before going inside, Angel pulled the scarf from her head and got her story ready. It was easier than she expected, because the woman who had opened the account for them remembered her and permitted the withdrawal even without identification after hearing the story of Beryl's mother. So Angel and Beryl ate, bought linens and returned to the hospital. They paid an orderly to look in on Beryl's mother, then took a taxi to Charley's house, which turned out to be four miles away. Rupert was returning from the customs office just as the cab pulled up, and Angel rushed out, creating quite a spectacle by running into his arms and embracing him. Only foreigners in Jamaica display such affection in public.

Tek caution

Neither of them had known such passion could exist. They had planned to be more circumspect, but now that Desmond was certain how Monica felt about him and knew Samuel Lawrence was no threat or competition, he abandoned caution and took to going to Monica every opportunity he got. The word spread like bush fire that he was planning to leave his wife for Monica. Miss Cotton summoned Monica and warned her about impropriety and flaunting what she had, but Monica merely laughed and asked what was the harm in enjoying life. Miss Cotton didn't have the words or gestures with which to answer Monica, but she felt the disturbance in her head. She wanted to still it, shake it loose, but her efforts were of no avail. Sometimes seeing was too much of a burden. Sometimes feeling was too much pain. Miss Cotton sat and waited, hoping she wouldn't have to wade in the river, but sensing she couldn't avoid the tears that would be spilled.

As a child, Monica hated Kristoff Village. There was no place she could wander without being known, without some adult correcting her behaviour, asking after her family, watching her, waiting for her to do wrong so they could put her right. She dreamed of a place where no one knew her or cared, where she could be herself. She could never be who or what she wanted to be if she remained in the village. These were her thoughts from as young as eight years old, and each year she made more firm plans to leave, to go somewhere far away. She hated school, mostly because by the time she walked the four miles, barefoot, she was tired, and the breakfast she ate was all spent, leaving her hungry until the eleven o'clock school lunch recess, when she would be given powdered milk, coco bread, and whatever little else there was, which was never enough. She wasn't bright, so was often flogged or sent to the corner to stand on one leg while holding the other behind. More than once she was made to stand in the centre of the class with the cone-shaped dunce hat on her head. She hated school and took no interest in learning, so after a while she was branded lazy and stupid. Teachers ignored her, made her wash the blackboard or do other errands for the class. She also hated being home because her mother never gave her a break. She had to fetch water, help with the washing, ironing, cooking. She was always doing something, never allowed to run wild or play like her brothers, to go fishing all day by the river, to hang out at nights with the boys who sat by the corner of the road or leaned on crates by the shop, listening to the men's stories, swapping their own, catching penewales and night flies.

Monica planned and waited for a time when she could be her own person, and when at fourteen one day she found herself home alone, she searched through her parents' room and found five pounds, six shillings. And she ran to Miss Cotton, her confidant and the only adult who listened to, respected and valued her feelings, and told her what she was planning. Miss Cotton gave Monica her favourite cream-soda and a bun and told her to make her own way.

She got as far as Montego Bay that day, and hid in the market. There she was discovered by several women from Kristoff Village, who scolded her. One even slapped her on her bottom. 'Fah worrying your mumma's heart,' she said, before ordering Monica to sit down beside her. Monica felt hopeless but not defeated; she was not going to return to Kristoff Village unless they dragged her bodily there. Early the next morning she heard someone outside the market, behind the stall where she had spent the night, talking about catching the bus to Kingston. She decided that was where she was heading: Kingston. She told the Kristoff women that she had to urinate, and once out of sight dashed from the market. She ran without looking back, and as she was running a bus pulled up alongside her. The side man, the conductor, said, 'Kingston, Kingston. We heading to de capitol.' Monica held up her hand, and the conductor pulled her on the bus. Her throat burned, but she didn't care. She was going to Kingston.

Where the bus stopped in downtown Kingston everyone peeled off with their baskets, boxes tied with rope, and other items. Monica waited until the bus was empty to disembark, feeling suddenly frightened by this venture. Kingston was larger, more noisy than she had imagined. She walked quietly behind a woman and her child who had gotten on the bus at Ocho Rios. Activity swirled all around her. Then she was thrust into a great open space with what seemed to be millions of buses. Music of various rhythms blared from every direction. Men stood on the street corners shouting sermons: one in a jacket and tie, with a sign hanging from his neck which read: 'Get Ready for the Day of Deliverance'. On the man's back the message continued: 'For the Almighty Lord is Coming to Claim the Holy Ones among Us.' The man had a book in his hand which he continually pointed to and banged on. But a woman hurrying by Monica spoke to no one: 'Koo mad Ezra in him suit with the Bible him thief from church. Him can't even read him name.' And she laughed.

Monica's head was throbbing; she was hungry, tired, with nowhere to go, had less than four pounds to her name and only the clothes on her back. She sat under a bus-stop shed and watched several buses go by. People got on . . . others got off. Still no plan came to her. How was she to survive?

Yet at fourteen Monica had the body of a woman. That was why her mother didn't allow her to go anywhere alone, fearful, like all mothers, that her daughter would be 'ruined'. Consequently, the clothes Monica wore were made like a child's, but ironically these simple garments only accentuated her body more. It was this mixture of innocence and sexuality that caught the pimp's eye as he hopped off the bus. A notorious womaniser with seven or more children from five different women, the pimp had a sharp eye, always alert for fresh prey. He particularly liked them young, liked 'to bruk dem in', as he joked with his men friends. He spotted Monica right away. Rather than approaching her immediately, he went and stood on the bank behind the bus-stop where he could observe her without her seeing him, and he smoked a cigarette, relaxed. He was working on a plan; he was tired of exerting himself for pittance and ill-treatment. He was planning to make a big move.

Six buses stopped then went without Monica. The pimp observed her anxious eyes. Evening was creeping on and still she remained. He decided finally that she was a runaway, probably from the country. She would be easy. He dragged on his cigarette, tossed it away, and walked over to her. He got straight to the point.

'Ah see you is a woman. Dat's why you run from home.'

'Is wha you want wid me?'

'Dat depends on how much of a woman you really is.'

'What you offering?'

He smiled; he was enjoying the game, but was admittedly surprised by Monica's forwardness. Monica herself was surprised at how bold she was being, but this route was one she had anticipated. She could come to Kingston and be kept by a man. The pimp, with his coal-black skin, white teeth, moustache, muscled arms, and smell of cigarettes, fit her image of a man. She was prepared to surrender her virginity to him.

'You hungry?'

'Is all day me been riding de bus.'

'Come den, mek we eat.'

He took Monica's hand, and she fell in step beside him. They ate, and her appetite was large. Then he took her to Rialto, to see her first picture show. Her dream of Kingston and a fun life had come through.

Run-away

She was daring. That memory suited the image she had of herself, and now as Monica watched Desmond sleeping, then glanced at the clock, she smiled, pulled the covers to her neck and snuggled next to him. His wife would just have to do without him because she wanted him, wanted him next to her in her bed, even though it was night and she had promised herself never to let any man pass the night with her here. But rules were made to be broken, and she was her own woman. She could do as she pleased.

Desmond threw his arms over Monica, pulled his body closer to her and breathed in her smell, kus-kus. He nibbled on her ears, threw one leg over her and used his foot to caress her calf. She giggled, turned to him, kissed his mouth then sucked on his bottom lip. Their hands and feet were intertwined, moving wherever a space made way. Contact sent pleasure. They were so engrossed in each other that not even falling on the floor interrupted their play, and it was a while before it registered that someone was knocking on the door and calling out to Monica.

'Good evening Miss Monica,' the voice said repeatedly, each time sounding less sure of itself. They held each other tightly, holding their breath. Desmond recognised the voice of his youngest son. They lay silent, becoming conscious of the cold tile floor. Monica got up, pulled on her duster and went to the front door. Desmond's son, Peter, a miniature replica of him, stood before her with a covered tray in his hand. She smiled at the boy, and resisted the urge to hug him to her breast. He did not look at her, rather looked over her shoulder or down at his feet.

'Good evening Miss Monica, mam. Mama seh ah to tek dis food fah Daddy and tell him don't boda come home.'

Monica's heart skipped a beat. She felt embarrassed, not so much for the child as for the mother who would subject her son to such an ordeal. 'Blasted coward!' she spat under her breath. Although not one to lie, she felt the child needed to save face. She took the plate from the boy's hand, made him look her in the eyes and said, 'Tell Miss Grace thanks for de dinner, and ah wish ah could help her locate Mista Desmond, but ah haven't seen him all day. You go home now.'

The boy gave Monica a sly smile then turned and walked out her gate. She stood watching him, then removed the beautiful embroidered cloth that covered the tray to see what a woman such as Grace would send to entice her husband home. She was impressed and took it into her bedroom where she and Desmond feasted on his wife's delicious meal of ox-tail, broad beans, yellow yam, boiled plantain, rice and a pitcher of carrot juice mixed with limeade.

'Grace is a good cook,' Monica said, wiping her mouth. 'Desmond, ah tink is time you go home. Is one thing dat Grace hate me, but me nuh wan you picknie dem fi hate me too.'

Desmond pulled Monica into his lap, wrapped her in his arms, and thought about what to do. He certainly didn't feel like going home to have Grace throw words and silence at him, but he also didn't want his children to think he was abandoning them. However, they were both saved from indecision, because Miss Cotton's granddaughter knocked on Monica's door, summoning her to Miss Cotton's side.

Peas in a pod

Valrie moved in with Arnella for two weeks to help her with Baby-Girl. Velma and Dahlia visited daily, each taking turns to rock the child in their old arms and whisper ancient secrets in her ear. She was beautiful, and even if she wasn't, she was told so in so many different ways, by so many varied voices that by seven days she was secure in the knowledge of her beauty. Her every yawn was a cause for excitement. The force and strength of her lungs were commented on when she cried; her slender fingers, the tips of which were the same even brown shade as her face, were admired. The glow of her black eyes, the length of her lashes, the sheen and tight curls of her full head of hair, her not-even-palm-length feet. Every part of her was examined and reexamined, assessed, admired, kissed, and declared perfect. Velma and Dahlia prepared her first bath, setting the basin in the sun to warm. Then they mixed bluing into the water, and a little bay-rum. Dahlia gently let blue water run over Baby-Girl's head, all the while whispering a prayer for mercy, long life, good manners and a pleasant personality. Velma took the child from Dahlia and anointed her joints with olive oil and rosewater and mumbled her own prayer for long life, health, beauty that was both inside and out, and a tongue that was light and quick.

Valrie would have been a painter had her world been different, if she had had access to paint and brush and canvas. But she hadn't, so she bought the same exercise books that children took to school to do their lessons in and drew whatever caught her fancy. Now, as she watched Arnella sitting in the rocking chair by the window nursing Baby-Girl, her hands itched. But as much as she searched she found no paper or pencil. A sadness that something important was being lost swept over her, and she quietly moved to the kitchen to prepare lunch. As she busied herself, she saw a large paper bag folded on the counter. She hastily turned off the stove, grabbed the paper bag and opened it, ripping the seams. She flattened it out and ran to Arnella, demanding a pencil. Arnella indicated her sewing-machine drawer. Valrie fetched a pencil and began to draw with intense concentration, glancing up every so often at her subject, Arnella nursing. Arnella hummed as she nursed her daughter, closing her eyes, both of them dozing from the sun and the sheer pleasure of their connection, and Valrie's fingers and eyes worked feverishly to capture the beauty and love she felt as a witness to her sister-cousin's motherhood.

Arnella awoke after a time under the concentrated silence of Valrie, who was on her knees on the floor adding details to the sketch. Arnella placed sleeping Baby-Girl in the crib, then stooped to see what Valrie was doing. 'Val! You drawing again? Memba how teacha used to say you was an artist?'

Valrie shook her head, and as Arnella stared at herself with baby-in-arms she saw Valrie's tears stain the page. Arnella's finger played with the wetness, smearing the lines that formed her body. But she did not look at Valrie, who she knew was now sobbing quietly, her body shaking. They remained like that for some time, Valrie's tears falling on the paper bag that she had turned into a canvas and Arnella crouched beside her catching the tears in her opened palm. Then Valrie collapsed on the floor and Arnella pulled her into her arms and rocked her as the tears continued to spill from her eyes and a moan deep and plaintive escaped her body, until they were both crying and embracing each other, afraid to let go, afraid they would drown in their tears, afraid if they were to let go they would continue to live with their pain and never let it be known how deeply their separation hurt.

Baby-Girl awoke to the crying and lay on her back, eyes wide; listening, but not making a sound.

Olive was at home in her kitchen cooking dinner when she heard weeping; she felt as if someone had reached inside her heart and opened a valve. She was so overcome by this feeling that she had to stop cooking and go and sit outside to catch her breath.

Velma, who had been asleep in her bed, woke and found her pillow wet, and when she reached up to wipe the sleep from her eyes, she found them wet and could tell from the feel of them that they were puffy and red. Her head felt light, as if she had been relieved of some heavy burden.

Milford was on his way home from the hotel; the soles of his feet ached. He was sitting in the middle of the bus, his face leaning out the window, and he felt something in his eyes. He reached into his back pocket and wiped away tears, looking around quickly to make sure no one else saw them. An image of Arnella and Valrie flashed into his mind: they were about five, and he had taken them to spend the weekend with his parents. The Sunday he went to pick them up, he took them to the beach where they ate fish and bammi. By the time they were ready to go home, they both said they were tired, so he hoisted one on each shoulder and walked to the bus stop. Everyone he passed smiled at him, said what beautiful twins he had, and a photographer who said he worked for the *Gleaner* had stopped him to take a picture of the three of them. The photograph came out about a month later in the *Star*, the three of them, with Valrie and Arnella's arms encircling Milford's neck looking like a single arm. Milford didn't know why that image came to him now, but it made him feel warm and soft and as proud as he had felt that Sunday, father of the beautiful twins.

◆

As Godfree sat fingering a piece of wood, he remembered the conversation he had with his grandmother, Dahlia, when he decided to marry Valrie.

'Nana, ah thinking bout marrying Valrie.'

She glanced at him, then continued what she was doing without saying anything. She knew that meant he had already decided and had probably spoken to Valrie.

'So wha bout Arnella?'

'She say she no wan marry; me fi marry Valrie.'

'So Valrie wan marry you?'

'She seh as long as Arnella no mind.'

Dahlia thought about this; her grandson's luck to have two beautiful women who would gladly share him. But were they sharing him? Everyone said and believed Valrie and Arnella were twins, very much alike, but Dahlia knew this not to be the case. They were very close, and would willingly die for each other she was certain, but they were two very different women. For one thing Arnella didn't want to get married while Valrie was willing. Arnella had returned from apprenticeship with the dressmaker in Montego Bay a self-assured woman. Rather than building a house in the same compound as the rest of the family, much to the protestation and consternation of her mother and aunty-mother she had taken family land that had belonged to her great-grandmother's sister, the one who had died alone in childbirth, a piece of land that hadn't been inhabited for too many years. And Arnella had found a love and a talent for sewing. Valrie had stayed home, chained to Velma's shadow, and had done nothing with her life all these years except grow more beautiful and more bound to her family. She had her parents' skill with cooking and baking, but she did nothing with it except prepare the occasional evening meal. She tended no tree like her grandmother, made no doily with her hand; her gift was her beauty that she kept for herself; she was an orchard yet to bear fruit. Dahlia wondered now if that would be enough for Godfree, who had not yet found his own talent. She, Dahlia, knew what it was, and she also knew the right woman could help him find it as she had helped her husband.

Godfree. She lost her two loves and gained him; now here he was, the recipient of two loves. Dahlia smiled to herself. Who was more deserving than Godfree, born an orphan to an old lady? She had loved both Valrie and Arnella since they were girls, and as she watched them grow, and saw them come flirting with her grandson, tempting him with their plum breasts and smooth skin, teasing him with their innocent open-toothed grins and swaying behinds, she had secretly prayed that he would choose not one, but both.

'What a brata!'

'Wha you seh, Nana?' Godfree said, looking at his grandmother.

Dahlia shook her head, admonished herself for thinking out aloud.

'So you gwane marry Valrie and keep Arnella.' It was not a question. Before he could respond she added, 'Mek sure you nuh bring contention at Brother Milford's house. Him is a private man. No shame me. It no matter how old you is, or where you live, you and me connected.' Dahlia paused and held out her middle finger crossed over her index, to demonstrate the bond that she and Godfree shared. 'No matta whe you go, or who you wid, you and me is one and whatever you do reflect pan me.' She spat, used the toe of her shoe to press the saliva into the earth, closing the conversation and sealing their commitment.

◆

Arnella and Valrie wiped each other's eyes, then laced fingers as they used to as children. Valrie now peered into her sister-cousin's eyes and confessed her pain.

'Nella, me did miss you so bad when you went MoBay to dress-making me decide fi die till you return. But whenever you return you neva tell me what you been doing; you neva come pull me so we could sit down unda a tree and talk and laugh like we used to. So each day you was gone, me would find a quiet place and sit down and bring you to me; dat's how me kept in touch wid you.'

Arnella interrupted. 'Me should a know was you a draw me energy, but me neva tink you did miss me like me miss you.'

'Me did miss you well bad. But even though me did pull you energy fi keep in touch it was neva de same as before when you and me used to share everting.' Valrie had spoken rapidly and her mouth was dry. Arnella poured her some water from the pitcher that was covered on the dresser, and she gulped it down, some trickling down her chin. The silence wrapped them like a baby swaddled in a blanket.

When Arnella spoke her voice came from a faraway place and her eyes followed. 'Ree, when Sister Olive tell me dat you and me not sisters, not twin, dat she wasn't me real mamma, dat Aunty Velma me mother, me felt like a big nail puncture me heart and right away it start bleed. It bleed so much me did tink me was gwane dead. Den when Sister Olive seh we couldn't share everything anymore, and

111

especially not Godfree, and dat since me de oldest me should set an example, me had to keep quiet to stop me heart from bleeding to death. And it just right dis minute stop bleeding; dat's why me can talk wid you again.' Arnella breathed through parted lips, still journeying to that place far away, where the river banks open into the ocean. Baby-Girl cried. Valrie picked up her niece-cousin, comforted the baby on her chest before handing her to Arnella to suckle. Both Arnella and Valrie felt light, giddy, a feeling they hadn't experienced for many, many years. After Arnella nursed the child, Valrie changed her diaper, and the three walked up the river, the salty air stinging their nostrils.

◆

Arnella made Valrie's wedding dress and Godfree's suit, as well as Olive's, Velma's and Dahlia's dresses and her own maid-of-honour dress. It was the largest wedding that Kristoff Village had ever seen. Feasting went on from ten o'clock the morning to late the next night. Two goats, a pig and several chickens and rabbits were killed. Olive made a four-tier wedding cake, and Milford cooked all the food himself. They all drank too much, and Godfree and Valrie spent their first and last time in a hotel, a gift from Olive and Milford's boss, a suite for the weekend. Valrie had wanted Arnella to come with them, but Milford, obviously shocked at her suggestion, said pointedly that the accommodation was only for two. Still, the Sunday night before they came home, Arnella met them in town and the three spent a glorious day surrounded by each other's love. They told no one of this venture.

◆

Godfree was a happy man. He had two sons and a beautiful daughter, and now to make his happiness complete, Valrie and Arnella were not only friends, but they were twin-like again, not listening to anyone who tried to separate them with small jealousies or tell them how they should live their lives. Individually they were both perfectly halved star-apples ready to be bitten, but when bonded they were a

112

complete, whole glimmering star-apple, almost too perfect to touch. Godfree felt their love pumping through his heart, and as his hand fingered the wood, it came apart in almost two equal pieces. He lifted the wood into his lap, pressed the pieces against his chest and caressed them. Then he smiled, hearing his sons' voices demanding that their great-grandmother tell them a story.

Valrie and Godfree's sons were sitting under Aunt Velma's lime tree listening to her end the tale about the time Anancy found a baby girl under the mango tree. Then Velma began a new story. Olive, cooking in the kitchen, heard her mother's voice, strong, ride the wind; she reflected on the time Velma had first told the tale, which she had not then realised was based on the real-life story of one of their maternal ancestors, Nel. But the story had achieved its desired effect. Olive shivered, remembering how frightened she had been. After that, no tempting by boys, including ones she liked, could persuade her to allow them close enough to put their hands on her body. It wasn't until after Valrie and Arnella were born that she figured out Velma's motive in telling her this story just after the onset of her period. She had later tried the same ploy with Valrie and Arnella, but it didn't work. They, especially Arnella, were more intrigued by the daring of this woman, Nel, than by the consequences of her action. Olive was certain that was why Arnella claimed Nel's land after she completed her apprenticeship in Montego Bay. At first Olive and Velma had feared Arnella would settle permanently in Montego Bay because she stayed longer than was necessary. But as it turned out she had been merely working and saving to make a place for herself.

Olive turned the stove down low, and drying her hands on her apron, walked over to Valrie's yard where Velma sat on her low stool almost touching the ground, and the boys sat on the ground at her feet. Velma's palms were opened in her lap; her hair was completely white, but her voice was as richly textured as cassava bread. Olive pulled up a stool and sat beside her grandsons, enraptured as Velma began the familiar tale.

'Time was old back then, so Time even older now. Time carried de weight and Time had de last laugh, and it wasn't always a happy laugh. Sometimes Time's laughter was bitter and frightening, like a sudden gush of wind dat blind you eyes. Dis is such a tale, when Time's laughter was de last thing you wanted to hear.

'Her name was Nel, Pretty Nel people called her. She was sister of you great, great, great grandmother, which would mek her your great, great, great second cousin, ah believe. She was pretty black with thick hair dat shun under de sun and she was full of laughter. After she died, people said Time stole her laughter but he could never mek her laughter his. Nel and her cousin were close and grew together, just like your aunty and mamma, but dem were never dat close and dem didn't love each other as much.

'Many men desired Nel and although she smiled at dem and when she went to parties spent the entire night dancing, no man had the pleasure of referring to her as his girl. She was a heart-breaker! Dat's what people said. After a while her sister got married and soon all her time was spent taking care she husband and she children. Nel was always a wanderer, liking to go off by herself, even at nights. Many times she was warned against such careless behaviour, but headstrong she neva listened.

'Well one night while she off taking one of her walks, she met upon a man. She had never seen such a handsome man. He was more than handsome. He had pretty, smooth skin like black velvet, almond-shaped brown-black eyes, hair black and tightly curled, a dimple in his left cheek; and he sported a beard. De man say hello to Nel, who stopped and talked to him; but even though she was drawn to him she didn't get too close. The fragrance of his breath was like cool mint. Nel felt her knees wobbling, her will failing, so she hurriedly bid de man a good night. As she was leaving, de very pretty man asked her to meet him de same time next evening. Nel ran off widout responding, but de next night she found sheself walking to de same spot, her heart skipping a beat. When she beheld her love waitin for her, her heart flew to her mouth and she was speechless. Dis was love fah true. Dem met every night fah a while, each meeting dem moving closer and closer like dem dancing, dem breaths, his mint, her honey, finally concluding in a kiss; Nel felt herself melting into his arms: the sky filled with stars that twinkled as on a Christmas tree. Birds sang and a cool wind caressed Nel's skin; she felt alive in a way she never had before. Then she was drowning, but could not save herself. De next morning Nel awoke on a gravestone; dat's when she realised she was in love with duppy. Duppy tek her heart. It was too late. She was possessed. She couldn't eat or sleep. Every night she went wandering, searching for dis duppy dat was her love, but she never found him.

'After a while Nel start to feel something moving in she stomach and she knew she was gwane have baby. Shame filled her. She no longer oiled her skin or plaited her hair. She pined for her love. Every time she tried to laugh it sounded like she was barking. Nel could not stand the sight of others so she ran from home and build a little cottage for sheself, right about where you Aunt Nella live.

'Den one bright full moon night she tek in. Dere was no one to call but she neva plan fi call anyone either because she knew she was having duppy baby. She lay down on the bare ground, rolling in pain. She call out for she love just as de baby born and de pretty man who is really a duppy appeared and said three times, "Come wid me, me sweet love; ah miss you more dan life itself." Nel reach out she hand and de duppy tek it.

'Is smell someone smell she. Dem find she and de baby rotten and bloated. De men dem who find she seh de baby was only half-human. No one did know Nel did pregnant cause she did shame and neva tell anyone. Everyone did warn her not to walk late at night and not talk to any man, but she neva listen. Her beauty didn't mean a ting. Time took it like him tek her laughter. Him had de last laugh. Time is like duppy, same way dem laugh like john-crow wid field rat caught in him throat.'

Rain clouds burst on Kristoff Village unexpectedly. People ran to cover, women hurried to gather in clothes that were almost dry. Children danced in the rain, running out of hearing range from their mothers; this was not a cold-getting rain, this was prancing rain, so sweet, so playful, a hose to cool the heat.

You don't say

Devil sweated even though he had done very little. He felt as if he was in a furnace, but he strolled around his garden, admiring the wonderful job the neighbours' sons had done. The deep green leaves of pink periwinkle that edged one fence shone under the sun; the cassin tree that grew by the front gate was in splendid bloom, its flowers like yellow clusters of grapes. In the back, creating a screen around the veranda, red and purple bougainvillaeas stretched up to the sky. Devil loved the riotous colours of the many flowers and trees. Seeing the red gingers shimmering near the fowl coop, he picked a handful, knowing how much She-Devil loved them. Then he turned the sprinkler high before going in search of his love.

When She-Devil glanced over her shoulder and saw Devil with a handful of red gingers she ran up to him, forgetting about the cake she had just put in the oven, and threw her arms around his neck. Tegreg would have found them like that, except Man-Stick in his excitement blew the horn.

Devil stomped his feet. 'Why dem must always disturb a man just when him . . .'

She-Devil cut him off. 'Noboda vex; just go see is who and tell dem we busy.'

Devil put on his 'Not Welcome' face. He was fed up with so many people losing their way and dropping in on him without warning; he was not a public servant. He just wanted to enjoy his wife. The Angels were more gregarious than he was, so from now on he was going to send uninvited guests to them. But he opened the front door and saw Tegreg, his baby girl, walking towards him. His mask of unwelcome dropped away and he jumped in the air and kicked his heels together. She-Devil, hearing Devil's delighted scream, smiled: her baby was home. She pulled off her apron and ran to embrace her child.

Tegreg loved her father's garden, and couldn't remember when she had seen it more beautiful than it was now, all the flowers and trees in bloom, colours everywhere, the grass cut and leaves raked. She remembered Man-Stick used to say her father's yard was the Garden of Eden. Her eyes didn't fail to notice the freshly painted rails and plant stands. Tegreg walked arm-in-arm with her father to the back yard where the bougainvillaea created its own enclosure from the veranda. They sat on the bench facing the sweet-sop tree, heavy with fruits, looked into each other's eyes and smiled. Tegreg realised how much she loved her father and missed him, their late-evening walks,

Devil pointing out all the trees, shrubs, birds, the names of which he knew. As much as Tegreg loved flowers and plants she couldn't remember the names, except for the most basic, like croton which grew wild in many different species, and which many people used to create a colourful edging to their homes.

Now Tegreg took on her little girl's voice and asked her father to identify some flowers. 'Daddy, what's that called again?'

Devil beamed with pride. Nothing made him feel more important than having one of his children ask him a question to which he had the answer; he felt especially proud because his Tegreg was asking about something which he grew and tended with his own hands.

'Dose anthurium. See dose small multi-coloured ones? A new experiment.'

Tegreg looked closely; sure enough a few of the smaller anthurium were a mixture of deep red, the most prevalent colour, and pink and white. She had never seen that before and was visibly impressed with her father's alchemy. She decided then and there that she would try her hand at a garden when she returned home, since Man-Stick was unable to grow even weeds.

'Daddy, will you give me some plants when I'm going home so I can start my own garden?'

Devil was so overcome, he could only nod his head in confirmation.

They walked into the kitchen where Man-Stick sat in front of an array of pastries, including fresh-baked bread, coconut frosting cake, which Tegreg could see her mother had just finished frosting, sweet-potato pudding, her father's favourite, and if her nose was working well, banana bread, her brother's favourite. Tegreg was overwhelmed by the different smells. A wave of nausea swept over her and her lunch came up right there in the kitchen. She tried to swallow, but still the nausea came up. She-Devil rushed to her daughter's side, and Devil brought her a glass of water.

'Sugar-Dumplin, you okay?' She-Devil, asked, worry in her voice.

'She all right. Doctor seh dat kind of ting normal for a woman in her condition,' spat Man-Stick, continuing to eat. Tegreg couldn't speak just then, but she wished she had put a piece of tape over Man-Stick's mouth. She gave him the eye, but he was too busy with his third slice of bread to notice. She had discussed this with Man-Stick

117

before they arrived. Tegreg herself wanted to be the one to surprise her parents with the news that in another six months they were going to be grandparents. But not in the kitchen. She had planned to wait until they were all seated for dinner because she knew her mother had probably planned a special meal, Tegreg's favourite food, and was going to have them all seated formally at the mahogany dining table with linen tablecloth and napkins. Now here was her bumbling husband, with no sense of tact, spilling her surprise like it was water running down the drain. Tegreg sighed deeply as she turned to her father, who had called her by his pet-name for her.

'Pretty-One, wha dis bout doctor?' Devil asked, not really having heard what Man-Stick said, and touching Tegreg's forehead to see if she had a fever.

She-Devil had heard, and momentarily was puzzled, but as she bent to wipe up the vomit, it dawned on her; she smiled secretly. Grandmother! What a blessing! She suspected that Tegreg wanted to tell them in her own way, so she tried to distract Devil. 'Stop questioning de child, and bring her some sweet-sop juice dat she love. Or is forget you forget what you picknie like.'

Devil scratched his head and moved to the refrigerator. Even before they heard the continuous trademark rhythm of Brimstone's car horn, Devil recognised the roar of the twenty-year-old Land Rover he had given to his son when he was seventeen. Were his ears fooling him? He hurriedly poured a glass of sweet-sop juice. When he turned around he saw Tegreg and She-Devil heading down the hallway to the living room, moving in the direction of the front door. He slammed the glass on the nearest counter, spilling some, and hurried behind them. Today was Friday, his lucky day. Both children home. Devil was beside himself. Maybe She-Devil had known. She must have; that's why she had the Angels' boys do the yard and the girls give the house a thorough cleaning.

Whereas Tegreg was lean and even-tempered like Devil, Brimstone was big-boned, colourful and bouncy like She-Devil, except his personality bordered more on the flamboyant side. Brimstone always thrived on attention and he knew exactly what to do to get it. Before the jeep had come to a complete stop, he jumped over the closed door, ran up to his mother, picked her off her feet, spun her around,

118

then kissed her long and loud on both cheeks. Seeing his sister, Tegreg, he did the same to her. Then he saw his father standing back with a big smile on his face. He ran up to him, tackled him by the waist, threw him over his shoulder and spun him around too. Then Brimstone looked at the three of them standing there, laughter all over their faces, and he threw back his head and shouted, 'It good to be home, man!'

The people in Kristoff Village were startled by what sounded like a squeal that broke through the sky.

She-Devil took her son's face between her hands and examined it closely, making his eyes meet hers. Satisfied with what she saw she released him to his father. Man-Stick sauntered over to them, a slice of pie in one hand, and slapped his brother-in-law on his shoulder before they embraced. The five of them stood with arms around each other's waist just looking at each other and smiling as if they were getting ready to play a ring game.

'Can we get out?' The child's voice interrupted their game, and all turned at once.

Brimstone broke loose, ran to the jeep, picked up a boy about eight years old and placed him on his back. Next he took out another boy about six, and hoisted him on to his shoulders. Finally, he lifted out a little girl of two and said, 'Come on; they won't bite!' before walking towards Devil, She-Devil, Tegreg and Man-Stick, who all stood with their mouths open. To their amazement they realised that Brimstone had spoken to a petite, sand-coloured woman with long braids, wearing a multi-coloured skirt with a red midriff blouse and sandals. Her toenails were painted gold and three of her toes bore rings. She was beautiful, and her smile revealed the most perfect, pearly white teeth they had ever seen. Even Man-Stick, who thought Tegreg was quite fine and daily thanked the stars for sending her to him, couldn't help but let out a breath. Tegreg gave him the eyes and he had sense enough to pretend that he had coughed.

Brimstone strolled up to his blood relations and announced, 'Folks, dis brood hanging all over and off me, and even dis beauty by me side, is me new family.'

At that point the gorgeous woman locked arms with Brimstone and smiled even more engagingly at them. Devil, She-Devil and Tegreg looked at each other, then at Brimstone with the children hanging from him like leaves on a tree, and then at the gorgeous woman. Nobody said a word. Man-Stick, who came alive in the most awkward situations, rescued the moment. He extended his hand to the gorgeous woman and declared, 'Welcome to our family. Please come in.' He took the boy sitting on Brimstone's shoulder on to his own back and started to lead the way to the veranda.

It wasn't until they were on the third step that She-Devil recovered and ran to join them, thinking as she went, 'Ah too old fah all dis excitement. First Devil wid his nonsense almost kill me, now me children giving me heart-attack. Me soon turn grandmother!'

They were all on the veranda and Brimstone placed the children on the porch swing. She-Devil was lost in her own thoughts. 'Grandmother! But what me saying?' she said out loud before catching herself. 'If me can count, look like me is grandmother three times over already. Lawd! Dis excitement gwane kill me.'

Somehow they managed introductions. She-Devil brought them all juice. The children drank it up, ran up and down the veranda, shouted, climbed on the railings, and swung in the porch swing so roughly that it knocked down one of Devil's anthuriums. All the while Brimstone held court, centre stage, filling in the family on all his various activities, drama in his every move. They were spellbound. Finally one of the children walked up to She-Devil and innocently asked, 'Can I call you Nana?' She-Devil smiled at the request and nodded her head, yes. Brimstone was still recounting his escapades, and his lovely lady seemed enraptured by his voice. The younger boy put his arms around She-Devil and said. 'Can we eat? Me hungry.' She-Devil was embarrassed at her negligence. She took the child by his hand and they went into the kitchen to warm up the meal and set the table. Before they were through, the lovely lady, who said her name was Tallawah, joined She-Devil and the boy, her son, who was called Anansi after the trickster spider. By the time the food was on the table, She-Devil had decided that she liked Tallawah and had silently approved the union.

Tallawah's name suited her; she seemed truly a spirited warrior, which was what it meant. She had married at seventeen, she told She-Devil, and bore her first son before her eighteenth birthday. Like most young wives, she had been more enamoured of the whole idea of marriage than of her husband. She submitted to him more than she should have. But she was a woman of varied interests. Always interested in theatre, she resumed acting after her first son was born. Her husband didn't object as long as it didn't get in the way of her duties, cleaning the house, having his meals prepared. By the time Tallawah was twenty-four, she had two sons and had miscarried a third. Her mind was restless. She decided to focus on another life-long love: writing. That's when the trouble started. Her husband said it was not natural for a woman to lock herself up and think and write. He disrespected her privacy, and always sent the children to barge in and interrupt her. He claimed what she was doing was unhealthy. One day after a successful morning at her typewriter, she produced six wondrous pages. She placed them on the dining table to proof later. Her husband came home hot and thirsty, and demanded something to drink. Tallawah got up and gave him some juice. He spilled it, but rather than getting a cloth to wipe up the spill, he took the six pages she had laboured over, and, ignoring her protest, used them to blot up the juice. Then, further to demonstrate his displeasure at her writing, he took the pages and tossed them away.

The tears made Tallawah's eyes glisten, but they did not spill down her cheeks. She would not give him the satisfaction. She thought of taking a knife and shoving it into his side, but decided he wasn't worth her anger. Within days of the incident, she discovered she was pregnant, and so it took six months. But one day, while her husband was at work, Tallawah packed up and left with a two-week-old baby girl and her two sons. She left her husband a poem which read.

> I am my name
> I will dance
> to the flame that
> beats in my heart.
>
> You tried to contain me
> but like the wind
> I'm elusive.
> I am my name.

121

And so she had been on her own ever since, acting and writing, three plays to her credit. But five months ago, at the preview of her latest play, she met Brimstone, and they fell in love.

The story warmed She-Devil's heart, and she embraced Tallawah, welcoming her to the family.

Dinner was splendid. Even though the children spilled food on the beige linen tablecloth, and Devil smacked too loudly, all were pleased with the sauté egg-plant (Brimstone's favourite), steamed swordfish (Tegreg's favourite), curried rice and fried green banana (Devil's choice), and stuffed cho-cho (She-Devil's speciality). Just before they were about to pry themselves from the table, Man-Stick knocked his spoon against his glass and said, 'Ah request everyone's undivided attention. Me lovely wife, Tegreg, has a very important announcement.'

Tegreg was taken aback, because what with Brimstone's stories she had forgotten her plans to announce her pregnancy. She felt somewhat shy, fearing that her news was not as thrilling as Brimstone's adventures, but Man-Stick was insistent. 'Sweet-Biscuit,' he coaxed, using his private name for Tegreg, 'is crime fi keep such news to youself.'

By now Devil was very intrigued, as was Brimstone, who went over to his sister, put his arms around her neck and urged, 'Come on now, Miss Fire-Mouth, tell us your news.' At that very moment, Tegreg felt as if she wanted to vomit, and panicked. She swallowed, and the feeling passed. She pushed back her chair, and looking directly into her mother's eyes she said, 'Ah go give you a grandchild in six months.'

Although She-Devil knew what Tegreg was going to say, hearing the announcement hit her. She covered her mouth and tears streamed down her face. Devil jumped into the air and let out a great scream. Brimstone hugged his sister and said, 'Me gwane be a uncle! You just made me a very happy man. Blessings, me sister.'

After everyone quieted, and Tegreg had been hugged by everyone including Tallawah's children, Brimstone said since the day was near to perfect, he was going to test his luck, and moving to stand directly in front of Tallawah, and looking first at his father then his mother, he cleared his throat and asked, 'Tallawah Christian, you de woman who has taken me heart, swept it clean, except of your enchanting fragrance. Will you marry me?'

A brief silence of surprise, followed by the excitement of a child's voice. 'Marry him, Mamma. Please! Him so funny,' begged Anansi. Brimstone smiled at the boy. Tallawah looked at all the faces staring at her. Then she bowed to Devil and She-Devil and addressed them: 'Mother, Father, if me allowed to call you so.' Then she turned and extended her hand to Tegreg and Man-Stick. 'Sister and brother, if me seh yes to Brimstone, me will be saying yes to all of oonuh too. Oonuh willing to accept me?' Tegreg's confirmation was an embrace. She-Devil went over to Tallawah, took her by the shoulder, and walking her over to Brimstone said, 'Today you came home, child. Now embrace you man.' The children clapped, and Devil with much pain shouted, 'Is fi me day dis! Is fi me day!'

Neither Devil or She-Devil could fall asleep that night. They tossed and talked and laughed and were very very happy like newly-weds.

The people of Kristoff Village sweated and due to the heat could not sleep; they cursed the heat of the day that refused to seek shelter at night.

All things made plain

Miss Cotton woke with a headache that kept her in bed and made her husband and granddaughter worry. She soaked a scarf in bay rum and tied it around her head. She sourly sent her granddaughter to boil her some fennel tea, which she drank without sugar, making up her face each time she sipped the bitter liquid. Her stomach was in knots.

She did not want to see what she saw. She didn't know how to prevent the inevitable. All day Miss Cotton locked herself in the room, not opening the wooden shutter to let in sun or breeze. Every so often Master Cotton, who was stationed by the bedroom door on his straight-backed chair, heard Miss Cotton humming; but it was such a deep painful humming that several times he found himself wiping tears from his eyes. Was she going to die? Several people coming to the store to purchase this or that item, finding Miss Cotton absent for the first time in memory, enquired of her; and when her granddaughter told them of her condition, they made their way further up the hill to her house and enquired of Master Cotton. He could not provide them with any satisfactory explanation so they waited around, called 'Howdy!' and shouted 'Feel betta' to Miss Cotton, then reluctantly moved off to their homes and chores. 'Something nuh right, a-tall, a-tall,' they mumbled, cupping their breath in their hands and throwing it over their shoulders to thwart any evil that was present.

While Beryl was at her 'piece of land', as she called it, she heard a woman's voice calling to her. At first the voice was pleasant, but the more she listened the more accusing the tone. She had woken with her head pounding; it felt as if someone had broken rock on it. She had got up and boiled fresh garlic, sweetened it with molasses, and drunk two cups full before she felt her strength return to her, but still her head pounded. She hadn't done much all day at the field, and now as the woman's voice faded with the wind, she felt all her energy leave her. She slumped on the ground and bawled, her wail scaring the ground lizards and inviting her faithful brown and white mutt, Two-Coloured, to raise his voice and howl with her.

Since their granddaughter, Baby-Girl, had been born, Velma and Dahlia had renewed their girlhood friendship, visiting each other and swapping stories. Restless, and finding no comfort under her lime tree, Velma walked to Dahlia's house. As is the custom, just as she approached Dahlia's house, Velma called out, 'Who dere? Anyone home? Aunt Dahlia? Is me, Velma, you friend.'

'Ah! Aunty Velma! Ah by de pipe. Come! Come rest you feet,' another voice rang out. When the two women saw each other, they fanned back their right hands in greeting, and Velma sat on the stool out of the sun. Dahlia was scrubbing the bottom of her pots with mud and gravel to make them shine. Velma watched her and remembered how much she hated scrubbing pots; but it was evident from Dahlia's effort that she enjoyed this chore. For some reason Velma thought about the man who twice had planted his seeds in her womb. She knew he wasn't sitting by the side of the road anymore, sharpening his machete. The thought made her giggle. She wondered how he was doing. But that was not what disturbed her.

'You feel it too. Ah tell you, ah couldn't sleep last night,' said Dahlia.

'Strange. Very strange. Ah can't put me finger pan anything. But ah feel it right here,' and Velma touched her heart.

They began to hum an old tune, the words of which neither of them knew, but it was layered and sounded like a chorus of weeping women. They stretched out the hum, trying to hold back the tide, but they didn't know from which direction it was coming. They just sensed it, and felt all the more hopeless because there was nothing they could do.

The two elders sat still, listened closely to all the sounds. They were two old women who had carried and buried their own crosses, and were now quite contented with their lives. Dahlia, more prone to questioning and disagreeing with nature and trying Devil's patience, turned to Velma, her voice like dry twigs being cracked and tossed on a heap to make a fire.

'Velma, you and me did know, you can't walk straight widout turning a corner.'

Velma nodded her head in agreement, and weighed whether or not to add her two-pence.

Desmond had not been able to work all day. He knew Grace deserved more, but he didn't have it to give her. For more than a week he hadn't slept at home, just going there to change his clothes and say hello to his children. The last time he was there Althea, his daughter, tried to talk to him, but Grace told her she better hurry since she was already late for school. Desmond had been relieved because he thought Althea was going to question him about not being home. Worse was Grace's behaviour. She acted like he was never gone. Every evening she prepared him food and sent it to Monica. They both ate it, laughing at her foolishness. But what was Grace to do? He wasn't being fair to her. From the very beginning she had always done as he asked, had always been supportive; she was just not what he wanted, and hadn't been for a long time. But it had never bothered him until Monica came. The thought of Monica made his heart race

125

and his blood boil. Desmond was like a bee trapped in honey, and he wanted to drown there. Maybe no one in Kristoff Village had ever divorced before, but there was no law saying he couldn't. 'Maybe dat would be betta. To come clean and break wid Grace. Den at least she free to do what she want and me picknie dem won't tink me is just anoda wukless man wid outside woman.' Desmond decided to go home directly after work and inform Grace of his plans.

Monica was still glamorous, and probably the only woman in Kristoff Village who regularly took pride in painting her finger- and toenails. Because the day was so hot, Monica sat in her panties and a cotton blouse in the living room, the front door wide open, her feet resting on the centre table as she painted her nails. The young girl who came in to clean, wash and cook had sent her little brother to say she was ill, so she hadn't been in for four days. As Monica blew on her nails, she saw the film of dirt on the tile floor and on the furniture. Feeling suddenly domestic, and not wanting Desmond to think her sloppy, Monica disregarded her wet nails, and went for the broom and dust cloth and began to clean her house.

She had a sensation that someone was at her shoulder, but whenever she turned around, the person was gone. She sweated under her arms and in her palms. The more fear crept on her, the more earnestly she dusted, even dusting the pictures hanging on the wall and moving furniture to sweep in corners. Still she couldn't shake it. She heard the voice.

'But is who you think you is, coming back here and throwing folks' piss in dem face? You don't have no shame? You won't mend you ways? Mek you tink you can live lawless among those wid rules? You tink you is man too? Plenty dirt pan you feet.'

It was her mother. Monica knew it was her mother, who had never forgiven her for running away, who had never forgiven her for spreading her legs freely to men. Monica heard the anger in her mother's voice, the anger of failure. The mother had not been able to keep Monica safely bound to Kristoff. While Monica was away, free from the voice of the community, her mother was trapped, having to pretend not to hear the malicious slander of her daughter, the whore. Her daughter the whore! A woman whose daughter was a whore had failed, and Monica's mother died with that pain. Now she came to tell her daughter that she would no longer walk behind her and watch over her. She was on her own.

Monica screamed into the empty room.

'Mamma, why you can't just accept me for what me is? Is what you want from me?'

She heard the shrill laughter as it floated out the window. 'Is no wha me want from you dat gwane hurt.'

Monica held her head in her hands and closed her eyes till she was certain her mother was gone.

She couldn't prevent the change that was occurring in herself. She was not going to give up Desmond. Damn, blast the consequences. She had always done as she pleased and she wasn't going to change now. Other women played by the rules, but she made the rules as she went along. She put away the mop and dust cloth and went to the bathroom. Before turning on the shower, she talked to herself in the mirror. 'Chow! Grace had Desmond all dis while and neva know wha fi do wid him. Is my turn now. Me no care who don't like it.' With a defiant turn, Monica ignored the small voices echoing in her head and took a long shower.

During the seven months of her pregnancy Marva had gained sixty pounds. Although miserable, she still kept stuffing food in her mouth. She looked like a bloated frog about to burst. She knew Ainsworth was disgusted by her appearance, although he was still attentive. But she also knew that his attentiveness was for the baby's sake. Daily Marva prayed she was carrying a girl. If it was a girl she was going to have her tubes tied. Her neck had disappeared, her skin was discoloured and blotchy, her nose was swollen, and the varicose veins made it painful to walk. Her hair, which had always been red, was dull and brittle. Marva hated herself. She resented Ainsworth for preferring to read rather than talk with her. Books were everywhere in their house. He would spend almost an hour in the bathroom – she and the boys would have to bang on the door, and he would be in there reading. Sometimes she heard him laughing and talking, and when she went to see who he was talking to, all she saw was his head buried in a book. He got more fun out of books than being with her.

Lately he was reading more, even at the dinner table, which Peggy said was poor manners. When she told him so, he said, 'Den go eat wid Peggy.' He never looked at her any more, or caressed her arms like he used to do in the mornings before leaving for work. Most nights he slept on the sofa or with one of the boys, because he said her gas was overpowering. Now every evening after dinner, he and his sons sat in a circle and took turns reading to each other. When she complained, he invited her to join him, even though he knew she read poorly; two of her sons read better than she. Marva felt Ainsworth wanted to embarrass her, make her seem small.

Then Ainsworth and Monica had become friends. Feeling jealous, and angered by Monica's acceptance back into the community, Marva had accused Ainsworth of sleeping with her, just like his friend, Desmond.

'Whe you hear man and woman is friend? Is idiot you tek me fah? You should a shame fuckin de whore.'

Ainsworth, with a tone in his voice Marva had not heard before, warned her not to speak to him in that kind of language ever again. He said, 'You have children, suppose dem hear you. If you don't respect youself or me, show dem respect.' And he went on to say, 'Me respect meself and our marriage. Monica is a friend. She like me reading to her. Ah haven't slept with her, nor do I have any intentions.' He ended using his business voice.

His words hurt Marva deeply. She was boiling and added the quarrel to the list of injuries that Monica had inflicted on her. She was convinced that Monica was the cause of the problems she and Ainsworth were having. She remembered the other morning when she was passing by Monica's yard and heard her singing at the top of her voice, 'Cordelia Brown wha mek you head so red?' Marva believed Monica was teasing her. The song made her remember her school days when the children had teased her about her hair, changing the name in the folk song to sing, 'Marva Hendricks, wha mek you head so red? You si-down inna de sun-shine wid nutten pan you head. Is dat mek you head so red?' Then they would laugh, and run away, leaving her crying.

'De damn whore. Change everything since she come back.' Marva was consumed with jealousy and anger.

The day was so hot, Marva's thighs rubbed against each other, chafing. She could not find a cool spot, so walked around like a woman possessed. At last she settled and decided to season the meat for dinner. Her craving for hot pepper had increased with her size. She walked to the side of her yard where a scott bonnet tree was laden with stinging peppers. She picked a large bowl of them. After seasoning the meat and cutting up two whole peppers into it, she decided to take some peppers for her friends. Peggy wasn't home, so Marva headed for Grace where she found Peggy comforting their mutual friend.

'Ah tell you ah don't know what else fi do. Desmond don't come home anymore, except to change him clothes. Ah cook him dinner every evening and send it to him, and him and him sweetheart, de one Monica, nyam up me food widout any shame.' Grace paused, stirring the food, but would not meet the eyes of her friends. Marva tossed the peppers on the table where she and Peggy sat.

The music from the radio was like a wasp circling their heads. Peggy snapped, 'Turn that damn radio off so ah can think.' She tapped her fingers on the table and called Grace to sit with them. Taking Grace's hands into hers as she would those of a child, Peggy said, 'Grace, forgive me for saying so, for God knows you is me friend, but you acting like a blasted idiot. Sending food to your husband at him sweetheart house. Of course dem eat. Dem know you too good to poison them. Besides, Monica can't even boil water. Now if it was Trevor, he wouldn't touch it because him know ah would poison him rass.'

Marva looked at Peggy in surprise, hearing her curse for the first time.

Then Marva offered her own advice. 'What de one Monica want is a good beatin.'

'A good tracing down would be more appropriate,' Peggy chimed in. 'We don't want to be too common.'

Grace spoke quietly, yet carefully. 'We not any match for tracin Monica. Ah sure she do plenty tracin in she life.'

'So what? You gwane just give up Desmond without a fight?' came the incredulous voice of Peggy.

'You all see if it was me? It wouldn't done so. Me would have fi

129

call Monica out she name. Me would fight she and tear off she clothes. Nutten too common fi do fi keep me man.' Marva spat and began fingering the peppers.

Children came home from school, did their chores, completed their homework and went outside to play until father came home from work or the field to have dinner. Grace's children sat alone, and none of them was given the unbearable task of delivering food to their father. Besides, he wasn't at Monica's. They hadn't heard his motor-bike. Their mother served their food and left the house without eating, giving them instructions to put away the left-over food and clean up the kitchen.

Ainsworth heaped a forkful of stew peas and rice into his mouth and gagged. His nostrils burned and his eyes watered. He reached for water and gulped the glass in one swallow. Marva sat chewing her food. The boys all began to cough and reached for their waters.

'God, Marva, mek you use so much pepper! De children can't eat dis.'

Their eyes were all teary. Ainsworth pushed back his chair from the table, grabbed his sons' plates and emptied one in the dog's dish. The dog swallowed the food greedily, then let out a yelp and ran to his water bowl.

'Marva, is what get into you? De food even too peppery for Stumpy.' Then thinking perhaps Marva was eating separate food, Ainsworth took the fork out of her hand and put a mouthful of her food into his mouth. His jaws puckered and his sinus unplugged. Shaking his head, Ainsworth went into the kitchen and made his sons and himself corn-beef sandwiches for dinner.

Cold feet bring grief

Darkness was beginning to cover the day, but still Desmond had not come home, nor had his wife sent his dinner. Monica had cooked steamed fish, rice, cabbage and carrots, which were cold now, and the table which had been set for two was unused. She was restless. She

130

felt as though ants were crawling under her skin. She tried to shake the feeling by watching television, but was too distracted. She was dressed in a lacy blue off-the-shoulder dress, had rouge on her cheeks and powder on her face. She looked pretty, but felt cheap.

'Is whe Desmond deh so late?' she said aloud, walking to her gate and looking in the direction from which he would come. He hadn't returned to Kristoff Village because she hadn't heard his bike. She paced back inside, flouncing her skirt as she walked and exaggerating the sway of her hips. How had she arrived at this stage in her life, waiting on a man? Someone else's husband, at that? She lay on the sofa and dozed. She did not hear them enter until she felt the scarf stuffed deep into her throat.

She started to laugh at their boldness, but caught sight of their eyes, and her breath stopped. They were angry. They hated her. Two marched around her, fingering her dress, jabbing her in the face and chest while the third stood behind and firmly pushed her down on the sofa by the shoulder. She knew them, they knew her; but this wasn't a game. The evening was suddenly cool and very quiet. She couldn't hear a mosquito buzzing or a cricket chirping as hard as she listened. She needed sound. They supplied it, threatening her and reviling her as they shoved her into the bedroom, pushed her on the bed. They wound rope around her wrists and ankles, attached the pieces around her hands to the window levers so she was spread across her bed, and the pieces attached to her feet to the closet door. They pulled her closet open, grabbed out her clothes, went into her dresser drawers, turned out her underclothes, emptied her many bottles of perfume, sprinkled powder in her hair and laughed. The first sound was her tears.

Then they closed in on her and one of them smeared her face with pepper, pushed pepper up her nose. They flung her dress over her head and ripped off her panties. One of them shoved her peppered fingers as deep into her womb as they could reach until the cup of chopped peppers was empty and her fingers were on fire. They didn't say anything then. They didn't look at her or one another. They couldn't hear her scream in her head or see her tears sealing her eyes. As they left, they turned off the television and lights and pulled the door shut behind them, leaving her to go silently mad.

131

Bitch! Whore! Man-stealer!

No stars warmed the sky, no moon held court. They walked in single file, shadowing the banking. Their steps were light, their hearts heavy.

'Night.'

'Night.'

'Night,' they mumbled as the first reached home.

'Night.'

'Night,' they mumbled as the second arrived at her house.

The third pulled the gate closed behind her. Swollen fingers were immersed in lime water.

You can't fool the devil

Her godmother and only true friend was frequently heard saying, 'All life begins and ends wid tears.' Monica never understood what the phrase meant, but as she lay tied to her pain she understood fully. If she survived the pain, and she wished to, she wanted another chance to make right her life. She would be more careful and respectful of others' feelings. She was not going to concentrate on the fire raging inside her most private place, for it would only consume her. She would focus on the only person who could save her, the person who always came to her rescue, who forgave her wrongs, rebuked and applauded her. Monica focused all of the little energy that she still had on Miss Cotton until Miss Cotton's face loomed over her. Then darkness spared her some of the pain.

'Jesus Christ! Merciful Lawd!' Miss Cotton screamed, sitting up in bed. Her husband, who was dozing by his vigilant post at the door, came awake and stirred out of the chair. Miss Cotton was pulling on her dress when he opened the door. She kept mumbling, 'No one deserve dat, no one.' She would not answer his questions. Instead she pushed past him and hurried down the steps without her lantern.

The night was dark and cool, and an eerie wind whistled as Miss Cotton hurried to Monica. She hoped she was not too late, but she was afraid; she needed help. As she turned into Monica's gate she smelled it, and cupped her hands to her mouth and shouted twice.

'Sista Beryl, oh! Sista Beryl, oh! Ah calling on you.' She didn't wait for response. If Beryl was alive she would arrive shortly. Miss Cotton stumbled on the bottom step that led to the veranda, but did not slacken her pace. She pushed the door open and tried to see through the darkness. She smelled it. What was it? With her hands in front of her like a blind person, she found the bedroom door, walked in, immediately felt grit and fabric slowing her path. She smelled it. Tears blinded her. Concentrate. She couldn't fall apart. Search as she did along the wall she couldn't find the light switch. Tears took her senses. Concentrate. She was shaking. She was too late.

'Moda Cotton? Moda Cotton? You in dere?' came Beryl's voice from outside. Miss Cotton couldn't speak but the light found her, and together she and Beryl discovered Monica – half dead from the fire raging in her womb. Miss Cotton buried her head on Monica's stomach and wailed while Beryl cut Monica free with her machete. They smelled it, but couldn't identify it. So familiar. Their nostrils flared and eyes teared. Beryl recovered first from the horror and ran and fetched a basin of water. Miss Cotton was still wailing, her head buried on Monica's stomach. The two of them couldn't do it alone. They needed help. But the others were too far; neither of them could leave. Beryl used Monica's ripped panties to wash the lips of her vagina that were swollen and blistered. Water was not enough. They needed helping hands. She placed the ripped, dripping panties in Miss Cotton's hand, and ordered her to wash the wound. Then, taking the lantern, Beryl ran out the back door, cut through a path in the back of the yard and ran the quarter mile to the nearest house. Out of breath she called, 'Daughta Angel! Cousin Rupert!' When they came out to her, she couldn't speak. Rupert brought her water and finally she managed, her eyes not focusing. 'Daughta Angel ah need to borrow you. Cousin Rupert, is oman business dis. Run go call Aunty Velma and Miss Dahlia. Tell them hurry come to Miss Monica's house.' Beryl grabbed Angel by the hand and pulled her along. Angel remembered the first night she arrived in Kristoff Village; it was such a night as this one. Her heart beat loudly with fear.

By the time Beryl got back with Angel, Miss Cotton had recovered enough to strip Monica and get her sucking a piece of cloth on which she had poured condensed milk.

Angel was devastated. 'Who?! What?!' she began, alarm rising in her voice.

Monica tried to dig inside herself, and Beryl and Angel struggled to keep her from tearing herself apart. She couldn't speak, or wouldn't.

When Rupert went to get Velma he found her sitting on Olive's veranda telling stories, Valrie's children leaning on the arms of her rocking chair. Olive acknowledged him and he went and whispered in her ear. She in turn whispered in his ear, and patted him on the back. Then Rupert headed for the path that led to Dahlia's house. Olive went over to her mother, touched her arm, and immediately the mother said, 'Story done fah tonight,' and rose from the chair. Olive called to Milford, who was dozing and watching television. 'Milly. Wake up. Aunty Velma and I gwane tek a walk. Come put de boys to bed.' Mother and daughter moved quickly down the road.

As Rupert turned down the track that led to Dahlia's house, he cursed himself for not bringing a lantern. It was dark, the path was almost completely blocked by foliage, so the ground was damp and slippery underfoot. He walked gingerly, looking down at his feet even though he could hardly see them. It wasn't until he was almost upon the figure that he heard it and stopped, his heart racing. The figure stopped too. Rupert heard his breathing and wondered if he should run? He waited. Nothing. Finally he managed, imitating bravery.

'Who dere?'

'Is me should be asking. Is only me one live down dese ways.'

Rupert smiled, recognising Dahlia's voice. 'Night, Aunty Dahlia. Is you me coming to get. Cousin Beryl want you at Miss Monica's house.'

'So is whe de light you bring fi light we way?'

Rupert laughed out loud; he knew Dahlia was teasing him. 'Ah was in such a haste to reach you, Aunty Dahlia, ah forget de light at home.'

'All right. Come tek me hand and help de old oman; me leg dem not so strong anymore, but walk fast.'

'Yes Aunty Dahlia,' Rupert replied, guiding the old woman by the arm.

When Velma and Olive saw Monica, Olive screamed out. Velma pinched her nose and sucked in her breath and both swore silently under their breath. Olive realised soon that Miss Cotton was too distressed to be of use, so took her into the living room as Velma suggested. Dahlia arrived at that moment. Olive left Miss Cotton in the living room and walked Dahlia into the bedroom. The old woman who had buried her husband and daughter and single-handedly raised her grandson looked at Monica and all the anger and sorrow that she had felt thirty-three years earlier when first her husband then her daughter died, surged up again and the tears she had refused to shed in defiance and stubbornness then, came forth now like a hose turned on. Dahlia fell on her knees, clasped her hands on her head and shouted, 'Jesus peace! Is who wicked so? Merciful saviour! Is who bad-minded so!'

Beryl and Angel had found it necessary to tie Monica's hands loosely at the wrist to prevent her from tearing out her hair. Her eyes were open wide, wild looking as if she was trying to see what she needed to do.

Velma spoke to Dahlia. 'It all up inna her. We have fi get it out or she gwane rotten.'

Dahlia quickly withdrew her hand when she touched Monica. 'She roasting up. We have fi cool her down.'

'Put her in the bath tub.' Angel's foreign-sounding voice cut through the room. Beryl and Angel carried Monica into the bathroom, and she collapsed into the tub. They ran the water and Angel ran back and forth to the kitchen for bottles of cold water and trays of ice to empty into the tub. She had to keep moving now or she wouldn't be able to move, not for a very long time, she was certain.

In the tub Monica started to moan, not like a person, more like a dog that has been wounded and has taken itself off to die or heal alone. Miss Cotton, who was sitting on the sofa, and whose tears had not stopped flowing, stood up when Monica began to moan, stomped the ball of her right foot into the floor and beat her palms together without the fingers touching. Olive could see that Miss Cotton felt better now, her sadness turning to rage, so she left her and went into the bathroom. Olive helped Monica out of the tub and patted her dry with a towel. As she turned to drain the tub, she saw tiny pieces of fleshy red pepper floating in the water. She swore under her breath, kissing her teeth. She knew that a lot more pepper was still inside

135

Monica, and they would have to douche it out. She grabbed Monica's hot water bottle, hanging on a hook on the door, as she guided Monica out of the bathroom.

'Beryl, go find pawpaw and fresh ginger,' Velma ordered.

'You,' Dahlia said, taking Angel's hand, 'go put water to fire to boil, then find some towel.'

Angel heard herself whisper 'Yes mam,' before hurrying to her task.

Olive and Beryl washed the green pawpaw, peeled it, then beat it into a paste. Angel grated the fresh ginger then tossed it into the pot of boiling water and stirred. Olive and Beryl took the pasty pawpaw into the room. Dahlia and Velma spread the paste on a clean piece of white cloth which they folded in three to make a pad about four inches wide and a foot long. They put some pawpaw paste in the hot-water bottle with warm water. Olive held one of Monica's feet, Beryl the other, and Miss Cotton held Monica's head in her lap. Dahlia and Velma struggled to find her opening. When they managed to force the spout of their improvised douche into her vagina, Monica's scream cut through the night. She wrestled to get free, but Olive and Beryl held her firmly. Miss Cotton stroked her hair and whispered soothing words.

Angel stood by the door, with the mug of ginger tea sweetened with honey in her hand, unable to move. She heard the mug rattle against the plate in her hand, but she could not quiet the anguish that rocked her body.

Monica appeared to fall into a deep sleep; Olive and Beryl released her feet. The old women looked around for chairs on which to sit; they shared the stool that was in front of the dresser. Beryl and Olive then took the cloth on which they had spread the pasty pawpaw and placed it over Monica's swollen vaginal area like a menstrual pad. Monica breathed deeply and slept. Angel took the ginger tea to Miss Cotton, who pried open Monica's mouth and spoon-fed her.

There was nothing else they could do but wait, and hope, and watch Monica for any sign of change. They sat around the kitchen table, sipping ginger tea, blowing into their cups and reading the steam for signs. They all ached. The crime was too violent for words. The lips of their vaginas throbbed in sympathy, their wombs ached, and their salty tears left stain marks on their faces. The three old women took up conference in the kitchen, and the three younger ones went to Monica's room, hung up dresses in the closet, folded clothes and put them in drawers, picked up empty perfume bottles, washed the floor and the entire room with rosemary water, then took the soiled linens and washed them too. The smell of pepper still stung their nostrils and burned the tips of their fingers; they soaked their hands in warm pawpaw-puree water.

Miss Cotton went outside, found two dried pieces of stick which she broke into four pieces; Velma connected the twigs into two separate 'x' shapes with a piece of vine she pulled from a tree. Dahlia found a bottle of over-proof white rum, poured a mouthful into her mouth, and through clenched teeth sprayed the x-shaped twigs. She then gave the twigs to Miss Cotton. Olive, Beryl and Angel stood by the kitchen door watching the elders. Miss Cotton led all of them to the front of Monica's house, where she mounted the three steps that led to the veranda, then, bending, placed one twig under the straw doormat with a few leaves that she took from her pocket. Then she walked to the back of the house and did the same thing. No one said a word. She made them all drink thyme tea without sugar or honey. Angel gagged, and it took all her discipline to keep the fluid down.

Dawn shone through the open window in a shiny silver-blue dress. This was usually the most beautiful and productive time of the day. Angel yawned. Velma made a pick-axe hitting-stone sound deep in her throat. Olive wound a few strands of her hair around her finger, a sure sign she was worried. Beryl massaged her elbow, and Dahlia stuck out her tongue like a lizard catching flies. Angel threw open the front window and glanced out at the first signs of morning. There was a tranquil beauty that soothed her aching heart and quieted her nagging questions. Miss Cotton thanked them all and sent them home, then she took up watch at the head of Monica's bed. Finally she dozed, and for a few hours silence fell over Kristoff Village.

◆

The birds woke him. Desmond squinted his eyes, moved his head and looked for the singing birds perched in the red hibiscus edging. He sat up and was able to locate their pretty forms among the flowers. He smiled at his discovery, but his head reeled. He wasn't sure where he was, on whose veranda he had slept. Turning, he saw his friend from the bar, still sprawled on the floor. How many flasks of rum had they consumed? He had lost count after the fifth.

Desmond had a big problem. He was a notorious coward who avoided confrontations and quarrels at all cost. Although he didn't want to continue living two separate lives, just the idea of confronting Grace and telling her he wanted a divorce had been too much for him. Yet he had to do something. The image of Monica pained him. He sensed she needed him now, but his immediate concern was finding the bathroom, and rinsing the foul taste out of his mouth.

◆

Ainsworth remembers clearly the night the light was turned on. Miss Cotton and Master Cotton invited the entire village to come out, offering free soda and crackers for everyone. People dressed up like they were going to church or a Christmas fair, and began to gather long before it was dark. When the lights came on without an announcement, Ainsworth, like the rest of the villagers, clapped. An old man standing beside Ainsworth repeatedly nudged him, saying, 'Dis light ting is magic; is true magic.' Ainsworth didn't understand how the light came on on its own, and kept asking his mother. But she either ignored his questions or told him to ask someone who was more book-learned than she was. At that moment, Ainsworth decided he would read all the books in the world so he could know the answers to all his questions. From that night reading became his goal. The Christmas after the first street light came to Kristoff Village, Ainsworth got his first book; he was five. He read it over and over, and begged his parents for others. But they couldn't afford to buy any books except for school, and even then books were a luxury. Ainsworth was thrilled beyond words when he discovered the library. He had never imagined there were so many books.

The night of the first and only street light began to slip away from him, but he pulled back on the memory. Miss Cotton, Aunty Velma and Dahlia sat on the landing just in front of the shop, Master Cotton and some of his friends stood by the door. The adults, babies and small children sat on the first step from top; below them, the older children and teenagers sat on the other steps. Ainsworth was sitting below his mother, his back resting on her knees; he was pressed in from side to side, and he remembered enjoying the feel of the other children's bodies against his own. He felt safe, connected to a larger life. Everyone had drunk their aerated water and eaten their crackers. Master Cotton had given the children sweeties, the hard Bustamante candy that stuck in their teeth but which lasted long because it was too hard to bite and chew. Ainsworth savoured his Bustamante and listened to the story that was being told by Miss Cotton, Velma and Dahlia. He remembered thinking it strange that they were seated like they were, no one really watching the faces of the teller, or even each other. When Miss Cotton began people shifted their bodies on the step and turned sideways, but they couldn't see her. Not that it mattered, because her voice had more details than a photograph.

This is not the story that Miss Cotton, Aunty Velma and Miss Dahlia told, but it is the story Ainsworth remembers:

Who knows the taste of tears? Tell me how it taste. Tell me how it makes you feel.

It makes you feel good? Yes? It cleanses you? Yes? Always it begins with tears? Yes?

Yes indeed. Everyone agreed, some bringing their hands together in a firm clasp, others shaking their heads, a few tapping their feet. They all agreed.

'How did it begin?' Miss Cotton asked.

'When?' they replied,

'In the beginning,' Aunt Velma said.

'Wid tears,' they assured her.

'Wid tears,' Dahlia chimed.

Ainsworth and the other children waited, but only silence responded to them. They were certain they had missed something; a few of them even thought perhaps they had fallen asleep. They asked those who sat beside them, but they could offer no explanation. Ainsworth looked at his mother and she was crying. He felt ashamed for her, but he noticed the woman beside her was also crying. He saw the faces of all the adults, including the men, and tears streamed down all their faces. The story was their memory. The story was the pain that produced tears. The story was what they had lived. The story was their petty jealousy that caused them to begrudge each other every minor success and plot ways to harm one another. The story was all that was lost to them because someone was too selfish to share, too mean to forgive, too blind to see the possibilities. The story was the beginning of their lives that had been told them over and over, but out of embarrassment they hadn't listened; so when the time came for those tales to be useful, they didn't know the details and groped in self-darkness. The story was in the first drop of salty tear that was shed for them, that they shed for themselves.

Ainsworth looked around at his mother and the other adults crying and felt cheated, until he found his own tears. Salty. Sticky. Inseparable from him, like the pain of birth. That was indeed the beginning.

IV

Remembering to remember

all things
come full circle
clouds bubble
the sky opens
the earth drinks
sun kisses moon
a petal opens ·
an ant tunnels under
you and i too
chase the wind

Go back, She-Devil can't help you

She-Devil was up to her elbows in flour and sugar. Three more days and her Brimstone would wed Tallawah. She-Devil and Devil had agreed to host the wedding since Tallawah's parents were deceased, and She-Devil was thrilled beyond belief. Her Brimstone had found him a woman who was not only beautiful and artistic, but spirited as well. Since meeting Tallawah, She-Devil had had occasion to observe Brimstone and Tallawah together and had come to realise, much to her pleasure, that Tallawah was not simply taken up with or taken in by Brimstone's verbosity and flair, but could match him toe for toe. Even better, when Brimstone got out of hand, which was often, and became so full of himself that he allowed no one else a word, Tallawah had a way of charging in, like jumping into a turning rope without breaking the flow, and getting Brimstone to tone down without losing face. She-Devil had to admit, she knew only one other woman beside herself so competent at handling a man, and that was her daughter, Tegreg. Tallawah was a woman after her own heart, and just the kind of woman she had been hoping her son would have the sense to marry. Tallawah couldn't have been more perfect if She-Devil had hand-picked her herself.

In three days, Tallawah and Brimstone would be wed at her home, in her house, and after much persistence from her son, She-Devil had agreed not only to make her famous black fruitcake, but to cook all the food as well. Once it was agreed that Devil and She-Devil would host the wedding of the year, they quickly went about soliciting the help of the Angel clan, who had very little to do and were often bored. The Angels gladly agreed, and soon Devil had the Angel boys raking and weeding, trimming and painting, and repotting various plants and flowers. He even managed to acquire the help of God, the Angels' father, who was known for being a rather sad-faced recluse. None the less, every so often when She-Devil looked through the window she

143

saw Devil and God engaged in conversation and God good-naturedly taking directions from Devil. She-Devil made a mental note to be more friendly with the Angels after the wedding. She would overlook their critical disposition and their insistence on perfection. They were useful, and now that the whole bunch of them had been working together for almost two weeks she heard laughter and merriment coming from them. Today, Sabbath, the Angels' mother had volunteered to come and help, saying she was quite adept at mixing a cake, and knew how to make the crust for patties and the other pastries She-Devil had put on the elaborate menu for the guest list of over five hundred and growing.

It was with all these thoughts swimming in her head at the break of day, and her elbows in flour, sugar and nutmeg, that She-Devil smelled Monica coming. Instantly her nostrils flared and her eyes watered.

'Kiss God and shame de Devil,' She-Devil muttered.

Quickly, she dusted the flour off her arms, spilling some on the floor as she reached for the towel to wipe her hands. She could feel the pepper steaming up her insides. She reached for and gulped down a glass of water. Angry words were not going to issue from her mouth, but steam emitted from her nostrils. She moved quickly to the veranda, then jogged to the gate. Standing firmly, with legs apart, she shouted at the top of her voice to the emerging figure. 'Listen here. Ah don't mean to be wicked, but go back. Ah can't help you today. Ah ain't ready fah you yet. You mek you bed so sleep pan it. Ah busy preparing fah me son's wedding.'

Monica faltered in her tracks. There were no tears left in her eyes. She stood, desperate, pleading for comfort. She-Devil, not insensitive, none the less stood her ground.

'Wha dem do to you is worse dan crime but don't give up. The fire will burn itself out. But ah done blame dem. Me have husband too, and some woman can be desperate. Sorry, me can't help show you de way today. Go back, your time not due yet.'

She-Devil turned and walked slowly back down the path leading to her house. She felt weary and suddenly old. She knew Monica was still standing there, hoping she would change her mind. But she was resolute. By the time She-Devil climbed the steps leading to the front veranda, Monica had turned around, moving like a wounded dog with its tail between its legs.

◆

Miss Cotton was jolted awake by the groan coming from Monica. She had fallen asleep in the rocking chair at the foot of Monica's bed. Now she hobbled out of the chair, moved to Monica's side, and saw her staring wide-eyed. All the water was sucked dry from Monica's eyes; they were like marbles, but Miss Cotton could tell she was weeping. Miss Cotton wet Monica's lips with the rag in the basin, spoon-fed her two tablespoons of condensed milk and caressed her arms. Monica seemed to fall back to sleep, but just as Miss Cotton was walking back to the rocking chair she heard a voice, raspy and pained, say, 'She send me back. Say is not me time yet.'

Miss Cotton nodded at the sleeping form and added her own consolation, 'Hush, de fire dying down. Hush, is all right.' Then she hobbled back to sit and think and be vigilant in the rocking chair at the foot of the bed.

◆

She-Devil had the first batch of cakes in the oven. She had designed the wedding cake like waterfalls, since Dunn's River Falls was Brimstone and Tallawah's favourite recreational spot. She sat to sip her cocoa, eat a salt-fish and onion hard-dough bread sandwich, and make her list of the many things to do that day before Sabbath and the Angel girls came over to assist her. She could hear Devil up in the bathroom, trying to sing as usual, and she smiled. She would yet have to boil some coconut oil and pour it down Devil's throat to help him keep a tune. Just as she settled, with her pencil poised, She-Devil heard a sound as if something had bumped into the gate. At first she ignored it, thinking perhaps that the Angels' blind cow had wandered off again, but then she heard rattling, like someone shaking the gate. She was exasperated. Today was just not going like she had planned. She flounced through the house, her feet banging loudly as she walked to the front veranda. At the gate she made out the form of a small woman, draped in a white gown that was opened in the back.

'Is who dat?' She-Devil hollered. 'Ah don't have time for fooling or talking dis morning,' she continued, before the person at the gate could respond. But the rattling continued. And for the second time that morning, She-Devil hurried to the gate. The rattling went on, even as She-Devil approached, kissing her teeth in both annoyance and disgust. All her thoughts were on the wedding, only three days away. She recognised the woman when she was five yards from the gate. Her posture slackened, and her face relaxed. She opened the gate, put her hand around the woman's shoulders, and as she led her through the gate spoke softly to her.

'Ah not ready fah you yet, but you time well due. Besides, ah turn away one woman already dis morning so ah have to tek you. Come. Ah just drinking a sweet cup of cocoa tea, ah will pour you a cup and fix you a little something to eat. Ah well busy today, so ah gwane put you to work. You can help me bake. Come. Mek we walk a little quicker, ah have cake in the oven.'

She-Devil led Miss Madge up the steps into the house.

◆

Beryl had not gone to bed since returning from Monica's house. What she had witnessed had frightened her, but it had also awakened in her a dormant rage. She had gone to sit in her favourite spot, in the left-hand corner of her veranda, in the old broken-down lignum vitae chair that her father had built for her twelfth birthday. She had lit her pipe and sat smoking in the cool night air before falling asleep. Now she jumped fully awake, the pipe falling to the floor. Immediately the three dogs started howling, almost in rounds. Beryl wiped her eyes and felt tears. Sensing that someone stood in front of her, she rose up and pushed back the invisible person. She felt as if her head was swelling. In that moment she knew. She covered her mouth and allowed tears to trickle down her face.

'Bye Miss Madge, bye Mamma,' she whispered, turning into the house, leaving the dogs howling.

*

For the second time in less than a hour, Miss Cotton was awakened. She heard the howling dogs, felt a whiff of air, then sensed her head go light. She got up and walked to the bed, looking down at Monica, touching her cheeks. The heat from Monica's cheek caused her to smile. Now she understood what Monica had meant about being sent back. Miss Madge, who had out-lived her time, having made right all of her actions that she could, had taken Monica's place so that Monica too could have the opportunity to make amends.

'Thank God and praise Devil wife,' Miss Cotton mumbled, walking to the kitchen. There she lit a match, turned on the gas burner and put the kettle to boil. She went and looked through the window that directly faced Beryl's house, although separated from it by thick banana boughs and other foliage. The kettle whistled and Miss Cotton turned to the stove, talking to herself.

'You mamma gwane, Daughter Beryl, but we is here fah you. She live a good and long life. She tired, and miss you pappy. Hush. Cry but don't cry too long. Life begin and end wid tears.'

Miss Cotton made herself a cup of mint tea, sweetened it with milk and went back to take up her post at Monica's bed.

'Valrie. Wake up and burp Baby-Girl. Ah just done feed her. Ah gwane down Miss Monica.'

'Lawd, Arnella, is mad you mad, gwane outside widout scarf pan you head. You want catch cold and dead?' Valrie said to Arnella, handing her a scarf that was hanging over the bed head. As Arnella carelessly tied on the scarf, they heard the howling dogs.

'Is who dead, Nell?' Valrie asked, clutching Baby-Girl close to her bosom.

'Sound like it coming from Miss Beryl's yard.'

'You tink Aunty Madge dead?'

'Could be. She did well sick. Burp Baby-Girl and oonuh go back to bed. Ah gone,' Arnella said, turning from Valrie.

A rooster began his cocka-doodle-do wake-up call. A few birds were rustling awake. The air was sweet and moist. A stillness permeated the air. Arnella took deep breaths, basking in the new day. This was her most favourite time; she wanted to walk further and linger longer, but she was already at Monica's gate. As she climbed the three steps to the veranda and reached for the door-knob, the dogs stopped barking.

Arnella put aside her reflections as she knocked on Monica's bedroom door.

'Who dere?' came the sure voice of Miss Cotton.

'Is me, Mamma Cotton,' Arnella replied, pushing open the door.

'Beryl's dogs dem mus fraid you. Dem stop howling just as you push the front door.'

The women smiled at each other, comforted by one another's presence. Many an evening when dusk had fallen, Arnella and Valrie had sat with the other children on Miss Cotton's steps, listening to her stories. However, Arnella was always the only one who heard the underside of the story and knew how to answer the questions Miss Cotton would ask at the end of the session. Since then, Miss Cotton knew that Arnella had eyes in the back of her head, and would be a woman who kept her own company most of the time.

'Ah been a poor soldier,' Miss Cotton now confessed to Arnella. 'Just haven't been able to keep sleep from me eyes.'

Arnella kissed the old woman on her forehead and patted her hair. 'Afta you help me wid Monica, you go stretch out in de guest room. Ah will stay watch for a few hours. Valrie will bring Baby-Girl when she ready to feed again.'

'No, ah must stay alert until Monica come to. But ah so glad oonuh is twins again; you and Valrie are strands of de same plait.' Miss Cotton heaved herself up from the chair and walked round to the side of Monica's bed.

'We need to go see about Sister Beryl. Ah think Aunty Madge gone,' Arnella said, moving aside the sheet covering Monica.

'Yes, she gone all right,' Miss Cotton replied. 'She did stop on her way to ask me to look in on Beryl. We will do de best we can.' The two women, old and young, paused, their eyes locked on each other, the older's eyes saying, 'Take heed daughter, you can do it.' The other's eyes said, 'Yes, although it hard, is my turn now.' Their eyes held and they buoyed each other as they silently acknowledged their roles as links in the community. Silence danced around them as they worked.

Arnella fetched a clean wash cloth and water. Miss Cotton gently squeezed the water on the blistering lips of Monica's private parts. Monica groaned and writhed on the bed. Arnella knelt on the bed. leaning over Monica's exposed lower half. Bracing on one hand, she brought out a breast, which was hard with milk, and began to express it all over Monica's swollen inner thighs and blistered vaginal area.

Miss Cotton caressed Monica's hand and began to croon a wordless song. When Arnella's breast was empty, she returned it to her bra, and climbed down from the bed.

'How is her fever, Mamma Cotton?'

'Not so bad, but she still a little warm.'

Arnella sat at the edge of the bed opposite Miss Cotton. Together they held Monica's hands and sang to her as if she was a tiny baby. Their voices were smooth and even. But for the sweat which covered their bodies, soaking their clothes, the veins like garland rope pulsing in their necks, one might have mistaken them for a photograph, so still were the three of them. Monica was breathing through her mouth and moaning, breathing through her mouth and moaning, moaning slowly, like a song gone sour in the mouth, a song that reminds the singer of a lover who fled or a child who died shortly after birth. Miss Cotton and Arnella kept working their eyes to discern all that they could see; kept working their love and all that they felt through Monica, and Monica kept moaning and moaning, and cooling the fire raging inside her.

Morning sprinted, the sun burst through the bedroom window like a rude child, signalling to Miss Cotton and Arnella that they were relieved of their task.

'We can stop now. The head of de fire is smitten. It will burn itself off,' Miss Cotton announced to Arnella before stumbling to the rocking chair. She slumped there, covered in perspiration.

Arnella sighed, relieved; she raised her legs on to the bed and braced her back against the frame. Squinting into the sun, she declared. 'It gwane hot today. More trouble coming.'

'We will do de best we can,' Miss Cotton muttered, trailing off to sleep.

After resting for a while, Arnella felt a pain in her other breast. If she did not express the milk, it would soon become engorged. She found two clean wash cloths and expressed milk into one of them until the cloth was damp, then she placed the damp cloth on Monica's forehead. Into the second cloth she expressed milk until it was soaked, then she folded it like a pad and put it between Monica's legs. Then, covering Monica, she tiptoed out of the house, heading for Beryl's.

At Beryl's gate the dogs started their barking. Arnella pushed the gate and shouted at them. 'Quiet oonuh noise and step out me way.' Then, changing to a solicitous tone, she called, 'Sister Beryl? You decent? Ah come to see if you hear anything?' She had not seen Beryl sitting in the middle of the banana trees that sheltered her house, so she jumped when Beryl responded.

'Ah don't hear any news yet, but ah know Mamma dead. She come stand up right in front of me, where me was sitting on de veranda dere sleeping.' Beryl pointed to the spot on the veranda where she had fallen asleep. 'Dis morning just before de dogs dem start howling.'

Arnella nodded, and walked over to where Beryl sat with tearstains marking her face.

'Ah did hear de dog dem too. Miss Cotton say Aunty Madge stop by on her way and ask her to look out fah you. Ah tink she gone. They will soon send telegram confirm.'

The other woman nodded. Silence, except for the whimpering of the dogs, the buzzing of flies and the gentle flapping of the banana leaves. Arnella walked over to Beryl and offered her a hand. Beryl consented to be pulled to her feet.

'Is mek you dress wet so! Look like you was working hard,' Beryl exclaimed.

'Miss Cotton and me help Monica out the fire,' replied Arnella.

'Praise be! From me born me neva see such wickedness.' Beryl heaved her chest and folded her hands in a gesture of defiance.

'Same here,' declared Arnella, spitting. 'Such wickedness mustn't go unchecked.'

'Is truth you talk.' Beryl nodded her head repeatedly as they stood in the middle of the banana plot, the sun reigning overhead.

Walking towards the kitchen, Beryl offered Arnella a cup of tea.

'So how Baby-Girl? She eating all right?'

'Yes, but me still have plenty milk. Is like me have milk fah two babies.' Pause. Only the sipping of tea and shaking of heads expressed their thoughts.

'So Beryl, wha you want us to do bout Aunty Madge?'

'She live long, would be seventy come her birthday September. And me know she did tired and want to go on. Ah can manage. She wasn't much company lately. Beside now me have Monica next door, and de American lady, Angel. She favour our ways well. Me and her did get on good, good,' Beryl said, dusting her hands.

'Good. Well ah gwane go cause ah feeling me breasts pulsing; that mean Baby-Girl want milk.'

'Walk good.'

'One love.'

Arnella rose, and immediately the dogs started barking and hanging by her legs. At the gate she met Sister Olive coming towards her with a tray of food. She waited and held the gate open, and as Olive passed through she reached over and kissed her on the cheek. Olive smiled at her, then warned, 'Go home and tek off dat wet frock before you catch you death of cold.'

Arnella smiled at her sister-mother's back and headed for home. Passing by her old house she called, without stopping, 'Daddy Milford ah saying good morning.'

Milford ran to the veranda and waved to her back. He shouted after her.

'How is me new grandbaby? What you doing out so early? You must rest, you know.'

Arnella waved without turning around. Milford watched her retreating back and smiled before going into the house.

Run, but time waiting round de bend

The village was wide awake. Mothers could be heard calling children to get up. Children were crying; men demanded breakfast, hollered about being late for work. Orders were issued to older children. Needs were being requested; everyone talking at once. Dogs were yapping, chickens cackling, goats maaing, cows mooing. Sounds

151

blared from radios, from voices, from animals, insects and plant life. The entire world was alive. The sky was taffeta blue, dotted with spongy white clouds. The sun was chivalrous and proud; the breeze coy but playful. The day was on, brazen with colour and texture, begging for mischief and indulgence.

On such a day as this Desmond returned to Kristoff Village after sleeping out for the second time in his sixteen years of marriage, without warning or prior explanation. As he turned into the junction leading to the village, he was not thinking about his wife, but rather his sweetheart, Monica. How to explain to her his cowardice. Rather than face Grace and demand a divorce or separation, he had chosen to get drunk and ended up sleeping on a friend's veranda. His head throbbed despite the two large mugs of coffee he had drunk this morning without even a pinch of sugar.

After swinging by his job to explain that he wouldn't be in (a small lie about his wife being sick), Desmond stopped at a little hole-in-the-wall and ate three fritters, four johnny cakes and a hot cup of milo. He was nearly feeling his old self by the time he joined the morning traffic, turning on to the main road away from Montego Bay. The wind blew life back into his body, but his head still pulsed, and as he neared the junction to Kristoff Village he felt as if someone had rubbed his clothes with pepper which burned his lips, stung his nose and caused his eyes to water.

The old woman who every morning loaded her glass case with snacks and sweets and sat by the side of the road selling her products to schoolchildren and workers, was there as ever, a sentry at the entrance to Kristoff Village. Desmond stopped to greet her and buy something sweet to get the pepper from his mouth. She looked at him long and hard, then said: 'So you sleep out last night. Well trouble tek you. You sweetheart pan fire.'

He searched her face for the meaning of her words, but her face was sealed. She took his money, gave him a coconut drop, then dismissed him from her presence by starting to sing a dirge, looking, it seemed, straight through him. Disconcerted, he revved his bike and rode slowly into Kristoff Village. Several people he passed greeted him oddly, quickly looking away. A few women all but pretended he was a duppy. Desmond didn't know what to make of it, but the closer he got to home, the more his heart raced, his nostrils flared and his mouth felt glued shut. He rode more and more slowly; a toddler could have kept up his pace. He began to sweat, but refused to let any images of calamity enter his mind. Just as he turned the last bend at the mouth of the village, he almost ran into Raymond, his older son. The boy was trotting, and sweat greased his face. Desmond stopped, dismounted.

'Why you just now going to school?' he asked in an even tone.

The boy panted, shifted his book bag, watered his lips, then answered. 'Morning, Daddy. All a we wake up late. Mamma didn't wake we.'

'Morning, son. Althea and Peter leave fah school yet?'

'No, Daddy. Althea say she wasn't feeling well, and Peter say him school clothes did dirty.'

Desmond stared at his son, trying to make sense of his story. Deciding he would soon get to the bottom of it, he patted the boy on his back and told him to hurry along. Then, on impulse, he decided to give Raymond a ride to the junction or he would miss the last bus and be forced to wait another hour or more.

'Hop on.'

Raymond smiled, and circled his father's waist. At the junction he hopped off, but stood looking at his father, seeming to reflect on a matter. Desmond believed his son was waiting for him to explain his absence last night, and became agitated.

'Gwane before you miss de bus.'

Raymond moved off, hesitated, then swung around to face his father.

'Daddy, last night something bad happen to Miss Monica. All night Miss Cotton, Aunty Olive, Miss Velma and Miss Dahlia at her house. Even now when I was passing Miss Cotton was still there. I think Mamma know what happen,' the boy said in one breath. Then he ran across the street to the bus stop. Stumped for a moment, Desmond stood looking at his son on the far side of the street. Then he mounted his bike and was off at a dangerous speed.

Before he was through the gate, Miss Cotton was standing by the front door, with one hand akimbo. Desmond didn't like the look on her face. Her eyes were like coal, and her lips were puckered.

'Good morning Moda Cotton,' Desmond greeted the elder, his head bowed.

'Tell me what you see good about de morning.' She did not stand aside.

'Ah come to tell Miss Monica a good morning.'

'Is who tell you she want you to greet her, and don't ah done tell you dat dis is not a good morning?'

'Yes, ma'am, but ah still want to see Miss Monica,' Desmond replied, standing his ground.

'But what a way you bright?' Miss Cotton declared, loud enough for people passing on the street to hear. 'You have two woman whose bed you can sleep in, but you is such a big man you sleep out. Whe you was when dem brutish women come in Miss Monica's house and assault her? Whe you was when she scream out wid pain, and cried fah de Devil to hold her hand? Whe you was? Her suffering is pan fi you hand.' And with that Miss Cotton gave Desmond her back and strode into the house.

Desmond slowly entered behind her. Miss Cotton stood, arms folded across her chest, like a guard by the bedroom door. He approached her, and politely asked, 'Ah begging you to let me pass.'

'You eyes big enough to see pain? You heart deep enough to catch tears?'

Desmond nodded. Miss Cotton swung open the door and followed at his heels. Seeing Monica lying so still on the bed, Desmond hurried to her side, and caught his breath as he saw her puffy, swollen face.

'Wha happen here?' he demanded, feeling Miss Cotton approach behind him.

'Wha happen here?' she echoed. 'De truth have not yet come to light, but it will, and many casualty will fall in de dawning of de truth.'

Monica moaned and turned, partially pulling back the covers. Miss Cotton tugged at Desmond's arms, pulling him towards the foot of the bed, mumbling and talking as she moved him. 'You eyes have only see half de truth.' And so saying, she pulled back the covers, exposing Monica's nakedness, showing her pubic hair trimmed, her labia bubbling and blistered. 'See what you carelessness mek dem do her? See? Is your fault,' Miss Cotton spat accusingly.

154

'Rass! Rass! Rasscloth!' Desmond could find no other words to give voice to his shock. He fell to his knees, hugged Monica's feet and wept.

Miss Cotton left Desmond with Monica and went to breathe the morning air. It was going to be a long day, and an even longer week. She sighed, feeling weary and used up.

◆

She-Devil had completed her list, fed Madge and Devil, and was steaming some more currants, raisins and prunes to make more black fruitcakes when she heard Sabbath and the three Angel girls coming. They came in silently; they were always silent until she gave them chores and a song to steer their way. Just as She-Devil had established a rhythm, Tallawah and her youngest son Anansi turned up, bringing food and serving trays for the wedding.

She-Devil surveyed her soon-to-be-daughter-in-law, and had to declare, 'Girl you more than guava-cheese on jelly. You sweet bad.' Tallawah was wearing a shocking orange top that stopped just short of her knees, revealing a see-through, gold and black skirt that flared at her calves. She had rings on three toes of each foot, and her nails were painted orange. Birds of paradise were stencilled on her big toes. She-Devil had never seen a woman more gorgeous, more in the world to celebrate the beauty that was herself. Seeing Tallawah did She-Devil's spirit good. She beamed while introducing her to Sabbath.

'She-Devil,' Tallawah started, after exchanging pleasantries with Sabbath, Madge and the Angel girls, 'tomorrow I'll be done making corrections on my play, so I'll be by real early to help. And ah don't want to hear you can't use my help, although it looks like you have plenty hands, fah true. Well?' Tallawah said, her voice high and musical as a mocking bird's, her body forever in motion, hands and hips and legs swaying here, there and everywhere all at once. 'One more hand will make one less job.' Then she turned, calling for her son. 'See Anansi dere, up in dat tree. Ah neva see a boy could climb. Anansi, come down out Grandpa Devil's Julie mango tree. Mind you fall and bruk you behind. Mind you manners and come say howdy to Grandma Devil.'

155

Anansi scampered down the tree, a mango in one hand, another bursting the seam of his back pocket.

'Kiss, kiss, Grandma Devil,' Anansi said, pursing out his lips for She-Devil to kiss. She-Devil smiled at the child with the spirit of his mother and kissed him, then hugged him to her. After hugging her back, Anansi freed himself and ran to peer into all the pots, taking time to savour the aroma coming from each one.

◆

Left alone with Monica, Desmond wept and admonished himself for getting drunk. 'If only me did come home last night,' he said repeatedly to himself. Monica awoke begging for water. Hastening to fetch her some, Desmond stumbled over his own feet and fell on all fours. Composing himself as best he could, he quickly crossed the distance to Monica's bedside, raised her head and spoon-fed her a few drops of sweetened water from the bedside table.

'Monica, ah did well sorry, ah well sorry,' he whispered.

Monica clutched his hand; but although her chest heaved, no tears trickled from her eyes. They looked at each other, and silently agreed to forgive each other of any wrong. Then Monica fell back into an uneasy sleep. Desmond rested his head on the bed near her stomach. He was afraid to ask who was responsible. He was afraid of what he would do. Last night he had failed to come home because he hated confrontation, but his action had left the way clear for someone to attack and deeply hurt his love. At that moment, Desmond was as certain of his love for Monica and his desire to be with her as he was of his name. He moved to the bedroom window facing the side yard and watched Miss Cotton pacing around the mad-red monkey-tail plant. A doctor-bird flew by Miss Cotton's head. Desmond smiled at the sight, until Monica's snoring pulled his attention back inside the room. He sat momentarily in the rocking chair where Miss Cotton had sat, but it was too hot. He got up and paced. Every time he turned, his eyes fell on Monica and he wanted to ask her forgiveness and curse her attackers. He sat back down on the edge of the bed.

Involuntarily his hand moved to caress her stomach. She moaned and pulled away at his touch. He stopped, waited, then again touched her stomach lightly, feeling it, rubbing it, sending her his love. Love was all he could give her in her present state, and he was confident his love was strong enough to make her well. He wanted her well, to love strong and passionately over and over again. Then he pulled back the sheet, moved aside the cloth soaked in milk that Arnella had replaced between Monica's legs and stared down lovingly at the womanhood from which he had derived so much pleasure.

His love directed the gentle massage of his tongue as he bent to slowly lick the remaining pepper from the folds of Monica's labia and the mouth of her vagina. He blew his love-breath and ran his tongue over every space, every fold, every membrane of Monica's private self, and imagined that he felt her healing under the moist attention. When she shivered, then mewled, he kissed the inside of her thighs before raising his head. The fire was now inside his mouth, but he knew how to extinguish it. As he took out his handkerchief to wipe his lips, Miss Cotton called him to come to the kitchen for a cup of tea. Handing him the cup, she looked him straight in the eyes and said, 'You did well love her to taste de fire.'

Desmond did not respond. Neither did he concern himself about whether Miss Cotton had seen him between Monica's legs. The fire was calming him.

They listened to the radio, his tapping on the table accompanying her humming. Soon the voice on the radio receded from both their minds and only his tapping and her humming were real. She would tell him when their rhythms matched. Desmond continued to tap, and Miss Cotton hummed. The breeze was playful, swirling dust and leaves. A host of butterflies, black with orange-golden wings, fluttered by the sweet-sop tree in the back yard. They heard nayabinghi drumming in the distance. Desmond kept tapping, sending all the other sounds away, until he recognised Miss Cotton's song, and accompanied her, moving in and out, up and down, with the tune she was weaving like straws being braided into a basket.

'Two days now ah been seeing dis gwane happen, but couldn't see it clearly. Sometime, ah might as well be blind, fah seeing but not being able to prevent. Ah took to me bed, trying to still it, struggling to hold it back, but ah couldn't. Ah tell you, sometimes seeing is more trouble dan blindness. Is why ah can't have eyes just like others? Is why ah must always see de water before it come but not be able to hold it in me mouth? Dis seeing. Dis seeing is a plague and a blessing.'

Miss Cotton paused, leaned her head on her hands, shook it clear, then continued.

'Monica was like me own daughter. Ah did love her from she was a little girl, before she run off. Me encourage her to run. Knew if she stayed here she would marry and end up sorry and mean-spirited like so many others. Then when she come home, me look into her eyes, and was happy because ah know she done lived her life, and was ready fah rest and quiet love. Then you walk into her house. You tink ah don't know how you seduce her with de damn light-blue shirt dat bring out de glow of you skin. Ah don't see any woman more wise and yet so simple as Monica. A damn blue shirt. Chow!'

Miss Cotton caught Desmond's eyes as he smiled. He was thinking of his attraction to Monica's white teeth against her mauve gums. Her fibrous hair, untamed yet proud after they tossed in bed. Her plump, meaty thighs; her round, high behind. He was an experienced man caught by the everyday wonders of a woman. 'Wise yet simple' could also apply to him. He had not set out to fall in love.

'Well you know de rest, de both of you carrying on like young puppy, flaunting oonuh sex, even in broad daylight. You riding back from Montego Bay to Kristoff Village like you is baby in need of his bottle, or something. Making all kind of noise, loud and non-caring, carrying on, de both of you, like oonuh is de only one know love. Ah did warn her. Ah say, "Monica, Grace might be foolish and fraid her own shadow, but she is woman too, and even de mildest woman can be prompted to sting or bite or kill." Ah did warn Monica because ah did see dis, but didn't see all of it. Ah did feel it, but didn't feel de pepper of it. Lawd, it beyond wicked . . .' and again Miss Cotton cried, tears spilling onto the table.

Desmond stopped tapping. For a brief moment there was an eerie calmness; then they heard a voice screaming for help. Desmond sprang up; the chair fell to the floor. He stood, his body frozen on the verge of flight. Miss Cotton stood too, clutching the table. Her head pounded, her hands felt like ancient paper disintegrating on contact with air. She let go of the table like it was hot and stood there, frozen in alarm.

Desmond recovered, ran to the front, and recognised his youngest child, Peter, the one always sent on difficult errands. He was shouting for help, screaming something unrecognisable. Desmond leapt the gate and ran to meet his son. Holding him tightly by the arms, he ordered him to calm down.

'Daddy. Mamma killing Althea. Mamma killing Althea.'

Desmond released Peter suddenly, causing the boy to fall, turned and sprinted toward home. Already a few people had gathered and were inching their way towards the house. He pushed through them, bursting inside and the wetness that smeared his face was his daughter's blood. Grace was on top of a bleeding Althea beating her alternately with a thorn stick and one of Desmond's leather belts and cursing her at the top of her voice. All Desmond could make out was, 'Is you father and him whore's fault.'

Desmond sprang at Grace and grabbed at the belt. She reared at him like a tigress, hitting out and spitting. He freed the belt but she held fast to the stick, poking at him. He saw out of the corner of his eyes that Althea was naked, and blood flowed down her back. He kicked at Grace, tripping her; she clung to his feet and he felt her teeth trying to saw through his skin. They rolled around on the ground. Only a firm blow to the side of her face caused her to let go of his leg, but she took with her a piece of his flesh. She began to scream and tore at her hair, shrieking, 'Peppa! Peppa! Peppa!'

Milford and Godfree ran in and held her between them. The rage went out of her and she hung limply between the two men. Olive threw a sheet around Althea's body and guided her swiftly out the door.

At Olive's home, Olive and Velma sponged Althea down and rubbed warm olive oil mixed with aloe vera on her welts and bruises. The girl's entire body was battered. Her face was swollen, and she had a large gash on her back which they judged would need medical attention. By the time Desmond arrived, limping, Althea's wounds were dressed and Olive had slipped an old nightie on her. Desmond hugged Peter, who was sitting sniffling on the steps of the veranda, then took him inside with him to see about Althea. Althea, always a daddy's girl, reached out for her father and clung to him; Desmond held his hands away from her body, not wanting to hurt her, not sure where it was safe to embrace her. Olive offered Desmond and his children fruit juice, then left them to go and attend to Grace.

Attracted by the commotion, Valrie, Arnella and Baby-Girl had made their way to the Burton place. Dahlia, Rupert and Angel, who were consoling Beryl, also headed for Grace's house when the disturbance started.

Everyone gathered agreed that Grace had lost her mind. Master Cotton, who had hobbled to the scene, said they should take her to the river to calm her down, but that they should be careful that in her state she didn't drown herself. Olive said Althea needed to be taken to the hospital to see about the gash on her back. Milford showed Olive the piece of skin that Grace had bitten out of Desmond's leg and suggested that perhaps Desmond too might need to see the doctor – as, surely, did Grace. But since only Master Cotton's car was available at the moment, they decided that Althea and Desmond were in immediate need, and that Grace would have to wait. A few of the other village women offered to take Grace to the river. Milford promised to take care of Peter and keep track of Grace, and Olive went with Desmond and Althea to the hospital. Velma went to keep Miss Cotton company and watch over Monica.

Such a day as this Kristoff Village had never seen, and hoped not to see again any time soon. Everywhere the smell of pepper permeated, wafting on the air. Women walked with their legs pressed closely together, distrustful, contrite, feeling wronged. Wickedness had taken hands and feet. It was no longer a curse said in anger or a silent wish whispered then quickly retracted, or a plan for revenge that diminished as time passed. Wickedness was a woman, could be any woman wronged or believing she was wronged, any woman who separated herself from her clan, any woman who forgot that she wasn't invincible, any woman who didn't know that if you spit in the sky it was bound to fall on you.

The river was a woman and when the village women took Grace to wash off her madness the river rose up, wetting the banks that had long been dry in this the drought season, rumbling and roaring and frothing at the one moaning 'Peppa! Peppa! Peppa!' The older women, with a wisdom born of experience, feared neither Grace nor the river.

They knew that they had to help cool the wickedness giddy-upping in Grace's head, for they had time and time again put aside their own desires for revenge and gone on with living, gone on with forgiving. The older women hoped that the young, hot ones, with new ideas and romantic notions, with possessive ways and individual agendas, would see Grace and learn forgiveness. They also prayed that the young women would mark Monica's flamboyant actions and learn discretion. The river frothed at Grace, and it cooled the fire storming in her head. She made an attempt to drown herself, but the women wrestled her, water-logged, out the river. Grace's voice was finally stilled in the afternoon's heat.

Such a day.

But the day was not over yet.

Eternal Valley was experiencing its own share of excitement as the preparations for the wedding gathered pace.

Wade in deeper, but try to stay afloat

Ainsworth had not been able to sleep. After finding a dozen peppers scattered on his pillow he had gone to sit on the veranda. That was when he remembered why there were tears, not the kind that Marva with her peppery food was making his eyes produce, but real tears, so salty they were sweet. He couldn't reach Marva. He suddenly realised that he had not loved her for a while. That rather than growing softer with the love of her children and his dedication, Marva was growing more mean-spirited. He didn't understand what motivated her. Nothing satisfied her; the more she acquired the more resentful she became of others. Perhaps, Ainsworth reflected, his father had been right when he had advised him not to marry her.

Meeting Marva for the first time, Ainsworth's father had taken an instant dislike to her, telling his son privately, 'Dere something hard about her. No juice. She like dry-coconut, after all de milk evaporate. Rancid. Woman supposed to be jelly, soft and sweet. She hard, well hard.'

Ainsworth had listened respectfully to his father, and when he was done, after reflecting on his father's words for a moment Ainsworth had come to Marva's defence: 'If she hard, is de rough life she had had to survived dat make she tough, but I see softness. Is shy she shy so she put on a tough face. You'll see. She soft like St Vincent yam.'

His father had not looked convinced, but he said then, and he had been true to his word, that if Ainsworth chose Marva, he would never again say a word against her. Ainsworth's father had always been polite and considerate to Marva, especially after she insisted on naming their second son after him.

A few days after Monica returned to Kristoff Village, Ainsworth went to visit her, and they went for a long walk through the bush. And though branches scraped her, and the path underfoot was uneven, Monica never complained. In fact, when they returned to her house, she told Ainsworth how much she had enjoyed the walk, and invited him to come walk with her again. It was then she told him that the two things she missed most while she was living away from the village were walking in the bush and reading. The next time Ainsworth went to walk with Monica he brought his worn copy of *West Indian Poetry* which he kept secure in his shirt until they came to a cool spot with trees that seemed to form a circle. When they stopped to rest, Ainsworth pulled out the volume and started to read. The delight on Monica's face was sheer pleasure to Ainsworth, whose memory of Monica was mostly from the stories Miss Cotton constantly told of her daring. Every time he ended a poem and suggested they return, she begged him to read another, and they passed an hour like that, so that he was very late that Sunday for afternoon dinner and Marva railed at him. After that, every time he visited Monica he brought a book, usually poetry, and read to her. Once he requested that she read to him. She protested at first, but then she took the book that he thrust in her hand, flipped through the pages, and read a poem in a schoolgirl tone. That was also when she complained that all the poems he read to her were written by men.

'So wait! How come me no see no women name in this book? Women no write? Me use to write, you know. Ah probably still have a few exercise books with some of me original poems.'

Ainsworth's interest was stimulated and he pressed Monica to show them to him. But she said she wasn't ready. The Monday of the next working week, Ainsworth rushed to the bookstore during his lunch break and was very happy to find a collection of Louise Bennett's poetry. On their next walk, he presented her the book, wrapped in brown paper. She was so happy, she pulled him to her and kissed him loudly on both his cheeks. They didn't walk very far or for long that day because Monica was too excited, reading the poems along with him, leaning over his shoulder.

Ainsworth had just got out of the shower when he heard the dogs howling. At first he couldn't determine the direction from which the sound originated as many dogs were howling, almost in rounds, but when he put on his clothes and stood on the veranda he heard only one set of dogs and knew they came from down the lane where Monica and Beryl lived. Once he pinpointed the location, his heart skipped a beat. For a moment he thought perhaps Monica had died. Earlier that same day, he had gone down to Monica's house with his book, intending to read to her. He knew Miss Cotton was deeply concerned about Monica, and she had no answers to his question as to whether Monica was going to be all right. In fact, standing on the veranda at that moment listening to the dogs' howling, Ainsworth remembered Miss Cotton's exact response, even the timbre of her voice. 'Who to say whether tomorrow gwane be a good day?' Then she had started rocking, with a closed look on her face that said, 'Don't disturb me with any question.' He had lifted the stool at Monica's dressing table and put it close to the bed; then he had begun reading some poems that he knew Monica liked.

'Monica not dead.' Ainsworth repeated this to himself like a mantra, as if his words alone could keep her alive. He walked down the lane in the direction of the howling dogs. But it was only when he stood by Monica's gate that he felt relief. She was not dead. Beryl's dogs were the ones waking up the entire village. Since he was so close, Ainsworth proceeded to Beryl's house. When he reached her gate two of the younger dogs, one of them only a puppy, left off howling and ran to the gate, jumping and barking at him. Ainsworth shooed them away, pretending to fling a stone at them so that they scampered off as he pushed the gate open. Beryl's door was wide open, but there was no light inside, so he sounded a warning.

'Beryl, you in de house? Is me, Ainsworth.'

No answer, save the dogs' incessant howling. He continued slowly up the path, again sounding his voice.

'Beryl, you in dere? You all right? Ah come to see about de dogs howling.'

He heard a nose being blown. Feet moved towards him, then he saw Beryl standing in the doorway, strapping yet unsure, like a gig that is losing its balance.

'Beryl, you all right? You hear any news about Aunt Madge?'

'Is dead she dead. You no hear de dog dem howling? Is dead she dead all by sheself in de hospital; me wasn't even there fi hold hand when death call pan her.'

Ainsworth saw Beryl's body jerk though no sound came from her. He walked to her and put his arm around her. The weight of her body met his, and with her head on his shoulder, she cried. He could feel her tears soaking through his shirt, her soft tears, her warm, rough tears. Ainsworth didn't know how long he stood in the doorway holding Beryl, but when she finally pulled away from him, the sun was out and the dogs had ceased barking. She seemed almost ashamed of her vulnerability because she only mumbled thanks, then turned inside her house, closing the door behind her. Ainsworth ambled home, not seeing the colours of the crotons or hearing the chirping of the birds.

Ainsworth knew from the quietness of the house that his sons were still asleep. He would help Marva with their breakfast before waking them for school. There were still three weeks remaining until her delivery date even though she had been as big as a house for over two months. Whether or not this baby was a girl, they would not have any more children, Ainsworth determined, no matter how she insisted that she needed female company in the house. With five boys already, even though he earned a good salary, things were not easy. Were it not that his father still grew and supplied them with much of their food, he would not have been able to indulge Marva's determination to compete with Peggy. He wished Marva had worked as hard at keeping a helper. They had had three this year already, and the year was not even three-quarters over. Marva, although she had grown up very poor, or perhaps because of it, was brusque and insensitive to the young girls she employed to help with domestic chores. She was often rude, and was very critical of all their actions, sometimes even accusing them to their faces of stealing or planning to steal from her and threatening them with terrible reprisals. All of them soon got disgusted and left, and the last helper, almost a month before, had cursed Marva shamelessly. Aunt Dahlia had whispered the full story in Ainsworth's ear a few days after the incident.

Entering the kitchen, Ainsworth saw Marva standing by the sink, the bread knife in one hand, the other fingering a cluster of peppers by the butter-dish. He had been actively working not to think about who might have attacked and violated Monica. Miss Cotton had spat, 'Dem low-down, worst dan animal, she-brutes!' when he had enquired, suggesting that more than a single person was involved. Although Ainsworth did not know the details of Monica's violation, he suspected it was more horrible than he cared to imagine, considering it solicited the gathering of all Kristoff Village's most spiritual women.

'Morning, Marva,' Ainsworth greeted his wife, his tone unintentionally harsh.

'Is morning?' she replied, smirking at him, then kissing her teeth.

Ainsworth decided to ignore her. He filled the kettle with water and put it on to boil. Then he got out a pot to make the oatmeal porridge his sons loved. He was thinking about what sandwiches to make them for lunch when he glanced at Marva. His mouth flew open. She had smeared some bread with butter and had cut up and spread six large peppers over the bread, seeds included, and made the whole thing into a sandwich. Ainsworth couldn't believe his eyes as he watched Marva bite into the pepper sandwich. Only one small pepper was needed to make a large pot of curry goat so hot that glasses of water were required to cool the heat. But there stood Marva in front of him eating no less than six, seeds included. Yet her nostril didn't flare and her eyes didn't water. Ainsworth held a glass under the faucet and gulped it. His mouth felt as if it was on fire just from watching Marva. He couldn't hold his tongue any longer.

'Marva, is mad, you mad? How you can eat the scott bonnet pepper like dat? What get into you?'

'Is fi me mouth, and is fi me pepper. Me de one grow dem.' Marva cut her eyes at Ainsworth, flounced over to the cabinet, opened it and fished out the red-hot picka-peppa bottle. She separated the bread and shook picka-peppa on to the sandwich until both sides were sopped. Then she put them back together and finished eating.

Ainsworth held on to the oatmeal box, counting silently to himself. He would not look at Marva. He would fix his sons breakfast and get them all out of there, leaving Marva to her unusual cravings.

◆

Around eleven in the morning, Charley drove up to Beryl's gate. He had a slip of paper in his hand. Rupert and Angel were sitting on the bench that circled the guinep tree at the front of the house. They rose when Beryl opened the gate for Charley. This, they knew, was not a social visit. Charley's family could not afford for his taxi-cab to be idle when he could be making a fare. Angel remembered that when she and Beryl had taken Miss Madge to the hospital, the hospital staff had insisted on an address in town, the home of someone they could locate in an emergency. Charley, although not related to Beryl, was close enough to the family to be considered so. Besides, he was the only person she knew living in Montego Bay with connections in Kristoff Village; so they gave his address with his consent.

No one spoke as Charley entered Beryl's yard. They just nodded their heads in greeting and mouthed words that never left their lips. Charley had his cap in his hand, which he twisted along with the slip of paper.

Angel couldn't take it any more. She needed confirmation of Miss Madge's death. When the dogs had started their howling she had not been asleep – had not been able to sleep since returning from Monica. Nothing in life – save being rejected at twelve years old by the woman she had thought was her mother – nothing had affected her like what had happened to Monica. She had thought she knew wickedness and evil, but the attack on Monica showed her how very little she really knew about the destructive and mean-spirited ways of humans. Did everyone but she know who had peppered Monica?

Angel realised that much of her outrage centred on the fact that no one accused anyone of the crime, no one was demanding retribution or justice. Who were these people she had come to live with, and with whom she had been feeling so much at home? They were silent. Closed, seemingly accepting. They measured all their actions by some aspect of nature; saw messages in the stars, heard news in the wind, received pronouncements from owls and barking dogs, sought counsel with the bushes. A voice inside her head told Angel, 'Pack your bags and return to civilisation, the good old USA.' But another voice laughingly said, 'You home, child, you home. You just don't know it yet. Tek it easy.' It was the Jamaican voice, she suddenly realised, taking the slip of paper from Charley's hand.

Turning to Beryl, Angel spoke. 'Beryl, I believe this is for you. Is it okay if I read it?'

Beryl nodded yes. Angel unfolded the slip and read, first silently to herself, then out loud. 'Regrettably this morning, approximately 5 a.m., patient Madge Gordon died. Please come and identify and claim the body. Signed, Matron on duty.' Angel felt her hands trembling. This was her second experience of death, the first being that of John Fairbanks, the man she had believed was her father.

She remembered when he died. That evening, on John's insistence, Cindy had taken Angel to see him. He was as white as the sheet he was clutching, wrestling with death. She remembered how for the first time on that last day, after visiting him about once a week for a three-month period, repulsed by the foul smell of him and the fact that he was withering away, she had finally realised that John, the man she called Dad, was dying. Cindy couldn't bear to see him, and each time before she went to the hospital she took pills to calm her nerves. Angel hadn't wanted to visit her dad that evening; she had wanted to go with her friend to the ballet instead. But Cindy had said no, her father wanted to see her.

His eyes were closed when they entered the room, Cindy pushing Angel ahead of her. They stood by his bed for a long time, and finally Angel said to Cindy, 'Can we go now? He isn't going to wake up.' That was when he opened his eyes, and Angel could see that he was trying to smile. She hated him in that instant. Spittle had settled on the corner of his mouth. His skin looked like he had dandruff all over it, it was so flaky. He was an old man, and Angel wondered who he was. When he called them closer and told her to kiss him, she started

167

to cry. She looked at Cindy for help, but Cindy was already crying. She heard his voice again, unfamiliar yet familiar, say, 'Come kiss your dad?'

'Do I have to?' Angel wanted to ask Cindy, but she felt Cindy nudging her from behind, pushing her closer to the sheet-white, dandruff-faced man on the bed with saliva pasted on the side of his mouth.

Angel never did kiss John Fairbanks that day, the last time she saw him alive. He got hold of her hand and held her firmly, almost hurting, pulling her close to him.

'I'm your father. Remember that.'

Then he released her and closed his eyes. She and Cindy stood there until the nurse came in and checked, first his pulse, then the bottle of water-looking liquid dripping down through the tube that was attached to his hand. They left shortly afterwards, and Cindy stopped at their favourite ice-cream store and bought them both hot-fudge sundaes, which they ate, licking the whipped cream from the spoons. The next morning when Angel woke, Cindy told her that her dad had died in his sleep during the night. She had felt responsible, and vowed to herself never to eat a hot-fudge sundae again. And she hadn't.

Trembling, Angel walked over to the bench under the guinep tree. She heard Charley in the background, saying over and over, 'Ah sorry Beryl, ah truly sorry,' like a broken record.

'Her time did come,' replied Beryl, who took Charley's offered hand, and together they walked over and sat beside Angel. Angel looked at her watch. She sprang up.

'Maybe the people in Kristoff Village are right and duppies are real.'

As an option in her undergraduate education Angel had taken a course in African religion, and she remembered reading that many of the West African native groups believed in ancestral spirits and worship. The longer she lived in Kristoff Village, the more the bits and pieces of information she had picked up seemed to fit together.

Sandwiched between Beryl and Rupert, Angel's mind reviewed her short stay in Kristoff Village. Short, but it nevertheless seemed like a lifetime. She would never forget the darkness of her first night or her

168

fear. It had teeth and feet, and pursued her endlessly, until – exhausted – she had succumbed. Now darkness was her ally, and she walked unafraid in its black cool coat, feeling serene and creative. Beryl was much like the night, Angel reflected. Her hue was its colour and her disposition conjured its presence. Both were enigmatic: frightening and comforting. Beryl was the first person in the village with whom Angel had become intimate, and as the two of them got better acquainted she discovered Beryl's grace and youthful manner. Often when Angel went with Beryl to the field and they spent the day working, mostly Angel watching and listening, Beryl would speak as if she was a high-school girl. Angel wondered what had happened back then in Beryl's school days to cause her to stop really living. However, Beryl seldom spoke about her inner feelings. Whereas other villagers were willing to share intimate details of their lives, Beryl never spoke of any love or desire or pain.

Angel remembered Arnella saying once that she believed Beryl must have swallowed some great pain that was choking her, and that it would take a great calamity to dislodge it. Sitting now pressed up against Beryl, Angel was both repelled and comforted. Something about Beryl was so familiar, yet elusive. They were friends, and Angel valued talking to Beryl about most things, except sexual matters. Once, Valrie had remarked, 'Beryl sex starved; look how she sour all de time. It nuh natural fa woman to deny herself man. She cork-up, man; she need a good unplugging.' Angel had smiled, agreeing with Valrie that women needed to be loved regularly to feel good. However, Beryl had become her family, and was her and Rupert's mainstay in the village.

Tears trickled down Angel's cheeks. She sniffed, and Rupert put his arms around her. Beryl and Charley got up to pick some jelly coconut. As soon as they were out of earshot, Angel turned to Rupert. 'Mother Madge was like a grandmother to me. She was my friend. Every day she saved me some of whatever she or Beryl cooked and insisted that I eat it. Why is life so unfair?'

'How you mean? Aunty Madge did old, and tired. She live a long while. Beryl said she would be seventy come September. Dat is not a little time on this earth,' Rupert coaxed.

Angel nodded. She knew Mother Madge was weary of life, but

foremost in her mind was her own selfish desire to belong, to have a family to embrace her.

Angel remembered meeting her dad's mother, who lived in South Carolina. They had seen each other only twice, and both times it had been painful. It had been obvious the senior Mrs Fairbanks did not like her. She was five the first time they met, and she had asked her father, 'Dad, why doesn't Grandma like me?'

'Nonsense,' John Fairbanks had said, avoiding her eyes. 'She loves you . . .' Then his voice had faltered. 'You're just not accustomed to her.'

But Angel felt somehow that no lack of understanding accounted for her feelings. Every time visitors came, her grandmother told her to run and play. She remembered it being the longest ten days she ever spent. The second visit was worse, almost a year to the day before her father died. Even he could not deny or excuse away his mother's behaviour. Some distant cousin about Angel's age was also visiting, and Angel observed how her grandmother openly doted on the child, caressing her long silky hair. Her dad had said, 'Mother doesn't like to hug and kiss.' But Angel had seen her grandmother hugging and kissing the cousin.

The tears that trickled down Angel's cheeks now were partly for herself, for the pain of that memory she had buried. Her 'grandmother' hadn't liked her because she was black. That was why she sent her away when company came. Now Angel wondered whether that grandmother was still alive; she would be eighty, or close to it.

Cindy's mother, Grandma Ruth, had been different. She had lived in Manhattan, near them, and often came to visit, taking Angel on walks and to buy treats. Then she went on a cruise and never came back. At least that was what Cindy, eyes red, had said. How sad, Angel reflected, to die at sea, without any family. Angel had forgotten about Grandma Ruth, who must have died when she was around four years old. Yet the old woman had not forgotten about her. A few months after she graduated from Howard, vowing never to take money from Cindy again or have anything to do with her, a week after her twenty-first birthday, she had received a cheque for twenty thousand dollars. When in her self-righteousness she had sent back the cheque, Cindy had returned it with a copy of Grandma Ruth's will which clearly stated that each of her four grandchildren should receive equal parts of her estate when they turned twenty-one. Angel had been struck dumb. She couldn't even remember that woman, didn't even have a picture of her. But she swallowed her pride and called Cindy, apologised, thanked her, then asked if she had a picture of the old lady that she could send. A few days later, a small box arrived, with a five by seven photograph in a silver frame of a jolly-faced yet regal-looking white woman, holding in her arms three-year-old Angel, a dripping ice-cream cone gripped in one chubby hand. Angel still had that photograph. It was her one remaining image of that other life. For the first time in years she thought affectionately of Cindy, and wondered how she was. Just before she and Rupert left to come to Jamaica, Jasmine had written to tell her that Cindy had cancer and was undergoing surgery.

'I should write her,' Angel said out loud.

'Who?' Rupert asked.

'Cindy, who used to be my mother,' Angel replied, and it didn't hurt any longer.

Charley and Beryl picked half a dozen coconut jellies, and Rupert chopped them open. Both Beryl and Charley teased him that he hadn't gone to America and grown soft or forgotten the ways of his roots. They all laughed, and Angel wasn't sad any more, not about Mother Madge's death or about Grandmother Fairbanks or Grandma Ruth – not even about Cindy's rejection. She supposed, with great relief, that Kristoff Village was healing her and that it didn't matter that Beryl and Mother Madge weren't related to her by blood; they were related by spirit, and that was all that mattered.

'Listen oonuh ave to hurry so ah can drop oonuh into town. Ah ave to mek some fare to pay de mortgage come month end.'

'Let me pull on another dress and change me shoe,' Beryl declared, going into the house.

'I'm ready, ah just need to get my purse,' Angel chimed.

'Me will get it,' offered Rupert. 'For me have to get something from de house and change me shoes, too.'

Charley brushed the dust from his pants, rubbed his hands together, and smiled at Angel.

'So Miss Angel, how you liking de little village? You sounding more like we.'

'Charley, you don't need to call me Miss Angel, and me liking Kristoff plenty-plenty.'

They both laughed at Angel's mimicking the Jamaican habit of repeating words for emphasis.

As they passed in Charley's car, Angel saw Desmond's motorbike parked at Monica's gate. She would have given anything to be a fly on Monica's wall. The four of them were quiet, each preoccupied with their own thoughts. Rupert and Charley were up front, Beryl and Angel in the back. Once they were on the main road to Montego Bay, Charley started whistling. He apologised that his car radio was broken, adding that he hoped to have a new one by the week's end, as one of the higglers who sold wares in front of the craft market had gone to Cayman and had promised to sneak him in a good one.

'Why she has to sneak it in?' Angel enquired.

'Because it expensive bad-bad, man. If the customs people find it, it gwane cost more to pay de taxes dan it worth. Tings well rough out in Jam-down, Miss Angel. People have to lie and thief just to get by.'

Two completely different worlds, thought Angel, glancing back to see if she could still see the road that led to Kristoff Village. The village was cool, serene and lush, a place that could be compared to paradise, a place where everyone knew everyone else, where people still left their doors open, greeted each other daily, looked out and cared for one another. What happened to Monica was an aberration, something gone bad. Or was it? Angel didn't allow her thoughts to dwell on this. Kristoff Village was a world of its own, and somehow, although many of the inhabitants travelled daily or weekly to Montego Bay, they left the disease that was eating that city and the rest of Jamaica at the junction. Their values and ways were ancient and, Angel suspected, could be found duplicated in many small villages throughout West Africa, where colonisation had not laid its infected hand.

They were in the city now with its noise and stifling heat; people jostling; men on bicycles swinging dangerously in and out of traffic; a few stray goats wandering unconcernedly, eating from the open gutters; choking exhaust from buses and trucks; honking horns, angry voices, confusion, desperation, hustling. Angel sighed. She wished she had stayed and seen about Monica, or gone and offered her help to Arnella and Baby-Girl. But seeing Beryl's closed palms on her lap, she reminded herself why she had come, and knew she had made the right decision.

They were caught in the mid-day traffic jam. Angel felt perspiration trickling down her breasts and sweat spreading in her groin, making her underclothes damp and uncomfortable. Charley turned about and glanced at Beryl.

'Beryl, now dat Aunty Madge dead, you tink you gwane come live in town again?'

'Town not fah me,' she replied curtly.

Angel was surprised to learn that Beryl had once lived in Montego Bay and wanted to ask her when. But Rupert said suddenly, 'Charley, let we get out here so you can mek some fare. De hospital not dat far. We will stop and get something to drink, den walk to de hospital. We gwane stop by you house so check wid we bout four o'clock.'

Rupert was out of the car, opening the door for Angel before she could collect herself. Beryl hopped out from her side, thanking Charley, who hurriedly waved to them and made a dangerous and surely illegal turn in the middle of the street, miraculously missing people, goats and piled-up goods.

For a moment they stood by the side of the road, people hurrying by them, men and women and even young children hollering out the names of various foods or goods they were selling. Beryl stopped the whistling peanut man and purchased four small brown bags of freshly roasted peanuts, still warm in the shell. Further on a woman with a basket on her head called out, 'Shrimp! Shrimp!' Rupert hailed her, saying how much he missed shrimp, remembering that he had not had any since he returned to Jamaica. The red shrimp were in plastic bags, and when Rupert opened the bag, Angel could smell the pepper and see the seeds mixed in with the shrimp. Her stomach turned, but she swallowed. Beryl reached over her, pulled the bag from Rupert's hand, flung it on the ground and stepped on it.

'Ah don't want to smell, see or taste nuh peppa for a long while!' she declared before Rupert had a chance to protest. He turned away from the two women, suppressing his anger and disappointment.

Beryl took Angel's hand and pulled her along. Angel glanced over her shoulder at Rupert standing where they left him. She could tell he was mad. Although he had not seen Monica she had told him the whole story in graphic detail. He should have understood, Angel thought, squeezing Beryl's hand.

They slackened their pace, and when they got to a park-like area, rested on a bench and waited for Rupert to catch up with them.

'Sorry,' Beryl spoke up as Rupert approached them. 'Is not you peppa Monica, but ah just don't want smell any peppa now.' He nodded. Angel tugged at his hand, and pulled him to sit between Beryl and her. They sat for a long while, enjoying the cool breeze and watching people go. From habit, Angel looked at her watch. Finally, Beryl said, 'Let we go eat. Ah know a place not far from here.' They followed her lead, Angel feeling beaten down by the heat and marvelling that people actually worked, especially outdoors, in this oppressive atmosphere.

After about five blocks and several turns they entered a small passageway that opened on to an enclosed garden with tables and chairs threatening to be overrun by red and purple bougainvillaea. Angel smiled at the unexpected surprise. The whole of these last six months in Jamaica had been a bit like that: a refuge in the middle of pandemonium. They took an empty table and were immediately greeted by a young woman with the prettiest smile Angel had ever seen. The waitress pointed to the menu board on the wall and read out the specials of the day; then she rattled off seven different kinds of juice that were available. Angel ordered cherry juice, Beryl tamarind juice, while Rupert ordered a stout-back. The waitress grinned in his face. As she made off to fill their orders, Beryl touched her on the shoulder and enquired, 'Is Miss Mazie here?'

'Yes ma'am. She in de back.'

'Tell her Beryl, Miss Madge's daughta, would like to have a word with her.'

The waitress smiled and turned away. Reggae music was playing softly from two speakers. By the bar a fan whizzed wildly. Angel counted ten other tables, each with four chairs. All but two tables were empty, the others occupied by people who looked just like them. Angel kicked off her shoes under the table and sipped her water. No one spoke about their destination or the arrangements that had to be made.

A handsome woman, large and round, burst from the beaded curtain through which the waitress had disappeared, heading directly for their table. Angel was the only one who sat in direct view. She nudged Beryl, who glanced up, smiled broadly and pushed back her chair. The two women met half-way in embrace. Angel had never seen Beryl so animated.

'Gal is wha bring you to dis God-forsaken town dat you swear off?' Without waiting for an answer, the woman turned to look at Angel and Rupert, enquiring, 'So is who dese people you wid?'

'You memba ah used to talk about me cousin Rupert who went to America, well is him dis, and dat's him pretty wife, Angel.'

'How oonuh do? Please to meet you. Let me wipe me hand pan de apron before ah shake oonuh hand. Please to meet you. De name is Mazie, Mazie Jean McFarlin.' When she offered her hand, Angel found that it was warm and firm. Then Mazie turned her full attention back to Beryl. 'You see how you skinny friend get fat; dat's what having man and picknie do to you. So how Aunty Madge?'

'She dead,' Beryl said flatly.

'Oh God, wha you a say to me? When?'

'Early dis morning. We on de way to de hospital.'

'You mean she been here in MoBay and you neva stop tell me? Me neva even know she did sick.' There was outrage in Mazie's voice. Customers stopped eating and stared.

'Is two weeks now me and Angel bring her in. She had a stroke. Everything happening so fast.'

'Hush. Me did well sorry. So when de funeral?'

'Ah figure ah might as well bury her quick,' said Beryl. 'So Sunday de funeral.'

'You notify you cousin Carol? You know she working in one of them fancy new hotel in Negril,' said Mazie.

Beryl shook her head, indicating that she didn't know.

'Lawd God, Aunty Madge dead,' Mazie cried dramatically, placing both hands on her head. The few customers shouted condolences and Mazie thanked them. Then, taking Beryl's hand and leading her through the beaded curtain, she said, 'Come, ah have to cook people's food before dem cuss me and storm out. Come chat wid me while me cook.' Angel heard her voice trail off. She felt cheated out of some stories.

By the time Angel and Rupert finished eating their lunches they were the last ones in the restaurant. Beryl had not emerged, but every so often Mazie's loud voice rose in exclamation.

It was three forty-five and they had not been to the hospital. Yet they had told Charley they would be by his house at four. Angel held her wrist up to Rupert's face and indicated the time. He shrugged. Angel was becoming anxious. Why did no one seem to pay attention to time here? she wondered. She simply did not understand what was going on. Charley had brought confirmation that Beryl's mother was dead at eleven in the morning, and here it was almost four in the afternoon and they had not yet been to the hospital.

'Rupert, don't you think you should get Beryl so we can get to the hospital? It's almost four o'clock.' Angel tried for her most even tone.

'Wha de rush? Aunt Madge dead already; she nah go nowhere.' Rupert tapped his hand to the music playing softly. Angel slipped on her shoes and stood up. She didn't want to argue with Rupert in a restaurant over his concept of time or his aunt's death. She pulled her hair back with her hands, stretched, then strolled around the small room with its white wrought-iron tables and yellow and white chairs. She considered the fact that all the fights and quarrels she and Rupert had had, even when they lived in California, were over time: his obliviousness to time and her obsession with it.

Just as Angel decided to go and find Beryl herself, she appeared, followed by Mazie who offered to drive them to the hospital. At the hospital, they were directed to the morgue. A sour-mannered, prune-dried man took them inside, and after pulling out several trays, found the one with Beryl's mother. At the sight of her laying there stiff, one hand balled at her side, and her mouth slightly apart, Beryl, Angel, Rupert and Mazie all burst into tears. Both women put their arms around Beryl and they cried loudly. The sour orderly kissed his teeth several times, said they should call him when they were leaving, and mumbled loud enough for them to hear as he left, 'People dead every day and not a drop of tears gwane bring dem back.'

Rupert wiped his eyes and finally pushed the tray out of sight. Beryl was weak so Mazie and Angel held her up. When they stood outside and leaned against the door, Angel let out a breath that she had been holding in for what felt like forever. It was the first time she had been that intimate with death. She had seen her dad only once after he died, at the church, lying in a silver-blue coffin and wearing a navy-blue suit, white shirt and lipstick. He didn't look anything like the man who used to lift her above his head when he came home in the evening, or who used to pull her to sit on his lap and read to her. The corpse had resembled the washed-out, white, withering man she had visited on his deathbed.

Angel had met Mother Madge on her first day in Kristoff Village. She and Rupert had gone to Beryl to borrow something, and Beryl had invited them to breakfast. At first Angel hadn't noticed Mother Madge, who was sitting on a stool by the coconut tree near the kitchen. But Rupert had seen her. Mother Madge had taken his hand, held it for a long time and asked him a lot of questions, mostly about people Angel had not heard of. Then she had turned to Angel, told her to come and sit by her, and had taken the young woman's face in her hands and looked closely, like she was searching for the image of someone. Finally Mother Madge had turned to Beryl and said, 'What a way she did favour us.' They became good friends in that instant, and throughout the six months that Angel had been living in the village, not one day had gone by that she and Mother Madge didn't visit. The old woman asked many questions about America and Angel's people. Angel found herself talking overtime just to cover the silences that fell on Mother Madge when she heard that Angel was alone in the world.

'She look just like she did when she was alive,' Angel now declared.

'Is true,' Mazie agreed.

Beryl wiped her eyes, stood on her own feet, and indicated that she was ready. Rupert called to the orderly, who was sitting under a mango tree whittling on a stick.

'We leaving.'

'Tek it easy,' the orderly shouted, not moving from where he sat. 'When oonuh coming fa de body?'

'Sunday morning,' Beryl announced.

'Well me same one gwane be here. Don't fret-up youself now. Evening.' The orderly turned back to his whittling.

Angel hadn't known what to expect, but she was surprised at the informality of the whole affair. Beryl had to sign one piece of paper and that was it.

It was five thirty when Mazie dropped them off at Charley's house. Charley's wife had dinner waiting for them, but they were not hungry after the large lunch at Mazie's. Before Mazie left, she said she would send word to Beryl's cousin Carol and that Beryl should come and spend Saturday night with her. That way they could get to the hospital early to dress the body. Sis, Charley's wife, told them that Charley had checked by, but hadn't stopped because a passenger was in the car. However, he had said they should wait for him; he wouldn't be more than an hour. Angel wanted to know how long ago that had been, and when Sis said she wasn't sure, a woman's voice from inside the house said three thirty, for the announcer on the radio had mentioned the time just as Charley blew his horn. Neither Beryl or Rupert appeared put out that Charley had not yet returned.

The moment Angel sat down, the mosquitoes took to her legs and arms. She kept up a constant clapping of hands and stomping of feet. Rupert went for a walk down the lane. Beryl went to sit in the back and talk to Sis while she worked. Angel was left alone and she felt abandoned for the second time that day. At the restaurant Rupert had been with her, but the women had deserted her. She had felt like an outsider then, and she felt the same way now. She didn't like the sense it gave her of having been singled out.

At six thirty, Charley returned. He left the cab running as he ran inside and gulped down a tall, cool drink. Rupert had just got back from his walk. Charley grabbed him, saying, 'Come man, come. We have to get a coffin measured for Aunty Madge. Let we go before Godfree and Nathan close up.' But seeing Angel sitting by herself Charley suggested as he jumped back in his cab, 'If you wan lie down, plenty bed inna de house or go a back and keep talk wid Beryl and Sis.'

It took a while for Charley's words to sink in. Then Angel chided herself for not thinking about inviting herself to join the women in the back. She knew they had not forgotten about her because every so

178

often one of Charley's children came to her and enquired if she was 'All right' or whether, 'You want anyting Miss Angel?' – always followed by a little giggle.

Angel rose and strode to the back where she heard voices, easy in conversation. Sis, who was sitting over a basin of fish that looked still alive, asked if she needed anything. Angel said, 'No, but I hope you don't mind if I sit here with you and Beryl.' Sis was all apologetic for leaving her alone, but added, 'Charley bring dis basin of fish dis morning. Ah put dem to soak in lime water but if ah don't gut them now and put them pan ice, dem gwane go bad.' Then without pausing she hollered, 'One of oonuh children bring Miss Angel a chair.'

Before Angel was comfortably seated a woman next door stuck her head over the fence. 'Evening Sis, Beryl, sorry to hear bout you moda.' She turned her eyes toward Angel. 'So Sis, is de American woman dis dat Charley cousin bring from America?' Sis nodded confirmation. The woman beamed, stuck her hand across the fence and in her most proper voice said, 'Please to meet you Miss Angel.' Angel got up and shook the woman's hand.

It was eight fifteen by the time Charley finally drove them back to Kristoff Village. Lanterns were lit by Beryl's gate and they could see from a distance that people had congregated. When Angel disembarked from the car she saw that there were several women, some of whom she did not recognise, sitting on and around Beryl's veranda on benches and on stools, and that the entire inside of the house was lit up. As soon as Beryl stepped through the gate the women started singing. Aunty Dahlia greeted them. Godfree stood by the gate, poured some rum on the ground, then invited Rupert and Charley to have a glass. Charley, who had promised his wife that he would not linger, agreed to but one glass; even so, Angel noted that it was ten o'clock when he left. Aunt Dahlia and Velma explained to Angel that they were preparing the house for the dead. Angel asked what that meant. They said they had to take out Aunt Madge's mattress and other bedding and wash the room, so just in case she felt like returning to haunt the living she would be disoriented. Angel nodded as if she understood, but was enthralled by all the activities. Rupert had warned her not to drink any rum, but Angel accepted a glass from Dahlia. She figured if Dahlia and Velma who were very old could drink it without getting sick, then so could she. Before long, though, she felt her head spinning, and the next thing she knew she was undressed, alone in bed, her watch removed from her wrist. Her head felt too heavy for her body so she fell back, asleep.

Stand steady mek ant crawl over you

Ainsworth had not been able to work all day. He took a two-hour lunch break, combing the three bookstores near his job, trying to find Monica a collection of poetry by a Jamaican woman other than Louise Bennett. He came away empty-handed.

As much as he tried not to think about Marva and the child that she was carrying, she was constantly on his mind, her image fixed as he had seen her that morning, at the table eating a pepper sandwich. At three o'clock, after sitting at his desk, his mind wandering, he closed his folders and informed the receptionist that he was gone for the day. As he strolled along the street, deep in thought, he heard his name being called.

'Mista McKenzie, howdy. Mista McKenzie.'

Ainsworth looked around and recognised one of the women from his village. She was walking fast, a loaded hamper on her head, and carrying a small basket in one hand. She stopped directly in front of him and used the back of her free hand to wipe away the perspiration that was trickling into her eyes.

'Plenty trouble come to Kristoff these last two days. Someone body chop up Mista Desmond and him daughter. Me here see dem in de hospital dis very minute.' Then the woman turned and started to move very quickly.

Ainsworth spun around several times before he got his bearings. He hailed a passing taxi and told the driver to take him to the hospital. When he got there he recognised Desmond and Sister Olive coming down the steps. One of Desmond's pant legs was rolled up and a fresh bandage was visible. Ainsworth hurried over and greeted them.

'We was just going to find a little place close by to get a bite to eat,' volunteered Olive. 'We tired and hungry, but have to wait for Althea.'

They found a snack-shop and while they ate Olive related all the events of Grace's attack upon Althea, and how she had bitten out a piece of Desmond's leg when he intervened. Desmond remained silent, seemingly turned in on himself. Ainsworth ate without tasting the food. He wanted to talk with Desmond alone; he enquired about Althea, his goddaughter.

'Grace did beat her well bad,' said Olive. 'She got fifteen stitches pan her back, four on her left hand, and seven on her right leg. But de doctor say dem want to run some test to mek sure she all right. You and Desmond sit here awhile ah go check pan her.' They readily agreed.

Both men sat for a long time, unsure of how to begin. Ainsworth wanted to speak to Desmond about Monica but couldn't find the beginning of the thread.

'Beryl used to be a pretty woman you know,' Desmond declared, as if reading Ainsworth's mind. 'Didn't you used to like her bad-bad?'

Ainsworth smiled, remembering his boyhood when he and Desmond were best friends. It was only in Desmond that he had ever confided his love for Beryl.

When he was thirteen Beryl tutored Ainsworth in maths; he had long had a crush on her. Many evenings when she came to tutor him, Ainsworth found he couldn't concentrate. He liked her big white teeth that she frequently used her tongue to polish. Mostly he liked watching her walk. Her purple-hued skin, under the sun, glowed in royal richness. Her neck, the length of a giraffe's, her legs long as a flamingo's. She walked like the ground owed her some special honour. Wide-hipped, big-boned, not an ounce of fat.

Many nights Ainsworth went to bed dreaming of her. Several times he tried to sneak up to the river when he thought she might be bathing. The grass and insects had more luck than he. He remembered clearly the day when she jokingly knuckled her index finger, pressed it to his head, and said, 'You head tough you know; you fi concentrate.' All the next day he kept touching his head in the spot where she touched him and he heard her voice, flat but how so smooth, repeating in his head.

For endless days Ainsworth had practised telling Beryl that he loved her, but he never found his voice in her presence. Besides, he saw how the older boys and some of the grown men looked at Beryl whenever she passed. He heard some of their whispers; he knew he would never have a chance.

At the celebration held in honour of Beryl passing all her exams and being accepted into teacher's college, Ainsworth, an unsure adolescent, stood back, afraid to go and congratulate her, afraid to be too close lest his actions reveal his puppy-love. Beryl was a great dancer and all night held centre stage, dancing with men young and old. After everyone was gone save himself and his mother, who had promised to help clean up, Aunty Madge had said. 'But wait! Beryl, you been dancing all night and not one dance me see you dance with you first student.' Pulling Ainsworth towards Beryl, Aunty Madge had bade them dance. They danced, and long after the music stopped he did not let her go. His mother pulled at him, saying, 'How comes a big boy like you fall asleep when you dancing wid such a pretty young lady?' Ashamed to the core, he crept home with his mother, still feeling Beryl's warm, high-chested body pressed against his.

Desmond's voice interrupted Ainsworth's memory.

'What you think happen to her, man? She return to Kristoff two years after leaving fah teacher's college, beaten, having dropped out of everything it seemed.'

'Who knows?' Ainsworth replied. 'Life is sure strange.' Silence, then Ainsworth decided to speak openly to Desmond: 'Level wid me, man. Wha gwane on between you and Monica and Grace?'

Desmond's tone was defeated. 'Me and Grace living we life, then Monica return looking brand new. Now this thing happened to her all because of me; Grace lose she mind, almost kill she only daughter. Who know anything anymore?'

'So what you gwane do?'

'Ah love Monica. Long time now things just so-so between Grace and me, but she still is de mother of me children. But look how she beat Althea, and although ah don't want to believe it ah suspect she have something to do wid what happened to Monica. She and me ova, done.' Desmond said it with finality, rising. Ainsworth stood up too. He remembered that the food Marva had cooked yesterday was so peppered even the dog couldn't eat it. She had left the house hotly. He suspected that she too had something to do with what had

182

happened to Monica. Marva was as jealous of Monica as she was of his reading.

The two friends headed for the hospital. Ainsworth became anxious when he saw how badly Grace had beaten Althea; his mind turned to his own children. He wondered if they were safe, considering the state of mind Marva had been in. He had just decided to tell Desmond and Olive that he was heading home when Master Cotton returned with the car.

All the way to Kristoff Village, Ainsworth's thoughts swung between Beryl and Marva, on the one hand trying to imagine the cause of Beryl's resignation and on the other worrying about Marva's state of mind and her possible role in Monica's injury. Was Marva Grace's accomplice? Ainsworth's head throbbed.

He found Marva where he'd left her, in the kitchen, looking as if she hadn't bathed. He asked after his sons.

'Dem at you daddy's house,' Marva spat. 'You think ah don't know dat dem trying fi poison me picknie dem mind against me. Ah know dem don't like me.'

Ainsworth sat at the table with his wife, trying to find the right words to communicate with her. 'Marva, how you feeling? Ah hope you thinking about de baby. You need to rest, and ah don't think you should be eating all dem peppers.'

'Since when you turn doctor? Since when you so concern about me? You betta save it fah de one Monica, you sweetheart. Is she need doctor; she need plenty doctor if what me hear is true.' Marva ended with a sarcastic cackle. Ainsworth's banging on the table stifled her laughter.

'Marva, ah need to know, for you actions could have serious consequences – did you go with Grace to Monica yesterday evening?'

'First you posing like doctor, now you tek up barrister's coat? Don't come home harassing me. Why you nuh go ask you sweetheart who pepper her?' Marva ended, releasing a loud, long burp.

Ainsworth left her still sitting at the table and went to his parents' home to see his sons.

Monica was much improved, but Miss Cotton still insisted on keeping up an around-the-clock watch. However, Arnella persuaded her to leave her, Valrie and Baby-Girl to watch over Monica while she went home, bathed and rested. Reluctantly Miss Cotton agreed, and was just returning home when the car pulled up with her husband, Olive, Desmond, Althea and Ainsworth. As was her way, Miss Cotton took charge, ordering Desmond to bring Althea to Monica's house, 'So ah can look afta de both of dem. Besides, ah already have some tea boiling fah Althea to drink.'

Olive took Althea inside Monica's house while Desmond conferred with Mr Cotton. Grace was still home, in the care of a few women of the village. Their youngest son, Peter, was with Milford, where he had Valrie and Godfree's sons to play with. Desmond asked about Monica and wanted to see her, but Miss Cotton advised him to go and look after his wife first. Mr Cotton accompanied him on his task.

Arnella was feeding Monica some clear soup when Olive brought Althea into the room. Valrie covered her mouth to suppress a cry of alarm upon seeing Althea. Arnella left off feeding Monica, who had slept through the morning's events. Miss Cotton appeared and immediately began undressing Althea, ordering Olive to bring a basin in which she could sponge her down. Miss Cotton examined every inch of Althea's body, shaking her head gravely as she did so.

'Shame, shame,' she concluded, smacking her lips. 'A low-down shame.'

Olive, returning, said, 'Miss Cotton, dere is something else you must know. Althea about four months pregnant; dat's what did set Grace off.' No one said anything. Althea hung her head and started to cry.

'Please don't tell Daddy,' she pleaded in the midst of the silence. Still no one said anything. Miss Cotton threw a few tamarind leaves into the basin of warm water Olive had brought, then took a small brown bottle from her pocket, opened it, sprinkled some of the contents in the basin and began sponging down Althea.

'Arnella, you done feeding Monica? Then get a towel and find a nightie for me to put on this child.' Althea still wept silently.

Valrie took Baby-Girl into the living room and turned on the radio. After getting the towel and nightie for Miss Cotton, Arnella went to get Althea some food. Miss Cotton was humming, just humming, one of her wordless songs. Althea looked at no one; she had in particular avoided looking at Monica. She wasn't sure how she felt about her.

184

'Miss Cotton,' came Monica's weak voice. 'Is who beat up Desmond's one daughter so?'

'Her mother.'

Monica moaned, but not for herself. 'Ah sorry, Althea. Ah didn't mean fah none of dis to happen. Ah didn't even mean to fall in love wid you daddy and provoke you moda.'

'Well sorry too late now,' interrupted Miss Cotton. 'It all happen already. Now you have a daughter who have baby coming so hurry up and get well.' Miss Cotton patted Althea dry, rubbed some ointment over her body, and led her to the bed to lie next to Monica. The child complied. Baby-Girl began crying. Valrie brought in food and fed Althea like a baby.

When Desmond arrived later Miss Cotton told him that he could sleep in the rocking chair and she left to go to Beryl's. In the bedroom, Desmond found Monica and Althea asleep side by side. He had explained to his son Peter as best as he could, what had happened, before leaving him at Milford's to spend the night. He had been home to find that Grace, in a little girl's voice, kept calling to the women who were looking after her, 'Mama, come plait me hair.'

Mind over matters

She-Devil and Devil's day had been full. The Angels were good workers, but needed constant supervision. The cow, goat and pig had been killed and skinned. The wedding cakes had been baked. The house had been dusted and cleaned, save the cobwebs in the corners. The yard was almost ready. The outside of the house had been painted. The garden had been pruned. Both Devil and She-Devil were feeling very tired but satisfied: they collapsed on opposite sides of the bed. Then they both sprang up almost at once. She-Devil exclaimed first.

'Ah forget to go try on me dress. Ah have nothing to wear to de wedding. What a calamity.'

'Calamity,' shrieked Devil, known for exaggeration. 'Is a catastrophe! Is you and all dat cooking why ah can't get into any of me clothes dem. Is wha me gwane wear?'

'Listen here, man,' said She-Devil, 'don't vex me dis night, ah too tired. Besides, is who always begging me to cook dis and cook dat?'

'What I beg you fix? You de one always running about de place, telling me ah need to eat, ah need to eat . . .'

Before She-Devil or Devil could apply the brakes they were into a full-scale argument, each forgetting the point they wanted to make. Their quarrel came to an ending as sudden as its beginning when Devil poured his bedside glass of juice down She-Devil's blouse. She of course made him lick her off clean.

Memory is better than luck

Ainsworth was the last to leave Beryl's house. As he walked her to Rupert and Angel's house, where she would spend the night, he offered to help make the arrangements for her mother's funeral. She thanked him and went through the gate. Ainsworth closed it behind her; then he leaned on it, calling after her. She stopped and just before she turned he thought he glimpsed the Beryl he had been in love with when he was thirteen. She waited for him to say something. He suddenly felt unsure, like the thirteen-year-old-boy who had been visiting with him on and off all day. Finally he asked, 'Beryl, why you never become de teacher you always wanted to be?'

Although it was dark he could feel that she was staring deeply at him.

'You really want to know?' she asked.

'Yes.'

'Den ask me again after ah bury Mamma and ah not so tired.'

Before Ainsworth reached home the rain began to fall all at once, without warning. He started to run but then stopped, enjoying the feel of the rain on his body. As a boy there were few other things he had enjoyed more than playing out in the rain and trying to drink it as it fell. Now he stuck out his tongue and was surprised at the sweet taste of the rain on his tongue.

As Kristoff Village slept, the rain poured down and washed away all the pepper and all the anger.

V

Walk if you have feet

they sometimes forget
but time reminds them
that every story start in a pan
that has a hole
from which some peas spill
but still
jackass can't walk
on two feet

Not every cutlass can bill grass

Rain that comes without causing flood and landslide, rain that doesn't wash away people's crops or houses is a cleansing rain, a healing rain, a welcome rain.

The day after Beryl's mother died; the day after Grace almost beat her daughter to death, bit out a piece of her husband's leg, then quietly returned to her childhood, hanging on to her mother's dress; the day after Desmond confessed his love for Monica; the day after Ainsworth remembered his puppy-boy love for Beryl; the day after Arnella came into her own as a healer, helping Miss Cotton extinguish the fire raging inside Monica; the day after Angel remembered that she had a beginning and forgave the white woman who hadn't been big enough to raise a black girl; the day after the inhabitants of Kristoff Village felt as if the outside world had finally invaded their quiet and was causing confusion and dissension; the day after everyone had left Beryl's house to prepare it for the dead, and Ainsworth had tasted the sweet sticky rain on his tongue; that day the people of Kristoff Village woke to find the earth moist, and all the heaviness in the air washed away.

Arnella decided it was time to take Baby-Girl to the river. She had sent Valrie home on the previous night to look after her sons and to keep their husband warm. She packed a change of clothes for Baby-Girl and herself, then headed for the river before even the roosters were up. The colour of the day was silver-blue, and the air was sweet, like the last drop of limeade in a jar. Baby-Girl whimpered, Arnella hummed to her, walking fast as was her custom. Arnella didn't descend to the river at the place where the women washed and the young children bathed; instead she stole through tall ferns and grasses, holding Baby-Girl completely wrapped in a blanket. The path she made was thorny and tedious, but she kept up her fast pace, as if she had a date, making sure that Baby-Girl was nestled to her bosom. She heard the scurrying of mongoose and wild rats, the scuttling of lizards, the chattering of birds and the rustling of leaves. After more than a mile, Arnella came to a dense area that required her to bend and push back overhanging boughs; then to an opening sheltered by bamboo branches. At last she stood on the bank of the white river that flowed mildly that morning. Baby-Girl started to cry; Arnella looked around for a place to sit and nurse her. The air was still cool from the rain the night before, and the ground was moist; but she found a stump on which to sit. As she nursed her daughter, cooing to her, she became lost in the singular beauty of the place, and closing her eyes to imprint the moment in her mind she drifted, hearing the songs of the wood in her head.

Then she felt the wood on her bare breast, wood that was sanded but not to smoothness, wood that was still new and pungent. The wood pulsed, pressing slightly on her full breast, and the milk dripped down to her waist. She threw back her head, and she felt the wood that caught her head at the neck and nestled it; she felt the wood caressing the top of her chest and she didn't dare open her eyes with Baby-Girl still feeding. She flung off her slippers and rubbed the soles of her feet over the moist soil and knew it was too soon for her desires to be met. Now the wood was pressing her shoulder blades, moving up and down her spine, massaging her lower back. She felt Baby-Girl pull free from her breast, asleep. She could hear the river like a flute tune, and she wanted to suck on the wood, taste its bitter greenness in her mouth, have the wood touch her all over and roll in the moist earth.

He had a blanket with him which he spread. She placed Baby-Girl on it and covered her with towels. When she turned, his nakedness was a gift that propelled her to her knees. Her dress was caught under her, but she quickly freed it; he pulled it over her head, and his wooded-textured hands and her fabric palms met in greeting to the sun. They were dancing to the rays, and her arms were a fan above her head, and his fingers were like feathers tingling from her palm to her armpits where they played in her hair, caressing the sides of her breasts that released milk freely. He laid her on her back, kissing her stomach, massaging it; his hand was a plane on the side of her thighs. Finally their lips met and she sucked greedily, before his tongue found

190

her tongue and her fingers joined his, sliding up and down, up and down, in and out, in and out.

They were awakened by the heat of the sun on their sweaty bodies.

Baby-Girl awoke. Godfree went over, picked her up, kissing both cheeks. Arnella pressed against his back, rested her head on his shoulder. They tried to determine which traits of his and which of hers the baby had. He undressed the baby, handed her to Arnella, then dove into the river ahead of them. Arnella quickly took off her underclothes, walked to the edge and handed Baby-Girl to her father. Then she stepped into the warm, milky river. With Baby-Girl pressed between them, and their arms around each other's waists, they circled and bounced, circled and bounced until the child started to cry.

'Dat's enough. You stay; me will dry she off quick-quick.' Godfree clambered out with Baby-Girl held up in front of him. He quickly patted her dry, dressed her and bundled her up.

When he turned back to the river, he could not see Arnella. He put Baby-Girl down and ran to the bank, searching. He felt as if his heart had jumped to his throat. He dove, his eyes open. His lungs contracted, he came up for air, then went down again and came up. Nothing. Eyes like charred wood, he looked around – and saw Arnella slouched on the opposite side of the river. Godfree stood panting, not daring to look at her. He swallowed his panic. He crawled out, dressed slowly, kissed Baby-Girl and disappeared as quietly as he had appeared among the bamboo canes.

Arnella collected Baby-Girl, the towels and the blanket and walked home. Daddy Milford was waiting with breakfast that Aunty Velma had sent. Arnella made him feed her as he had done when she was a little girl. After he left with the dishes she went to sleep, a smile on her face.

Kristoff Village spent the next two days recovering from the events of Wednesday night and Thursday morning and in preparation for Madge Gordon's funeral. Although not a prominent member of the community, and although she had withdrawn gradually over the years, Miss Madge was nevertheless expected to have a good showing. She had been respected for her frankness and generosity, and for raising a hard-working, dedicated daughter. Since Beryl was an only child, as both her parents had been, there were almost no relatives to speak of, save a few distant cousins such as Cousin Carol. Only cousin Carol and her family, eight in all, had come Saturday evening. Some of them stayed in Beryl's two-room house, some in Rupert and Angel's cottage. Beryl had invited Angel to spend the night with her at Mazie's house in Montego Bay so she could accompany them the next morning to dress the body. Rupert decided to spend the night at Charley's, in order to meet Beryl, Angel and Mazie at the morgue with the coffin.

Ainsworth, Desmond and Godfree made arrangements for the grave to be dug in the valley of Beryl's land, quarter of a mile from her house, right beside the grave of her father, and where Beryl herself planned to be buried in time. Since Miss Madge belonged to no church, Mr Cotton would preside over the service which would be held right in her yard.

As for Grace, arrangements were quickly made for her. Trevor Campbell, Peggy's husband, had been away for the greater part of the week on a vehicle-parts-seeking expedition which took him all the way across the island. Thus he had missed the dramatic events. Upon his return on Friday afternoon, without being given an opportunity even to kiss his wife or see if his side of the bed had remained cold in his absence, he was drafted to take Grace to her mother's village. Initially, Grace had been taken to the hospital in Montego Bay, but they released her due to a lack of psychiatric space. They suggested she be taken to Bellevue Hospital in Kingston. A telegram was sent to her parents, who demanded she be brought home.

Peggy Campbell was, of course, expected to attend Beryl's mother's funeral. However, she had been keeping her head low since the night of the attack on Monica. Marva had been visiting with her back and forth, and Peggy's helper told someone, who told someone else, that Peggy had been heard complaining to Marva about Trevor, who was a notorious womaniser.

'Ah fed up of Trevor slackness. Him think me is fool,' Peggy shouted, ripping several of Trevor's shirts off the clothes-line and trampling them in the ground. 'Is why him always have fi go all the way to Kingston to find parts for de vehicles. Him must tink me is damn fool. Ah know he has some woman somewhere, and if he doesn't watch himself . . .' At this point her ranting turned to sobs that racked her body. She covered her hands and cried, 'I go tell Daddy to cut him off. Him park me in this back-o-wall village while he runs around.'

Rumour had it that Peggy and Marva were plotting against their husbands. However, since the community knew about their violation of Monica, they were marked and therefore not feared.

The morning of the funeral Marva said to Ainsworth, 'Ah don't think ah gwane mek de funeral. Ah not feeling too well.'

'Even if you were feeling well, Beryl told me to make sure you neva cross foot through her gate again,' Ainsworth replied, pulling a white shirt from the closet and not missing a beat. Marva kissed her teeth and left the room.

Angel had not thought much about dead people before. Although she had agreed to come and dress Mother Madge's body she hadn't been quite sure what that meant. The morning they arrived at the morgue, and the same sour orderly greeted them, Angel asked when the undertakers would arrive.

'Is who dem?' Beryl asked her in earnest.

Angel fished for words, but Mazie rescued her.

'Is only rich people use undertaker, me dear. We country folk tek care of we own.' And Mazie pushed open the door of the morgue. Inside the cold room Mazie nudged Beryl and, laughing, said, 'What a way de orderly fava mango seed dat you suck on den throw weh.' They laughed; Angel missed the joke.

Fear gripped Angel when the door closed behind them and they were left alone with the body of Mother Madge. Mazie and Beryl went to their task as if it were as natural as brushing one's teeth. Angel could not explain her fear, and tried to talk herself out of it. Mother Madge was dead, and the dead had no power. But she wasn't sure any more, living in Kristoff Village with everyone's constant talk of duppies. Duppies visited their dreams, spoke to them, even tried to do them harm. Angel stood well back, watching Beryl and Mazie undress Mother Madge and sponge her down. Not only did she not want to look upon the dead face of Mother Madge, but she certainly felt funny about looking on her nakedness. Angel turned her back, but there was no window through which she could look. She supposed she could go outside and wait for them, but she was certain that the orderly would be sitting there and would have something, perhaps not too complimentary, to say. She had to do this. Why had she volunteered to come if she wasn't going to be of some assistance?

'Miss Angel,' Beryl's solicitous voice broke through Angel's internal debate, 'you can go outside if you not feeling too comfortable.' Beryl had not called her Miss Angel since the day of their first meeting. Angel felt a pang at the distance that her inaction was interposing between her and Beryl.

'No, I'm all right. I just needed to catch my breath.' Angel glanced from Beryl's face to Mazie's and saw their doubt. She steeled herself; took a few deep breaths, then walked over to the table and forced herself to look at Mother Madge.

'She seem so small,' Beryl offered, patting her dead mother's arm.

'But she happy. Look how peaceful she face is,' Mazie submitted.

Angel looked closely into Mother Madge's face and saw serenity. Suddenly her fear was gone. She caressed the old woman's face then asked what she could do to assist with the dressing.

They dressed Mother Madge for her funeral in a simple white dress with embroidered lace around the collar. She held a white handkerchief in her hand, with a capital B embroidered in a field of yellow and red roses. Beryl and Mazie argued about whether to put the white hat on her head, or tie her head in the traditional way she had preferred when she was alive.

'De hat will look betta, more dignified,' Mazie concluded.

'But Mamma didn't like hat,' Beryl protested.

Angel found herself interjecting. 'Why don't we place the hat on Mother Madge's stomach, drape the white lace cloth that Beryl brought above her head, and just rebraid her hair like she often wore it?' In the minute it took Beryl and Mazie to make up their minds Angel bit on her bottom lip.

'Dat's a good idea, don't you tink Mazie?' Beryl said, turning to Mazie, who nodded her head in agreement. They asked Angel to braid Madge's hair. Just as she finished, and the three of them were inspecting Mother Madge, Charley and Rupert arrived with the coffin.

It was a simple coffin, made from pine and varnished to a sheen. The shape, however, made it unique: like an egg resting on a round-cornered rectangle, with banana-shaped leaves etched all around its parameter. The interior of the coffin was draped in lemon satin. Placed next to this colour, Mother Madge appeared the essence of calm.

Ainsworth and Trevor arrived. Ainsworth handed a bunch of yellow windflowers to Beryl, who sniffed at them before thanking him. Then she placed them next to Mother Madge. The whole effect – Mother Madge in her simple white dress, the white lace draped above her corn-row braids, her hat placed just below the hand holding the white handkerchief embroidered with B in a field of yellow and red roses – was striking. However, she was barefoot, although her feet were covered by her dress. Angel was surprised by this oversight and asked about shoes.

Mazie explained, 'We nuh want her to wander bout de place.'

Angel did not quite understand, but had become accustomed to the talk of duppies and other visitors from the spirit world.

The procession to Kristoff Village was a simple one. Mazie, her husband and three children, Beryl and Ainsworth squeezed into the car which led the procession. They were followed by Trevor's mini-bus in which the coffin rode, accompanied by Angel, Rupert and four of Cousin Carol's relatives in a tight squeeze. Bringing up the rear were Charley, his wife and mother-in-law in the front, and their five children and the next-door neighbour in the back. The first car had a sombre air, silent to the point of suffocation. But the middle car, bearing the coffin, had reggae music blasting loud. Trevor blared his horn at everyone, frequently stopping to tease or ask after someone. This caused Angel to pull her lips tight, and she wished she had opted to ride with Mazie rather than relinquishing her position at Beryl's side to Ainsworth.

Once they turned into Kristoff Village, Trevor had the good grace to flip out the reggae tape and put in a religious one. Cousin Carol's old people, sitting behind Angel, immediately began to sing along with the music and a mournful air ascended. Angel could see people standing by Beryl's gate. Trevor honked the horn, even though Mazie's car was ahead of his and had come to a stop. Rupert jumped out of the mini-bus, then helped Angel. Her black and white rayon dress was wrinkled. It did not have a funeral air, nor should it have, since she had purchased it about three years ago to attend an evening soirée. The crowd was swarming around the mini-bus, everyone trying to get a glance at the coffin.

Angel rushed ahead and followed Beryl into the yard, surprised to see that a big tent had been erected. All around the front of the tent chairs, arranged in a semi-circle, were already occupied by elders, mostly women wearing white, a few in black. Beryl wore a simple black and white loose-cut cotton dress with lace around the sleeves and collar. As Angel made her way through the sizeable crowd at Beryl's side, they were stopped every step of the way by people offering condolences. Angel could see Beryl's eyes watering, and she wanted to shout at people, for all their good intentions, to leave her alone.

Mr Cotton, who was presiding over the ceremony, approached Beryl. 'How you holding up, Daughter Beryl?' He patted her hand. 'Everybody just about here. Best to be done wid de burying, den everyone can eat, drink and remember Sista Madge with joy.'

'Gi me five minutes, Mista Cotton,' Beryl replied.

Then, pulling Angel's hand, Beryl dragged her down a path away from the crowd, and there she whispered, still holding on to Angel's hand: 'Ah fraid Angel, ah fraid. Ah don't know wa fi do wid meself now dat Mamma gone. Me too old fi turn teacha, plus me nuh qualify. Me life ova. Me fraid.'

Angel embraced Beryl and allowed her to cry on her shoulder. She wished she was wise and could offer some sound advice, instead she simply held the woman who had come closest to being the sister she had always wanted.

After a few minutes Beryl turned to Mr Cotton. 'Ah ready to bury Mamma.'

Mr Cotton called the crowd to order. Monica and Althea arrived quietly, escorted by Miss Cotton. Their presence sent a ripple through the crowd. The lid of the coffin was raised, and immediately people stood up to view the body. It seemed to Angel that the entire village, including young children, had come to view Miss Madge. Some people were crying, and many stopped to say a personal goodbye. A few commented to Beryl on her mother's serene appearance. 'Miss Madge look really-really nice, Beryl.'

'Ah like how you do her hair, and drape de white lace above her head.'

'Not a pain in dat face. Same way me wan look when me dead.'

'Her soul resting fah true.'

'Have a good travel, Madge, me soon join you.'

Finally, after what seemed like an inordinately long time, Mr Cotton asked permission to have the coffin closed. 'Praise be!' came the consent of the mourners.

Beryl rose and moved to the coffin. She stood holding on to the side, staring down at her mother's face. Her chin trembled, and from where Angel was standing she could see her lips forming words that died before she could give them life. The mourners, almost in unison, mumbled, 'Is all right Daughter Beryl, is all right. Tek it easy. Sister Madge resting in peace.'

Tears streamed down Beryl's face. Angel approached her, gently touching her arm. Beryl turned to her, eyes pleading. Angel draped her arm over Beryl's shoulder and spoke soothing words, the source of which she didn't know.

'Is okay Beryl, it's okay. Mother is going on another journey.'

'But she dead and me neva tell her,' came Beryl's moan.

'She knows already,' Angel assured her. 'She knows and she understands.'

'All right, Mamma,' Beryl cried, turning to the coffin. 'Walk good. Walk good and me sorry me disappoint you and neva finish me teaching certificate.' She wiped her eyes and moved back to the chair with Angel's help.

Songs were sung, and speeches were made by several good friends of Miss Madge. Angel heard it all vaguely. She kept glancing at Beryl, who seemed distant. Finally, Mr Cotton declared it was time to march to the burial ground. The pallbearers came forth and started the descent east to the site. The mourners spread out, some singing, others humming as they moved along. Finally they were at the grave site. Angel stood facing the deep, gaping hole in the earth. She half swooned, and it was Beryl's turn to offer support, steadying her on her feet. Angel had never seen a body lowered into the ground.

Ashamed of herself, she vowed to be brave and to support Beryl rather than the other way around.

Everyone, including children, went to the burial site. Many people were openly crying, others quietly sniffling. As hard as Angel tried to control her emotions, she felt tears streaming down her cheeks. She wanted to wipe them away and conceal her grief, but Beryl held one of her hands and Rupert the other, and they both were crying, so she relaxed and enjoyed the warm, salty release her tears produced, realising that where she was she was not required to put on a brave exterior. Grief was not a shame to be experienced in private or concealed from the rest of the world. So Angel cried, for all that she had missed, for the biological mother and father she never knew and probably never would, and for finding love with Rupert who had brought her to his village where she felt peace at last.

Mr Cotton cleared his throat, spread out his arms into the opening circle, surveyed the mourners, gazed at Miss Madge's coffin, then began.

'Sistas and brodas we here dis balmy day to bid farewell to we friend, Sista Madge, who lived a good, decent life.'

'True, Broda Cotton,' a woman proclaimed from the rear.

'No one can say dat Sista Madge wasn't kind to dem, didn't give dem help if dem came to her. She was a good oman, and she raised a good child who is now a oman standing in front of oonuh, witness of her mother's blessings.'

'Praise be!' another voice intoned. Mr Cotton continued as if uninterrupted.

'Sistas and brodas ah want all of oonuh to remember to be kind to Daughter Beryl from dis day on. She is widout moda or pappy, but not an orphan because all of we gwane watch ova her; she is widout husband and children but not childless because we have too many children who need a special aunty or godmother. If you agree wid me dat Sista Madge was a kind oman who didn't mind oda people business, den pass on her kindness to her daughter.' Then, pointing to the coffin and changing the tone of his voice, Mr Cotton continued, 'Dat is not de same Sista Madge you know in dat box dat we about to put into de earth and cover up. Sista Madge long rose out dat ole body and is probably sitting somewhere where dere is a party. Sista Madge didn't dance, but she loved to watch people have a good time, so ah bet you me walking cane, she sitting somewhere watching dancers. She was well ready to leave dis life and find another one, and ah tink a betta one. Ah want all of we to tek up a handful of dirt, kiss it to our lips and seh we last farewell to Sista Madge.'

Beryl and Angel held the soil in their hands long after kissing it, reluctant to release it. Some of the women started singing the traditional burial song, 'Rock of ages cleft for me/Let me hide myself in thee.'

Mr Cotton's voice rose above their dirge. 'Ashes to ashes, dust to dust, cova de dead and mek way for de living.'

Rupert and Ainsworth took shovels and began to fill in the grave. Then Rupert passed his shovel to Angel, who still clutched earth in her right hand. Ainsworth came around to where Beryl was standing and handed her the shovel. She refused to take it. Very softly, as if talking to a baby, Ainsworth said, 'Come Beryl, Aunty Madge waiting. Come.' Still Beryl stood, tears streaming down her face, falling on the collar of her dress. Ainsworth moved to Beryl's side, pried her hands open, put the shovel in her hand, and with his hands over hers helped her shovel soil into the grave. She heaved a sigh, held her face to the sky and leaned back, bracing against him. The other shovels were passed from hand to hand. The singing increased, accompanied by hand clapping and foot stomping. Beryl dropped the shovel, Ainsworth squeezed her shoulder and said, 'Ah ready to hear dat story whenever you ready to tell me.' They stood shoulder to shoulder. A faint smile crept over Beryl's face.

When all the soil was heaped into a great mound, Beryl planted a banana sucker at the head of the grave and Velma planted a small lime tree at the foot. Velma, voice tight like a wisp of wind on a very hot day, spoke to Beryl.

'Daughta Beryl, Sista Madge did like limeade. Every time she visit me ah had to make her limeade. So wid dis little tree at her foot she can have all de lime she need.'

'Thanks Aunty Velma. Mamma won't thirsty or hungry. She did like boil green banana too.'

Everyone was gone, except for a few women who were laying

flowers around the grave. When Velma was done, she looked at Beryl, bowed her head once again and said, 'Everything in its own time, everything in its own time,' and started the slight ascent back to the house. Angel regretting that she had nothing to plant, vowed to find a frangipani plant, which she knew Mother Madge had liked, and seed it before the week was out.

◆

Peggy Campbell and Marva McKenzie were the only two members of the intimate circle connected to Madge and Beryl Gordon who did not attend the funeral. Marva had left Saturday evening, claiming her mother was ill; but the villagers knew she had been forbidden to attend and that was her way of saving face. Peggy Campbell was in bed with a hot-water bottle pressed to her stomach. She had awakened Sunday morning with severe abdominal cramps, although her woman-hood was not visiting her. She eventually sent for the nurse who lived by the junction. But the nurse offered no consolation, except to suggest that perhaps she had eaten something that didn't agree with her. While the funeral was taking place, Peggy was in bed doubled up in pain, sweat covering her body.

Monica, Althea, Arnella and Baby-Girl did not attend the burial site. Monica and Althea quietly returned home. Arnella said she would walk with them. Although Monica and Althea had slept in the same bed for the previous three nights, and both had been attended by Miss Cotton and Desmond alternately, they spoke but a few words to each other. Monica, who was not one to let things sit indefinitely, felt well enough to break the ice. But she wasn't sure how to go about it. She wondered if Althea blamed her for what had happened to her mother. What were her feelings about Monica carrying on with her father? These thoughts ran through Monica's head as they walked home from the funeral. When they got back to her house, Althea said she was going to go in, and asked if it was okay to watch TV. Monica said yes, then turned to Arnella and signalled for her to sit with her on the veranda.

They sat on either side of the open door, Arnella with her breasts exposed, Baby-Girl nursing on and off. Her mind was at the river with the wood touching her breast; she savoured the green, sweet-bitter taste in her mouth. The memory caused her to smile.

'Monica, you doing well now, but we need to go to de river,' Arnella said, tuning in to the rhythm of Monica's rocking, which was heavy, too fast to be soothing; indicating that she was perturbed. Monica nodded her head, but said nothing.

'We gwane tek you and Althea to de river fi healing oonuh.' Arnella spoke with authority, sealing a commitment. Monica's silence was agreement.

Inside, Althea sneezed loudly. Arnella and Monica in unison said, 'Guzum!' to her. Then Arnella spoke again.

'Ah tink it's best dat Althea stay wid you.'

'Me nuh tink she like me; she neva seh more dan, morning Miss Monica, thank you Miss Monica. Not a word pass she lips unless me seh something to she.'

'Is frighten, she frighten. She like you or she wouldn't stay. You have to be her moda now,' Arnella said with finality, raising Baby-Girl to her shoulder to burp. 'Ah going so de both of oonuh can talk. You need to talk to her so she know how you feel.'

Monica reflected on how much Arnella sounded like a young Miss Cotton. After Arnella left, Monica kept rocking, not sure how to approach Althea, but knowing that she could not postpone it indefinitely. Finally she arose.

Althea was watching television when Monica entered the living room. She shifted her attention to Monica and sat poised, waiting.

'Althea, ah want you to turn off de TV so we can go sit out back and have a little talk. All right?'

'Yes, Miss Monica,' came the girl's timid voice. She obediently complied, and followed Monica to the back. They stopped in the kitchen long enough for Monica to take two ginger beers out of the fridge.

The back of the house was cool and quiet; no noise carried over from Beryl's yard. A few chickens were loose, pecking at the ground. Monica hesitated now that the moment was at hand. She had never had a child; had lost one voluntarily and another through miscarriage. She had dismissed both losses with nonchalance: dead children meant fewer complications in her own life and no responsibility. Even now as she glanced at Althea, the daughter of her former rival, she wasn't sure she wanted the responsibility of a child, or whether the child wanted her. How should she begin? The more she waited the more uncertain she became.

Suddenly she felt her back grow hot, and sensed the presence of someone standing over her. She turned around, but saw no one. Still the feeling persisted. Then she felt her head expand, as if it was ballooning out, and she smelled her mother. She jumped up from the chair in which she sat and scampered off the porch. Althea, watching Monica, jumped up too, fright on her face. Then Monica felt a soothing hand on her arm and she breathed deeply.

'Ah sorry,' a voice said. 'Ah did love you too much. Wha mek you run away? Ah didn't mean fi curse you. Ah didn't mean fah dem to hurt you. Sorry. Do right now.'

Tears smarted in Monica's eyes. She felt as if a weight had been lifted from her. Her mother, at last, had forgiven her. Now she could go on and forgive herself. She rubbed her eyes dry, and waved a hand at Althea to sit down as she herself moved back to the chair. She took a deep breath.

'Althea, when ah did return to Kristoff, me tell meself me done with love and men. Ah did have an old friend who fix up dis house fah me. Ah didn't love him, but him was me friend, and him did satisfy to see me once a month. Ah come back here and me eyes fall pan you daddy. Ah know dat him married wid children. Ah told meself ah jus gwane taste him den leave him alone. But once ah taste him ah wanted more, until ah didn't care if ah hurt de whole world as long as me have him. Ah didn't mean fi hurt you moda, ah didn't mean fi hurt nobody. Ah don't know how you feel bout me. Ah will understand if you hate me, but if you hate me, know dat you hate me fah falling fah you daddy.' Monica stopped and waited but Althea said nothing. 'Now ah don't know if you know all of what dem do me, but even though me no blameless, dem no have no right fi do me so. You moda bring the madness on sheself cause she help.'

Althea covered her mouth and suppressed a 'Why-oh!', tears pricking her eyes.

Monica emptied the bottle of ginger beer. A few wasps buzzed near and she fanned them away.

'You can stay wid me if you like cause me no have nothing against you and you broda dem. Me no know much bout being no moda, but me is a good listener, me try to be fair, and me love laughter. Anoda ting – ' Monica sat forward, her voice defensive. 'Is true wa de rumour seh. Me was a whore. Plenty man pay fi sleep wid me. Me neva thief or cheat any out a dem money; dem come to me fah a service and me perform well.' She fanned herself with her hand, suddenly feeling very hot. Still Althea said nothing, but now raised her head and looked at Monica straight on, rather than from underneath her eyes. Monica didn't know what else to say or how to persuade the girl to respond, short of opening her mouth and feeding her words. She sat more comfortably in the chair and hoisted her legs on the railing. Her pubic area was still sore, and her insides still burned. She wanted to pull off her panties and spread her legs to let the wind cool her crotch; but she wasn't sure how Althea would react. Then, feeling stupid for being censored in her own house, she stood up and quickly pulled off her panties. She looked over at the girl and said, 'De day too hot, me need some breeze.'

Althea smiled, then at last spoke. 'Sometime when it did hot me used to tek off me panties, but one time Mamma find me widout panties and beat me seh me turning wukless.' She paused. 'Is okay if me tek off mine too?' Monica smiled and nodded her head yes, so Althea looked around, and confident no one was watching, quickly pulled off her panties, put them on the chair and sat on them.

'Me no know is who invent dem tings,' Monica said, smiling. They sat enjoying the breeze teasing their private parts. Momentarily Monica forgot about Althea, and sat remembering her mother, the rare times when they had enjoyed each other's company. She recalled one time, when she was about seven, when she had accompanied her mother to wash clothes at the river. On an impulse her mother had decided to leave the clothes and take Monica fishing instead. They had travelled far over rocks, and her mother had shown her how to catch cray-fish. They had caught a small bucketful, which they cooked and ate all by themselves. That evening they didn't return home until late. Monica's father was home from his grounds, and shouted at her mother about not having dinner ready. Monica remembered that her mother and father argued way into the night, until her father slapped her mother across the mouth and their little house had grown very quiet.

Sitting there on the veranda Monica realised that she had always blamed her burdensome girlhood on her mother. She had forgotten about that fight and the slap that ended it.

'Ah sorry ma'am,' Monica mumbled.

'Miss Monica, Miss Monica.'

Monica was so far in the past she didn't at first hear Althea speaking to her. Startled, she looked around, saw the girl staring at her.

'Yes, Althea.'

'Miss Monica, me no hate you, ma'am. Me would like to stay wid you if you don't mind. Me no tink Mamma gwane come back. She neva did like it here and always did fret afta she own moda.'

'Althea, you can stay here for as long as you like as long as you respect me and clean up afta youself.'

'Thank you ma'am. Daddy will tell you dat me is a good helper, Miss Monica.'

'You know ah neva did like when anyone call me Miss Monica, and you and me no same age so you can't call me by me name, but me no like dis Miss Monica business.'

Althea was silent for a while, then she said rather timidly, 'Is all right if me call you Aunty Monica?'

Monica considered, and decided that she liked how it sounded. 'Yes, you can call me Aunty Monica.' They both smiled and resumed their reflections.

Althea was wondering how to tell Miss Monica – Aunty Monica – that she was pregnant. She also was worried about her brothers, Peter and Raymond. She knew that Peter liked Monica, whom he said always smelled sweet, but that Raymond hated her and blamed her for messing up their family. Mostly, Althea was thinking about her father, whom she worshipped, and how he would react to her pregnancy. Aunty Olive and Mother Cotton had promised that they wouldn't tell him, but Althea didn't know how much longer she could hide it. Monica interrupted her contemplation.

'Althea, if you gwane live wid me, we need to be honest wid each other. Ah want you to know me not judging you, but me need to know. How long you did pregnant?'

Althea wanted to deny her condition, but realised it would be foolish.

'How you did know me having baby, Aunty Monica?'

'Child, me have eyes. Any woman can look at you belly and tell. You tink is yesterday ah born?'

'Me don't rightly know. Is almost four months now me womanhood don't visit me.'

'You tell you daddy?'

'Please don't tell him, Miss Monica. Daddy gwane kill me.'

'Ah don't tell you ah don't like dis Miss Monica business? Beside you daddy love you, and me wouldn't let him raise him hand to you. Dat won't happen in fi me house.'

Althea wasn't convinced. Her heart raced. She didn't want a repeat of what had happened with her own mother when she told her. She didn't want to lose her father's love. 'Please don't tell Daddy, Aunty Monica, please,' she pleaded, tears running down her cheeks.

'Is who fada de baby? You tell him yet?'

'No,' came Althea's trembling voice. 'Ah don't know how fi tell him. Him did promise me dat ah wouldn't get pregnant. Ah don't want him to seh is not his.'

'Is him one you sleep wid?'

'Ah neva sleep wid him, Aunty Monica. Him tek me down near de riva and we did lean up against a tree. Him tell me ah couldn't get pregnant if we no lay down.'

Monica sighed. She imagined how little Grace had probably told the girl about her body, or about getting pregnant. What was she to do?

'Is how old you be Althea?'

'Ah gwane be sixteen come me birthday, next month.'

'So wha gwane happen wid school? You know dem gwane throw you out once dem find out.'

'Yes ma'am,' the girl said, hanging her head, her tone sad and mournful. 'Me like school, Aunty Monica, and Daddy always seh how me bright. Uncle Ainsworth, me godfada, say me gwane go university in Kingston just like him.' Then her voice trailed off. 'But ah don't suppose dat gwane happen now.'

Monica didn't know what to say to Althea. She herself had not been interested in school, but she didn't think it fair that a girl's life should be ruined just because she became pregnant. She was reflecting on the unfairness of a woman's lot so deeply that she didn't hear Desmond enter until he called for them. Althea jumped from her chair and, turning to Monica, placed her fingers over her lips, the middle finger on top of the index one. Monica did likewise and nodded agreement. 'At least fah now,' she said.

Two legs dance better dan one

When She-Devil remembered about her dress, the night before Brimstone's wedding, she got back out of bed – after she and Devil had made up their differences – and went and knocked on the door of the tired dressmaker, waking her. The woman was too vexed even to bother with She-Devil's apologies. She left her standing at the half-opened door while she went and got her dress. Then, without even fully opening the door, the dressmaker handed She-Devil the dress that was pressed and hung on a hanger, and saying, 'If it don't fit, don't blame me,' she slammed the door, leaving She-Devil standing outside feeling foolish. Although She-Devil had planned to try on the dress the moment she got home, once there she was reminded of several things that hadn't been done and stayed up until three in the morning, even though Devil kept hollering for her to come back to bed.

'Everyone can sleep,' She-Devil said to herself, 'but ah will be damn and blasted if dis isn't de most perfect event fah de century. Ah nah sleep till every detail taken care of.' However, as she crawled to bed several hours later she muttered, 'Ah been round Sabbath Angel too long. Ah getting to be just as compulsive as she.'

Ten minutes before the wedding, when She-Devil slipped on her royal-blue dress, the same colour as the bride's, it fitted perfectly. Tegreg, who helped her mother to dress, complimented her. Devil whistled when he saw her, but said the v-line in the back was too low. She-Devil flirted with her husband, and his daughter scolded, 'You too possessive, Daddy. Mamma look like a knockout. Is fraid, you fraid some handsome man wink at her.' Devil dismissed them with a gesture of his hand and went to meet his guests.

Everyone in Eternal Valley turned out to Brimstone's wedding. When She-Devil walked on to the veranda and looked out, she momentarily panicked. Was there enough food, she wondered? Devil feared there might not be enough to drink. He quickly stole away and hid a bottle of rum-punch to savour with his love after the event. The entire yard was jam-packed, lined with people, so numerous they were rubbing against each other, music blaring, voices going, and jugglers and acrobats – Anansi's idea – weaving in and out. Everyone, from what She-Devil could see, was having a grand time. The colours were a riot. Devil remarked to Tegreg, whose arm he draped over his as he strolled along greeting the guests – both the invited and the crashers – that he had never seen the residents of Eternal Valley so splendidly attired. Tegreg had to agree. Her 'bun in de oven', as Devil referred to her advance pregnancy, showed beautifully, and she was looking particularly lovely; her hair was braided in corn-row, weaved with silver, gold and red threads, the colours of her dress.

Tegreg strolled with her father through his garden, complimenting him on the arrangements of flowers, the profusion of the blooms, the depth of colours, the abundance. All eyes were on them because Devil cut a dashing pose in his royal-blue buba embroidered in red and white. When She-Devil made her appearance in her matching blue gown there was a noticeable pause.

'Far too sexy fah a woman who is de mother of de groom,' Man-Stick remarked, swallowing whatever else he had planned to say when She-Devil cast him a look. Devil and Tegreg waited until She-Devil descended the last steps from the veranda, then Devil held his arm for her to take it. They walked among their guests, stopping to exchange pleasantries, and Devil was a peacock, reigning supreme. The most astonishing appearance was made by Sabbath and God Angel, wearing matching yellow brocade suits embroidered in black. Almost on cue, Devil, She-Devil and Tegreg's mouths flew open at the sight of the divine couple, arm-in-arm no less, ambling to the wedding.

Throughout the compound musicians were performing, poets were reciting poetry, plays were being enacted, dancers were dancing, and children were playing, up to pranks, incited by Anansi. The sounds of laughter, chatter, and glasses clinking characterised the day. From the upstairs window of Devil and She-Devil's house, Tallawah looked out amused, awaiting the right moment to make her appearance.

Grudgeful is worse than wasp sting

Since Marva had been told that she was not welcome at the funeral, and sensing the community's displeasure with her, she decided to visit her family. Although she had only planned to stay for a day or so, once there she decided she would stay longer in the hope of making Ainsworth worry. But to her surprise when she called him at work on the Monday to tell him of her plans to stay a few more days, he seemed rather relieved. She returned home the following Saturday, almost a week after the funeral, only because a friend from her village, who now, through marriage, resided in Kristoff, had made it her business to report all the details of the funeral to Marva, making sure to embellish Ainsworth's support of Beryl. That was the only reason Marva returned, vexed and ready to pick a fight. She had hoped to use the state of the house as an excuse, but she found it spotless. When she arrived no one was home, and when Ainsworth got back, although he asked after her health and family, he showed no enthusiasm for her return.

However, he supplied her with just the ammunition for the fight. He held in his hand six coconuts which he said he had just got from Beryl. Marva went off. 'You is worse dan dog. Image me big and suffering wid you child dat me soon drop, and you have fi go mek pass at an old woman who mumma just dead.'

'Marva, what's de matter wid you? First of all Beryl is not an old woman, and second ah didn't mek no pass at her. Ah have too much respect for her, for dat. Now if you want to fight, you gwane have to fight wid youself, for ah going down de road wid Desmond, Godfree and Rupert. De children wid Mamma, and some food cover up on de stove.' With that Ainsworth marched out, leaving Marva fuming.

At Mother Madge's funeral, Godfree had suggested that the inner circle of men, Trevor, Desmond, Ainsworth, Rupert and Godfree himself, go bird hunting. Milford, who was standing near the group of men at the time, had remarked that although he hadn't gone bird shooting since he was a boy of fifteen, and that was a long, long time ago, he was certain he was better than the whole lot of them. They decided to take him up on his bet, so they had all gone home and dug out their sling-shots and were now going to trample through the bushes in search of catch. Mr Cotton said he would catch up with them. Trevor declined the invitation, saying he had to find parts for one of his vehicles. Desmond warned him, 'Listen, partner, tek a lesson from me. Mind de parts expedition to Kingston don't explode in you face.' Still, Trevor declined, and his absence was noted by his wife, Peggy, who now spent her days on the veranda, watching all who passed and complaining loudly of the pain in her stomach.

The men walked slowly, spread across the road. The day was hot and sticky, and as they ambled along Godfree remarked, 'Dis is a day to find a shady spot and share wisdom.' They had walked about four miles when Godfree spotted a bird, aimed and watched it fall. In less than twenty minutes after the first he had brought down four more. Milford decided they should find a cool spot. Desmond said he knew a place not far from where they were, where some workers stored some pots. Rupert had matches and said he would collect some sticks. Ainsworth discovered a yam field. Milford set about cleaning the birds. Desmond returned with two pots and a bunch of green bananas. The men stripped off their shirts, and Godfree cried, 'Riddle me dis, riddle me dat, guess me dis riddle or perhaps not.' He paused to see if anyone was game. No one showed much interest, but he pressed on. 'Is wha woman have in front and cow have plenty in the back?' There was silence, until Godfree offered the answer himself. 'Chow, man! Dat is easy pickney stuff. Breast.'

This was a riddle from their boyhood days; Godfree knew much more up-to-date ones. But the men were not in the mood for riddles. As the fire caught and the water boiled, they heard whistling and saw Mr Cotton hobbling towards them loaded down with kites and carrying a bag packed with Guinness stout and ice. Milford greeted the senior elder and led him to a shaded spot to rest. For a while no one spoke. After resting, Mr Cotton called to Desmond. 'How Althea doing dese days? Ah haven't seen her since Sista Madge's funeral.'

Desmond looked up and threw down the sticks with which he was doodling. 'Ah guess she is doing as well as one can expect, but she not saying much.'

'She and Monica getting along?' Mr Cotton pushed.

Desmond shifted from a squatting position and sat. 'Ah don't tink Althea have anything against Monica. Ah ask her if she did want to stay and she say yes.'

Mr Cotton rubbed his beard, seeming to ponder Desmond's response. 'Well you big son who always at the shop talking to my granddaughter say him don't like Monica and dat she is de cause of everything. Ah tink you should have a talk wid him because him always at me granddaughter's ears, and me too old for dese things.' The implication was not lost on Desmond; it was not so much about Monica or Althea as it was about Mr Cotton's granddaughter's chastity. One thing more that Desmond didn't want to deal with. Diplomatic, Mr Cotton shifted his attention, and turning around to face Ainsworth bent over the pots.

'So, Ainsworth, how is Beryl doing dese days? Don't you tink she looking well?' Mr Cotton enquired, his eyes a mischievous twinkle. Ainsworth had had a great deal of practice talking to Mr Cotton, so merely nodded and grunted what sounded like concurrence.

Mr Cotton smiled and walked over to the fire, peering into the pots. He banged Milford on the back.

'Milford, you is de only man I know who can boil plain wata mek it smell good. Olive doing all right? You loving her enough?' Milford cackled. Mr Cotton teased further. 'Nothing like loving a woman to keep her satisfy. Dese young boys don't know de ropes,' and he slapped Milford on the back, turning again to Ainsworth

'Marva look like she ready to drop any minute now. Ah hope is de girl she want. When you plan on stopping, Ainsworth?'

'Dis one is it,' Ainsworth replied, seeing no way of remaining non-committal.

'Ah tink you right,' Mr Cotton said, patting him on the back. 'Ah tink dis is de last seed you plant.'

Godfree had left off his sculpture and was untangling two tails of kites that had got twisted together. He didn't wait for Mr Cotton to approach him, but spoke directly to the elder. 'Mista Cotton, sir,' he began. 'Ah see you and Miss Cotton have cold in de knee. Me hear dat body heat help.'

'Well boy,' Mr Cotton smiled at the challenge, 'ah not as young as you, and ah neva have two wife, although Miss Cotton is more than six of de best women put together, but Miss Cotton ain't lacking warmings come night.' And in the same breath, without even a pause, Mr Cotton continued, 'Arnella's house is a good walk from Valrie's, but you have new daughter down dere so ah guess you up to de walk.'

'Every man have to carry de load drop pan him door,' Godfree said, rising, having freed the kites. 'Ah feel a little wind coming on so ah gwane walk up the hill. Desmond come walk wid me man.' As Godfree moved away Mr Cotton smiled, reflecting how much he liked him.

Rupert sat a little distant from the group of men, feeling like an outsider. He alternately wondered how Angel was coping with the women and visualised the house he was going to build, so that he didn't hear when Mr Cotton spoke to him the first time.

'Rupert! Rupert! Boy wake up and stop dreaming. You always was a dreamer from you was a little boy. So how is you American wife? Ah see more of she dan ah have of you since oonuh return. What you up to dese days?'

Throughout all the years, Rupert hadn't learned the art of conversation. He shrugged and answered Mr Cotton briefly.

'Nothing much.'

'Ah guess nothing change,' Mr Cotton concluded, staring off into the distance. He pulled out his pipe from his shirt pocket, stuffed it with tobacco then pulled hard several times before igniting it. He savoured the bitter aroma for a few minutes before turning to Milford.

'So Milford, wha you mek of all dese changes happening in our village?'

'Ah don't understand not de beginning of dem. What Olive and Velma tell me don't sound right half de time, and what ah see, sure don't look right. Ah don't begin to understand any of it.' And he tossed a flour-corn dumpling in the pot.

Mr Cotton puffed on his pipe and considered his words. 'Well it all not too strange if you can read de signs, you know. Change is always nasty. De life we know is changing, dat's all. Some for de good, and

211

oder, well now, dat's a horse of a different colour. You got to be prepared for change, Milford, or it will come and run you ova.' Mr Cotton rose and headed for the hill on which Godfree and Desmond were attempting to fly kites. 'Ah want to hear what Desmond and Godfree, and even Rupert dere wid him tongue on hold, have to seh bout dese changes. We gwane talk much story later afta we fly kite and eat we belly full.'

After they had eaten and drunk, Mr Cotton suggested that each man tell his story. As the elder, he began, linking his story to the community. There were long pauses, and much shuffling, but each man in turn managed to come bare, and as they talked they discovered they weren't afraid to look each other directly in the eye, remembering when they were boys and shared intimate details naturally.

The saying was true after all, 'A donkey can carry more load in a hamper, dan just strapped unto his back.' The stories took them way back and they remembered what they had allowed themselves to forget: that they too were vulnerable.

River-mumma calling

Miss Cotton and the women rose early the Sunday morning of their planned excursion to the river. They knew their men were on a similar journey. Miss Cotton's knee was worrying her, so she walked with her cane. Arnella and Valrie carrying Baby-Girl led the way, followed by Beryl, Angel and Althea holding hands. Olive and Monica walked just behind them, and at the rear was Miss Cotton, in between Dahlia and Velma. The air was chilly, and the older women had shawls over their shoulders.

When they turned into the bush off the road, an owl hooted. The hair on the back of Miss Cotton's neck rose. She stopped. Waited. Searched the bushes for the owl, but could not spot it. When she heard the second hoot, a signal that the way was cleared for them to proceed, she switched her cane and walked on. They quickly came to the bank of the river, but Arnella suggested that they walk further. It was only when Olive shouted that Miss Cotton was out of breath after more than three miles of trekking that Arnella finally stopped.

She threw off her slippers and gingerly moved down the side of the bank, extending one foot to test the water. She frowned and shook her head, walking further up, every so often extending one leg to test the water, each time not satisfied. Finally, from about fifty yards beyond where they had first halted, Arnella waved for the others to join her. Miss Cotton walked to where she was standing, lay flat on the ground, and extended one hand into the river. A smile lit up her face. She turned to Arnella. 'Yuh did good. Yuh did real good.' Then to the other women she nodded approvingly.

The women undressed silently. Althea, the youngest, and not accustomed to undressing in front of others, especially since her mother had told her that nakedness was an affront, felt very awkward. She didn't want to look at the other women, all of whom where older, all of whom had known her probably since she was in her mother's womb. She called them aunt, mamma, sister, not being old enough to call any of them by their names. But mostly, Althea didn't want them to look at her because they would see her pregnant stomach. Even though she suspected they all knew, and Monica had only the day before remarked that she couldn't hide it much longer, Althea was still afraid. She was also shy, having been raised by a mother who felt her body was ugly and even a sin, and so had warned her to cover up and not let anyone look upon it. She stood with her dress draped around her body; she wanted to run back home; she felt out of place. When Miss Cotton spoke to her she jumped.

'Althea, you prove you is woman by carrying baby. All we here is woman. You not no little girl-picknie anymore. You tek up oman ways when you spread you legs. So tek off you frock and leave you mamma behind. Monica and Beryl and all de rest of we is oman. When one oman do wickedness against anoda oman, den she do it against all oman dem.'

The other women nodded their heads. Even Angel found herself agreeing. Olive and Dahlia made a velar click, indicating their agreement. But Miss Cotton's voice was still stiff like dried cassava when she spoke again to Althea. 'Tek off dat frock and come ova here so ah can rub dis ointment pan you body; we no have all day to dally.'

Monica, who now stood naked, went and helped Althea off with her dress, then walked her over to Miss Cotton, who immediately

213

began to anoint her body. The women all cupped their hands, taking a little of the lotion that Miss Cotton poured into their palms, rubbing it over each other's bodies. Then in single file they waded into the river.

The water was warm and milky. The air was still, and the rays of the sun cast golden sheaths on the river. Arnella cupped a handful of water to her mouth and drank. Each woman found her own space and splashed around. Angel and Althea, the youngest, and both shy, if for different reasons, stayed close together. After a while Arnella told the women to hush. 'Each of oonuh must search out oonuh own place in de river. Let her, de river, talk to you so she can soothe oonuh worries.'

Angel wasn't sure what that meant, but reluctantly she parted from Althea, and began her journey quest. She wandered in a direction away from the other women. Soon she could hear her own breathing, in tune with the soft murmur of the river. She found herself in a dense area where the water bubbled like air in a hot-tub, and it was much warmer than where they had all entered. Angel immersed her entire body, imagining she was baptising herself. Something pricked her right sole. She lost her balance and found herself blowing bubbles. The pain in her legs expanded. She tried to swim to the surface, but found herself being pulled under. Frantically Angel fought with whomever, or whatever, was holding her down. Something pulled at her legs. She struggled, hysterical, spinning around. Her lungs were full. She couldn't hold her breath any longer. She started to laugh, thinking this was all too funny, coming to Jamaica where her dream of a happy life seemed attainable, only to drown as a result of joining her new friends in a ritual observance of their ancestors' ways. Then Angel panicked. It wasn't *funny*, she thought to herself. She didn't want to die. Suddenly she was overcome with a desire to know her real mother; she could taste her salty tears mingling with the warm, sweet, breast milk that was the river water, and she allowed herself to surrender, feeling very close to the mother she never knew.

Beryl had no trouble finding a place. She waded to it immediately. An almond tree hung over the banking of the river like an S on its side. Beryl manoeuvred her way around the branches resting in the water and stayed there listening to sounds inside her head. She felt light. She knew her mother was happy, and she heard her telling her, 'Is your time now me one daughter. Is your time now. Don't waste any more time. Don't let one mistake scare you fah life.' Beryl hugged herself, her arms making an X that covered her breasts. She rocked from side to side, and the tears that trickled down her face were sweet and fresh. She was willing to unload, to forgive herself, to begin again to remember the early light of daybreak that was a sign of perfect beauty and hope. As she began to itemise in her head all the things she would begin to do again she heard the child calling her. Immediately her hands flew to her ears, trying to block the sound. She hadn't heard any voices for a long time, but now she heard the urgent sound of this child calling her, not accusing, not teasing, but pleading with her for help. Beryl felt trapped and powerless. She called out, 'Is where you deh? Is where you deh? Tell me, and me will come get you.' She removed her hands from her ears and forced herself to listen outside of herself. She waded out from where she was nestled by the almond tree. Once in the open stream, she turned around. She heard the voice more insistent. Urgent, yet fading. She tried to run, then realising where she was, she dove under the water, searching for what she wasn't sure. She came up for air and found herself in a bed of the river that was the shape of a perfect V. The water in her mouth was warm and sweet. She no longer heard the child, but she sensed her presence. Beryl dove again, and when she came up, she cradled a gasping Angel in her arms, and the sun was in her face blinding her.

After more than half an hour of soaking in the warm water that was like expert hands massaging their bodies, Miss Cotton called the women together. They formed a circle and Dahlia and Velma raised the song, 'Dere is a meeting here today, come along now . . .' Olive and Valrie pulled Monica to the centre of the circle and immediately all the women splashed water on her. Through the crystal sheet of water they created, Monica looked like a torso in the centre of a glass sculpture.

Arnella's firm voice broke through the spraying water.

'Call dem out. Name dose who peppa you. Name dem; dem not you sistas.'

The other women echoed Arnella's words, until their collective voices were a mantra for retribution. All the women cleared their throats and spat in the water. Even Baby-Girl appeared to join the women voices when she began bawling, as if to shout too, 'Name dem!' Everyone except Althea and Monica was shouting, 'Name dem; dem is not you sistas. Call dem out.'

Monica's tears paled in the streaming water; her body danced and shook. Miss Cotton and Arnella signalled the women to cease spraying water, and they freed Monica from the glass in which she was trapped. They spun her round, then Miss Cotton stood to one side of her and Arnella to the other.

Velma and Dahlia stepped forward. They laid their hands on Monica's left shoulder. With a forceful, downward sweep, they pulled off the burden Monica had been hauling around; they rinsed their hands before doing the same thing to Monica's right shoulder. They ended with a sound so powerful it thrust their chests forward. Then Dahlia stepped round and positioned herself behind Monica. She pressed her thumbs to the base of Monica's waist, just above her buttocks, and Velma cupped the flesh that cushioned Monica's stomach to her pelvic bone. Together they massaged and pressed. Monica's moans were a circle that enclosed the women, forcing each of them to release their internal frustrations and bottled anger. Monica began to throw up bile and the stench caused the other women to hold their breaths and widen the circle.

The women waded away from the stench, pulling Monica along. They were close to the bank where they had entered.

Miss Cotton cupped up clean water and fed Monica. Arnella poured water over her shoulders and massaged her stomach. Velma and Dahlia alternately intoned, 'Release it; let it go.' The other women picked up the chant.

Then Miss Cotton and Arnella stood either side of Monica again, and tossed her back and forth with open hands. Monica's body was like a weightless sponge, and each time Miss Cotton and Arnella tossed her, water spewed from her body, and she screamed, 'Ah gwane name dem. Mamma came to me afta Miss Madge funeral and say she forgive me. Ah gwane call dem out for Althea say she no hate me. Ah name dem for ah forgive meself.'

'Name dem,' Arnella demanded.

Monica began to weep anew, leaning forward, hugging her stomach. Miss Cotton put her arms around her. 'You have to name dem me child. Dem must face dem punishment.'

Dahlia and Velma again raised their voices, 'Dere is a meeting here today, come along now . . .'

Monica stood tall, cupped her hands for water and drank. Her voice was soaked and heavy when she spoke.

'Marva was de ring-leader. She de one carry de bowl of peppa. Dey stuff a scarf in me mouth. Den Grace suggest them strap me to de bed, and she hold me hand while Marva and Peggy tie me up. Marva flung open me closet door and pull out me dress dem. She kiss her teeth, den rip dem up. Den Grace and Peggy follow suit, dragging dresses from de closet, pulling out de drawers, dashing me things dem pan de floor and trampling pan dem. Den Marva stumble ova by me dresser, smell me perfume, den start to dash de powder and perfume everywhere. When dem did spend demself, and me tink dem did done, and was gwane leave me, Peggy come stand ova me tie up pan de bed; she seh, "Dat will teach you fi leave women men alone." Me want to tell her, dat Trevor is one man she no have to worry bout wid me cause him too wukless, but de scarf was in me mouth. Me smell de peppa on Marva, when she stand right beside me. She look inna me face and laugh. Den she seh wid her hand raised wid de peppa on it, "Mek me blind you, bout you want thief me man." Her hand was dis close to me face,' Monica indicated, bringing her hands less than an inch from her face, 'but same time Grace pull weh her hand, and Marva just smear me face saying, "Ah gwane show you how fi powda you face." She smear de peppa all ova me face, then push her index finger in me nose. Ah could neva be able to describe de sting, but more was to come. Grace start to beg Marva fi leave me alone, saying, "Ah tink she did learn her lesson; ah tink she will leave Desmond alone now." But Marva was just warming up. She turn to Grace, huffing and puffing. "Is why mek you so fool-fool, and fraid-fraid, you own shadow? She a sleep wid you lawful husband and you want fi have sympathy pan her." Grace neva say nothing more, just stand dere and wring she hand. Ah could tell dat Marva was worked up and couldn't stop. She start to rip me clothes off me, and afta a while Grace and Peggy join her, then she lotioned her hand in the bowl of peppa then push her hand inna me. Me throat lock and me blank out. When me come to dem did gwane and de house dark. Me decide to die, den me remember you, Miss Cotton. Ah figure if ah didn't die, only you one could cool the fire inside me, so me try nuh fi tink bout de fire eating me up and call pan you. And here me is now.'

The women were like poles stuck in the river bed. A cool breeze wafted around them. The heat of the sun dried their torsos. The taste in their mouths was no longer burning, but their saliva was flat and sticky.

Velma and Dahlia sucked in their breaths.

Arnella felt weightless.

Valrie, who was holding Baby-Girl, let out her breath.

For a moment the river had gone stagnant until Baby-Girl yawned, stirring it alive again. Miss Cotton was dizzy. Angel felt herself clinging to Beryl, unable to let go. They stood, waiting for directions.

Miss Cotton found herself, and blew breaths from deep within until she saw rainbow-coloured air sailing from her mouth. Then, pulling Monica close, she embraced her, pressing her healing hands into the younger woman's body, running her hands up, down and all over. Releasing her, she looked Monica in the eyes and asked, 'Is dat all of it, de whole story?' Monica nodded her head. 'Den walk around the circle and let's be done wid it.' Monica moved around the circle and each woman she passed cupped water, threw it on her shoulder, then used their hands to rinse her body. In single file they waded out of the river, as if enacting a children's ring game that disbanded when the circle disappeared.

Althea felt ashamed for her mother and for herself. Since her mother was unable to ask forgiveness for herself, Althea knew the responsibility fell to her as the only daughter. She couldn't, however, bring herself to look at Monica. She could never imagine, nor did she want to imagine, what pepper might feel like in her most private place. She couldn't understand how any woman, especially her own mother, could inflict such harm to another woman, no matter what her actions had been. Althea could think of nothing to say to Monica. She felt as if the other women, at Miss Cotton's instigation, had left her alone to face her punishment.

Althea stood, rubbing her water-shrivelled fingers together. The water no longer felt warm even though the sun was burning above her head. Why was Monica standing in front of her not saying anything? She saw out of the corner of her eyes that the other women were sitting on the river bank. Althea listened, as if the sound of the women's voices, her many aunts, could free her; still Monica stood before her not saying anything.

Althea thought of the child she was carrying. She had avoided thinking about the life growing inside. The first month her womanhood didn't visit her, Althea had prayed, thinking she could pray it to disappear. When another month passed and her womanhood didn't visit her, Althea decided to forget about it, hoping that would make it disappear. But still nothing happened, so she accepted her fate. Now, standing in the river, wishing she could disappear from before Monica, Althea thought compassionately of the life growing inside, and she didn't feel like a girl any more, nor did she feel hopeless. She rubbed her stomach, smiling; she was going to be a mother, and she would be a good one to her daughter. Althea felt brave then. She raised her head, and looking Monica in the eyes said, 'Ah gwane have a daughter and ah would like you to help me raise her.'

Monica stared at this girl who had come to her through her pain, and felt capable of accepting the honour bestowed on her. 'If ah gwane help you raise you daughter, den ah gwane be needing you blessing.'

Althea cupped her hand and rinsed off Monica's body. The sun was full and bright when they emerged.

The inhabitants of Kristoff Village came awake slowly, groggily. Somehow the village seemed bereft of its core vitality. A few women who ran out of needed items were surprised when they went to Miss Cotton and Mr Cotton's store to find it closed. They knocked, climbed the hill to the house in the back of the shop. But only barking dogs and fluttering chickens being chased by the rooster took note of their presence. They left empty-handed, perplexed, stopping at neighbours' houses to borrow the things they required and asking about the absence of the Cottons.

After the women had eaten their breakfast, Miss Cotton took Althea's hands, and patting them, said 'Child, you have to tell you daddy you in de family way. Dis is not something to keep secret. Him not gwane hurt you, Monica will see to it. Besides you daddy is a gentle man. True him gwane disappointed, but him not gwane love you any less. So ah want you to promise to tell him soon.'

Althea nodded her head; then, remembering that it was rude to nod her head at adults, added, 'Yes, Aunty Cotton.'

Then Velma called out to Miss Cotton. 'Miss Cotton, we not done here yet?'

'Still some things not said dat need to be said,' chimed Dahlia.

'Let we rest a while,' declared Miss Cotton. 'We not leaving till every shut eye is asleep.'

Charley drove all the way to Kristoff Village to invite Rupert and Angel to go with him and his family to pass the day at Negril beach. He was surprised to find the house open, but no one around. He stopped by Beryl's place and met with similar circumstances. Vexed with himself for driving all that way and not finding anyone home, Charley resounded, 'Back-side! Is whe dem could be dis hour of de morning?' He looked at his watch which indicated that it was a little after six. Dew was still on the ground. The sun had not yet yawned or washed the sleep from its eyes.

'Look like dis place tun into duppy back yard,' Charley said, making a speedy retreat.

Peggy woke with terrible abdominal pains. Her telephone wasn't working so she couldn't call the nurse who lived at the junction. Trevor had left early Saturday evening saying he was going to buy parts, and if he didn't come back, it meant he wasn't having any luck. Her helper no longer came on Sundays so that meant she had to get out of bed to fix her two sons breakfast. She called to the boys, but got no response. Then she remembered that Raymond, Desmond's older son, had come last night to say that he and some of the older boys were taking the younger boys fishing, and that they would leave early Sunday morning before the sun was up. Peggy remembered now hearing them leave. She looked out the living-room window that permitted her a view of Grace's house and could see the vacancy like mist rising.

'Poor Grace,' she sighed.

Then she shook her head as if to erase her sympathy, and with a harshness in her voice that surprised even her, she concluded, 'But she was a damn fool. Imagine teking sympathy pan de woman who steal she husband. Damn fool.'

Holding her stomach as if something was falling out of it, Peggy stumbled to the back yard, raised her voice and hollered to Marva, who she hoped was in her kitchen.

'Marva! Marva! You home? Ah begging you to come to de fence.' Peggy leaned on the fence that separated their yards, breathing heavily through her opened mouth. Marva's house was still. Not even the dog that was curled up on the back step stirred. Peggy clutched the fence and called again. 'Marva! Marva! Ah begging you to come here fah a minute.' She waited, breathing, one hand gripping the fence, the other rubbing her stomach. Still nothing. She felt as if she was in a daze. With great difficulty she bent down, found a stone and flung it, barely missing the dog lying on Marva's step. The dog raised its head, looked in her direction, then lowered its head and went back to sleep. Peggy felt her entire body wrung in pain. She wanted to scream out, but didn't have the strength. Crawling on her knees she made it back to her house and slumped on the sofa. She couldn't produce tears. She didn't want to die alone, without her sons, her husband, 'wukless as him be' she mumbled, without her friends, Grace and Marva. Her throat felt dry, but she didn't have the strength to crawl to the fridge and get some water or juice to quench her thirst.

Beryl felt eyes focused on her. Angel sat between her open thighs while Beryl plaited her hair. She had stilled the voice calling her; Angel would be the daughter she had lost. But immediately upon making this decision she heard a new voice, faint, creeping up. She completed Angel's hair and rose, walking back to the river. At the bank she searched the water as if looking for something. Miss Cotton called her to rejoin the group. Beryl looked at the women and smiled, still hoping to avoid her journey.

'You stalling, Beryl. You stalling,' Miss Cotton began. 'Now ah don't blame you. You left dis village a strong, beautiful young oman, and you come back a beaten old one, and not one a we come ask

221

you what happen. Well, we asking now. We all need to know.' Miss Cotton sat, her skirt covering her legs, her hands rubbing her knees.

'We just done bury you mamma,' Velma added, 'and we promise her we gwane look afta you. She dream me already, you know, Beryl.' Velma leaned forward and touched Beryl's hand. 'She say to me, "Sista Velma, find out what eating me child, and help her find peace." Ah tell her dat ah will find out. So ah asking like Sista Cotton.'

Beryl was not prepared to shed the tears, but they came, falling directly from her eyes into the ground. Monica reached over and touched her. 'Is your time now.' They waited. Beryl blew her nose, and wiped her eyes.

'All me life me did want to be teacha. Ah study hard. All through high school me come first in every class. When O'level come me sit seven subjects and pass all of dem, four wid distinction. Me breeze through A'levels and pass all four: math, English, biology and geography. Me apply to teacha's college and get accepted and even win partial scholarship. Mamma and pappa happy. Dem throw big party and everyone come and dance. Me dance wid all de boys cause me did love dancing, but me neva mek no boy touch-touch me breast or put dem hand unda me dress. Me was a good girl, planning to mek mamma and pappa proud when me get me teaching certificate.

'Summer come and me cousin Carol write and seh she could get me a job at a hotel cleaning room, and ah could mek good money. Me talk it ova with mamma and pappa and dem seh dem know me will behave meself, and is good opportunity since dem neva did have too much to give me come October when teacha's college start. Mazie mother invite me to stay wid dem since Mazie get work at the same hotel. Dat way me could save all me money and no have to spend it coming back and forth. Everything ready. Me feel so big and proud. Me kiss mamma and pappa goodbye.

'Everything gwane well. Ah save every penny, just tek some now and again fi buy peanut. De first time in me life me eva see so much white people. So-so white people at de hotel. Everything fancy and brand new. Every morning de manager warn we about clean up good and no steal de guest dem something. Me did vex ever time me hear him seh dat cause me wasn't no thief.'

Beryl paused. She knew they were listening to her every word, waiting for her to get to the point, but she wouldn't be rushed. She cleared her throat and continued.

'One day a whole group of people come to de hotel, mostly men. Me see how dem eye ah roam ova we body. Me hang me head, and gwane like me no even notice dem. A girl who been working at de hotel fah four years, whispered one day at lunch dat we could mek more money. All a we lean in and ask her how. She say, "Much foreign man like black woman." We kiss we teeth and left dat girl sitting right dere.

'Well dis day me knock at room 207. A man seh come in. Ah seh, "Is all right sir, ah will come back later." Me finish clean all de room dem, and knock again at room 207. Me no hear anything so me pop in de key and open de door. Just as me a go toward de bathroom, a big man, red like lobster pop out from de bathroom, in only him undapant. Me so frighten me scream. Den me tink, "Lawd God, look how dis man gwane let me lose me work," so me start apologising, telling how me knock and me neva know him was in de room, and when me look pan him, him smiling, den him seh to me, "Gosh, you're young." It tek me a while before me understand what him seh, den me find meself blurting out, "Me not so young sir, me is almost nineteen."

'Anyway de next day when me go back to room 207 me mek sure and knock loud several times before me enter. De man wasn't dere, but me see an envelope propped up on de dresser wid me name pan it written in black ink pen. At first me tink is someone else him know name Beryl so me leave it right where it is, but just as me done and was leaving de same man come in and ask, "Did you take the envelope?" "Envelope, sir?" me said. "Yes, the one on the dresser. Didn't you see it? Surely you can read. Your name is Beryl isn't it?" "Yes sir," me answer, wondering how him know me name. "Well take it," him say, walking in de room and handing it to me. Me neva know what fi seh so me tek it and push it in me pocket and back out de room. Me did forget about it until me was changing to go home. It drop out me pocket and me pick it up and open. Inside was twenty American dollars and a little note that read "Hope I didn't scare you too much yesterday. Would love to talk to you about your country." Ah didn't know what to mek of it. Anyway me put it wid wha ah already save fa me teacha's college.'

Beryl paused again and searched her listeners' faces. Was she going to tell them everything, including what he did to her? She wasn't sure even then.

'Go on, Beryl,' Arnella encouraged.

'Well de next day me see de man again and him ask me to meet him when ah done work so he could learn more about Jamaica. Me tell him de manager seh we not to fraternise wid de hotel guest or we could lose we work, and me really need de work to help pay me college fees. Him eyes brighten den, and him seh, "I could tell you were different from the rest. I see that you're intelligent." Ah smiled and thanked him.

'For de rest of de week, every day de man was in de room, no matter what time me go to clean it, and every day him left me a note and money, mostly ten American dollars. Me still refuse to meet him, but would linger in him room, answering little foolish questions him ask me bout Jamaica. Two weeks de man play cat and mouse wid me. Den de following Monday when me knock pan 207, me hear him voice say, "Beryl, is that you? I have a surprise for you." "All right sir, ah will come back later," ah reply, but before me can walk off, him fling de door open, and stand up naked as de day him born. Me mek fi run, but him grab me and close de door behind me. Him push me up against de door, cova me mouth wid him hand and say, "Beryl, I've decided today is the day I'll have some Jamaican meat. You've teased me long enough. I know about you black women; I've had plenty where I come from." Me no know wha de man plan to do wid me, but all me a tink bout is how him gwane cause me fi lose de work, and wha me gwane tell mamma and pappa. Den him remove him hand from me mouth and tell me if ah scream he will tell de manager dat him caught me stealing from his wallet, and den him push money in me pocket.

'Me start to cry. Me beg him. Me seh "Please sir me working fi mek little money fi go teacha's college, me will bring back all de money you give me if you just let me go." But him just smile. Me want scream out but me memba how a girl who used to clean rooms like

224

me was fire when she accuse a guest of freshing wid her. De man seh she was hallucinating and de manager fire her right dere, not even giving her de pay she did due. Ah tink is dat why ah did keep quiet, whispering to de man to let me go. Den him throw me pan the bed, pull off me uniform and rudeness me.

'It hurt like ah neva did tink it should hurt. And when him roll off me and me see all de blood pan de bed me start to scream. Him slap me cross me mouth and tell me shut up. Den him say, "Ah! a Jamaican virgin. A dying breed. I heard you girls all lose your virginity by the time you are twelve. Where have you been hiding?" Ah couldn't move. Ah just sit pan de bed wid me shame all about me. Den him shove some more money in me brassière and seh ah didn't have to worry about cleaning up de room, but ah should change de bed. Ah tell you de truth ah don't know how ah manage to change dat sheet but ah do it, den heard meself saying, "Anything else sir?" Him come over to me, push him mouth pon mine and say, "Make sure you come tomorrow same time, or I'll make sure you end up in gaol for stealing. I have four more days in Jamaica and I intend to break you in." Ah close de door behind me feeling like ah was sleep-walking, and walk straight into the sea and try to drown meself. Carol and Mazie pull me out. Dem was waiting on me since ah stay so long, but ah couldn't tell dem what happen, not until afta de whiteman leave de island.'

Beryl's lips trembled. Angel crawled over to where Beryl sat and hugged her; together they wept.

'He raped you, Beryl, he raped you,' Angel said repeatedly, her voice breaking with sobs. Miss Cotton was speechless, deep lines in her forehead. Her eyes turned inward. She was tired of these foul tastes and acid smells. There was too much evil in the world. Too many pains that could never be eased, too many memories for tears to erase. Beryl's pain was such a one. Beryl raised her head, drying her tears with her palms. She looked at all the women, her sisters, and knew they didn't fault her. She would tell the entire story.

'Ah don't know why ah go back to dat room, but ah did for de next four days, and ah didn't feel anything. Him did all kind of rudeness me neva dream bout to me. Him suck me down dere den force him hood in me mouth, but me bite him so him didn't force me

225

dat way any more. Den him was gone. Me cry all de time. Me couldn't bear fah mamma or pappa fi see me now dat me did dirty, so me neva come home.

'De first week of teacha's college me start to feel sick and throw up. Me memba how some pregnant woman throw up. Me run more dan three miles to Carol business school and tell her. Together we find Mazie who was working in a restaurant, and we pass de day at de beach planning what fi do.

'Me study hard, trying no fi tink about it. Mamma and pappa write saying dem miss me and me must come home, but me couldn't face dem. Mazie find a woman who seh she know what herb fi gi me fi wash weh whateva in me stomach. Me gi her one of the ten dollar de man gi me, drink seven cups of nasty-tasting herbs, had diarrhoea, vomit plenty, but three weeks later de same feeling return, and me know de baby still growing inside me.

'December come and me know me can't tell mamma and pappa any more story. Me not really showing because not a food could pass me throat. Anyway Mazie and Carol show me how to band me belly just in case. Me come home and all mamma and pappa talk about is how dem proud of me, and how dem know me gwane marry a nice man when me done teacha's college. Me bust out crying. Mamma ask me wha wrong? Me tell her teacha's college hard. Lots of pressure.

'Is Mazie moda same one write mamma and pappa and tell dem how de pressure of school was getting to me so she teking me up to her country in Jerico to stay wid her moda. Dat's where me have de baby, two days afta me first year of teacha's school. Ah can't even remember what day in June dat was. Mazie was wid me de whole time.

'De baby did white, white. Me tell Mazie is can't mine, look how me black, but is me one dere did pregnant, so me have was to accept it. But me couldn't look pan her wid any love. Every time me look pan her, me memba how me get her, and me heart just turn sour. Me wouldn't eat, and de baby just bawl all de time. Me wouldn't bathe her, and Mazie mother said if me didn't want her to give her way. She say she heard dat some American people come to Jamaica and buy babies fah plenty money.

'When de baby born me name her Angela. Two months later, Carol

226

come tell me dat the white man who ruin me was back at de same hotel. Somehow Mazie and her moda contact de man, trace him off and tell him how him ruin me life and leave me wid baby. She tell him if him nuh claim de child she gwane obeah him, and mek him nasty hood drop off. Ah guess him did agree for dem send to Jerico and get de baby dat we did register as Angela. Mazie moda seh if me sure me not want her. Me wouldn't look pan her, but me shake me head yes. A week later, me sign some papers. Mazie tek de baby to the hotel and she seh de man and him wife said how beautiful de baby was and dem was teking her back to America wid dem as their daughter. Mazie brought a big envelope of money, and which her moda tek me to de bank and put almost all of it in me name. It still dere to dis day.

'But ah didn't complete dat next year of teacha's college. Afta me gi weh me baby girl just cause dat whiteman did rape me, me couldn't concentrate. Me would hear her calling me. Ah used to still hear her calling me, but she stop. Ah hope it mean she forgive me.

'Afta dat me life just mash-up. Me couldn't sleep wid any man cause dat whiteman defile me so no decent Jamaican man gwane wan marry me afta dem know dat a whiteman mash me up. But de worst is losing me only daughter.'

Beryl ended her story dry-eyed. There was nothing more to say after all these years keeping it a secret. Miss Cotton hugged her, saying, 'Dat's a heavy load you been dragging around all dese years, Daughter Beryl. Come let me walk you to de river so you can dump it.'

Arnella pulled Miss Cotton to her feet and the three walked to the river bank, and there they stayed for a while.

'A oman's lot is hot coals pon open fire,' Arnella said.

'A baby coming fah you,' Miss Cotton said, comforting Beryl.

Angel had heard much more than she could take in; her head was heavy and aching with all the details.

Arnella suggested that they move to her house, where she had a store of certain herbs to put in a bath for Beryl.

The women gathered their belongings and slowly trudged along. Monica and Beryl with clasped fingers led the way.

They boiled the herbs and filled a tub with water as hot as Beryl could stand it and immersed her in there, draping a sheet over her head and the entire tub to keep the heat in. Beryl felt the steam enfolding her body. The herbs were pungent and familiar, yet she couldn't name any of them. After she had steamed for about fifteen minutes, Dahlia and Olive sponged her body, Valrie dried her off, and Miss Cotton anointed her body, telling her she was clean and unblemished again, fit for the best of men.

Beryl stepped into her dress and her body tingled. She wasn't going to look back any more. She pulled Angel to her, saying, 'Come me daughta, leh we go home and cook a pot.'

Deeds done in darkness shine bright in daylight

Marva woke, having dropped off to sleep after Ainsworth left with the other men. She had been having insomnia, but blamed the baby for her condition, including her heightened irritability. She slowly swung her feet from under the sheet and rested them on the floor. The backs of her legs and her feet were cramping. She bent as much as she could manage and tried to massage them, with very little success. Marva felt the full burden of her weight. The last time she went to the clinic she weighed in at one hundred and ninety-seven pounds, having gained sixty-seven pounds since her pregnancy began. That was a month ago. She stood up, glanced at her figure in the mirror and sighed. She was certain she had gained ten more pounds since her visit. She could hardly recognise her face, which looked like a bloated bulla-cake. Her hair had grown redder, and more dull. Her neck and face had blotches. Her fingers were like monkey banana. Her legs had varicose veins. She was disgusted at the person who looked back at her.

'No wonda Ainsworth can't bear look pan me,' she yawned, moving to the kitchen without even rinsing out the staleness in her mouth or washing the matter from her eyes.

In the kitchen Marva found no pepper. She cursed Ainsworth, who she suspected had been throwing out all the peppers, so that she had had to buy some at the market a few days before. She pushed open the kitchen door leading to the back yard, and had to shoo the dog, shouting at him and using her foot to prod him in the side before he sauntered off the steps and allowed her to descend. She searched the closest scott bonnet tree, but found not a single pepper; not even a green one. She walked further into the yard, near the chicken coop, and searched first one tree then another. At last she found three peppers, one half-ripe and the other two green. She picked them and headed for the kitchen. She stopped before mounting the steps and leaned on the fence, hollering, 'Peggy! You awake? Ah calling morning.' She waited, but receiving no response she went into her kitchen, cut herself two slices of bread, spread them thick with butter, washed the peppers, sliced them vertically and lined them up on the open bread. She then crushed the pieces of bread together in a sandwich and chewed, savouring each bite. Afterwards she took a shower and ate two oranges. Finding her sons' rooms empty and their beds unslept in, she cursed under her breath. 'Mek dem gwane tink dem can tun me picknie dem against me. But wait till me have me daughter. Not one a dem gwane come close to her. Mek dem gwane.' And so saying, Marva decided to seek out her friend Peggy, who she knew would console her.

Peggy, coming awake on the sofa where she had fallen asleep, had heard Marva calling her, but was still unable to move. She felt as if her insides were being turned tight with a screwdriver. She had to get help, she kept saying, rolling on the floor and slowly dragging herself to the front door. She was bound to see someone passing. Halfway to the door, darkness took over her eyes.

Marva stood in front of her gate looking up and down the main road, the only real road, of Kristoff Village. Something was strange but she couldn't figure out what it was. She turned to her right, heading towards Peggy's house. By Peggy's gate she stopped again and looked up the hill where Miss Cotton's shop stood. It was closed. Not a window or door was ajar. Marva looked all around, seeing no life. She turned in at Peggy's gate, climbed the step leading to her veranda, and again surveyed as much as she could see of Kristoff Village. It was particularly quiet for a Sunday. No elderly women, dressed in their Sunday best, could be seen walking to church with their grandchildren tagging behind. Not one child from down the lane was returning with buckets of water on their heads for their households. No singing, shouting and clapping could be heard from the

Pocomania church over the other hill. No singing of birds, no flitting of butterflies. No sound. No life. Marva noticed the absence, but couldn't think beyond what wasn't visible.

Turning to find Peggy's front door closed, Marva remarked loudly to herself, 'But what a way tings quiet today.' She knocked and waited. Nothing. She knocked again and called. 'Peggy oh! Peggy! Peggy, is me Marva.' Not receiving any reply, Marva thought it odd that no one should be home, for she had sat with Peggy only yesterday evening listening to her complaining for the nth time about Trevor's alleged mission to find parts for his vehicles, and threatening again to tell her father and have him cut off. Marva was certain Peggy was home. Besides, Peggy hadn't been feeling well lately, complaining of pain in her abdomen. Marva knocked again, pressed her ear to the door, listening. Just as she was about to turn away she heard a faint moan. She pressed her ear closer and listened. Again she heard the moan. She called out again, her voice loud with alarm, 'Peggy! You in dere? Peggy?' Nothing. She banged on the door, then she turned the knob. The door opened and she stumbled forward, almost tripping over Peggy, who lay slumped on the floor.

Somehow Marva managed to drag Peggy to the sofa. She reached for the phone but found that it was dead. She went on the veranda and hollered. 'Help! Anyone. Help!' She saw no one, and heard no reply to her call. She rushed inside. Peggy's eyes were open, and she clung gratefully to Marva's hand. 'Me nah go die alone,' she thought thankfully, giving Marva a faint smile. After a while the pain subsided, and Peggy breathed normally. She begged Marva to get her some water. She felt much improved after she sipped the water, and was appreciative when Marva offered to make her breakfast. As Marva turned to go into the kitchen, Peggy called after her, 'But no peppa,' and they laughed knowingly.

Peggy made a remarkable recovery after the breakfast Marva cooked and fed her, and she teased Marva that she was an obeah woman to rival Miss Cotton. They laughed at their brazenness, and although they had not spoken of the night when the pepper went to their heads causing them to forget their womanselves, they both privately hoped that the incident was done and forgotten since no one had come accusing them. After Peggy took her bath, she and Marva sat on the veranda drinking fruit juice and gossiping about everyone their tongues could find; everyone came in for attack, except for Grace. At last the conversation turned to Marva's pregnancy.

'So, girl, when you gwane drop dis baby? You look ready to pop.'

'Ah feel like ah gwane bust any minute now, but de doctor seh ah have two more weeks fi go.'

'Ah hope you get you daughter dis time because six picknie is plenty headache.'

'Ah sure is a girl, and a gwane name her after you.'

'Ah wouldn't have it any other way,' Peggy said, clasping her hand in satisfaction. 'Godchild should name after her godmother.'

They laughed, and Peggy rose and stretched. She glanced up and down the road, then, turning to face Marva, she commented, 'Is one of de quietest days ah can remember since living in Kristoff Village. It eerie bad.'

Marva nodded her head, but changed the subject. 'So Peggy, you give up on trying for a daughter?'

Peggy shook her head, sadly. She rubbed at her arms as if she was cold, and when she spoke her voice was even, her tone formal. 'To tell you de truth Marva, ah haven't give up, but me alone can't make baby. Ah feel so unloved, and ah shame to tell you dis, but is close to a year now Trevor don't touch me.' She turned again to look in the direction from which Trevor would appear. Marva didn't know what to say to her friend. She had suspected as much; but since Ainsworth had not touched her since he learned she was pregnant, Marva had been reluctant to raise the subject lest she expose her own quiet bed. As much as she considered Peggy her best friend, she had no intention of divulging such information. So she sat quietly sipping the last of the fruit juice, and thinking it was time for her to go before she too got the urge to talk about her unhappy marriage.

She rose with great effort, remarking that it was time for her to start Sunday dinner. Peggy nodded understandingly. Marva promised to return when she had finished cooking, and in her haste to escape, did not pull the straps of her sandals up on her heels. Her left sandal caught on the edge of the second-from-the-top step of the veranda and she slipped down the remaining seven, landing on her side. Peggy

231

had been so busy listening for Trevor's car, which she thought she heard, that she didn't see Marva fall until she hit the ground.

'Oh my heavens!' Peggy cried out, moving to Marva. But instantly a sharp pain shot through her stomach, causing her to double over. Peggy panted. Marva groaned. Marva felt wetness between her legs and assumed her water-bag had broken, except it was not a trickle like the other times. She touched herself and when she looked at her hand saw it was smeared with blood.

Marva hollered. 'Peggy! Peggy! Help me; ah can't get up; help me, ah bleeding.'

Peggy was slumped on the floor, curled in pain. She tried to move, to call out to Marva for help, but she couldn't talk; the pain racked her body.

The sun slipped behind a cloud. Marva shuffled over to the railing on the side of the steps and tried to raise herself. She called out again, 'Help me. Somebody help me.' Marva heard Peggy grunting on the veranda, and knew she would be of no help. She managed to get to her knees and saw the pool of blood, with flies already swarming around to feast. She tried in vain to fan them away, and cried out for mercy.

'Please spare me daughta. Don't punish her for me. Spare me daughta.'

That evening when Miss Cotton and the other women, exhausted but renewed, returned to Kristoff Village, they were greeted with the news of Marva's fall, and how she was rushed to the hospital by Trevor, who happened to return just in time. Someone added that Peggy had gone to the hospital at the same time, as Trevor had found her on the veranda, doubled over in pain. The group of mostly women and children congregated halfway between Peggy's gate and Marva's, all reluctant to leave.

Arnella enquired, 'How long now since dem leave?'

A few women talked among themselves, trying to measure the time. Finally one offered, 'Not two hours yet.'

Another confirmed this. 'Ah was just done wid dinner and getting ready to call de children; yes, not two hours yet.'

'Well oonuh might as well go home and do what oonuh have to do.

It tek at least twenty minutes driving at top speed to reach hospital in MoBay so we not gwane hear any news just yet,' Miss Cotton said, heading towards her home.

'Ah guess not,' someone agreed reluctantly.

But a brave person voiced what surely everyone else was thinking. 'If you expose you batty, fly with pitch pan it.'

Still another voice joined in condemnation, 'De higher monkey climb, de more him expose himself.'

'Spit in de sky it bound fi catch you.'

One by one the villagers spoke out, distancing themselves from Marva and Peggy, acknowledging that they deserved their lot.

Just as the crowd was dispersing, they heard a vehicle coming around the corner by Miss Cotton's shop at full speed. They shrank out of the road, pressing into the narrow verge. Trevor's mini-bus came to a screeching halt by Ainsworth's gate. He jumped out, his shirt stained with blood. Ignoring the women crowded around him, he banged on Ainsworth's door. Beryl pushed her way through the crowd and grabbed Trevor's shoulder. 'Ainsworth not home. Tell us what happen.' Her voice was firm.

Trevor looked about him, undecided. 'Lawd God,' he finally managed, stumbling to a chair on the veranda.

Beryl stood before him and demanded to know. 'Trevor, wha happen to Marva and de baby?'

Trevor threw up his hand. 'She dead; she dead not five minutes afta we reach de hospital; de doctor seh she lose too much blood.'

A common sigh went through the crowd. A few women spat; others fanned at mosquitoes. Beryl was not done with Trevor. Her voice trembled when she spoke. 'What bout de baby, Trevor? What bout Marva's baby?'

'Is a girl. Doctor say she all right.'

'Praise be!' Beryl shouted, and as she moved away from the crowd she was heard uttering, 'Praise be! Ah get another daughta.' Beryl hugged Angel and together they skipped, Beryl's tears flowing sweetly.

Peggy was admitted for observation and tests.

Broken wings can't fly

It was close to eight o'clock when Ainsworth returned with Mr Cotton, Milford, Godfree, Desmond and Rupert. They were full, and loud with singing, having relived a day of their youth. The crowd had long dispersed. Ainsworth's parents had been informed about Marva and had fed their grandsons and put them to bed. Ainsworth's father sat on the veranda with the lights off, watching for his son to return to tell him the news. Beryl sat with him, but they didn't talk, each occupied with their own thoughts.

Beryl heard the men first and sprang up, leaning on the banister, listening to their singing. Ainsworth's father stumbled down the steps. Beryl held his elbow. They walked to the gate and stood with it ajar between them. The men came to a quiet halt upon seeing Beryl with the senior Ainsworth. Ainsworth came forward. He thought of his mother and his sons.

'Mamma all right? De boys?'

His father nodded his head, abating his fears.

'What going on?'

'Marva dead,' his father said flatly.

Beryl hastened to add, 'But you daughter fine. Trevor sitting by Miss Cotton waiting to tek us.'

Ainsworth looked from his father to Beryl. Confirmation was printed on both their faces. Mr Cotton came forward and threw his arms around Ainsworth.

'Come let we walk wid you.'

Beryl stepped forward. 'Ains,' she said, his childhood nickname coming to her mouth. 'Ah coming to de hospital wid you. Ah gwane tek care of you daughter fah you.'

Ainsworth nodded, dazed and stupefied. He allowed himself to be led by Mr Cotton and Beryl.

They didn't return that night. The two telephone lines in the village were down, so no news was relayed until the next morning when the village market women went into town. By the time they returned the next afternoon the news was old, although a few details were added.

Trevor hastily reported that Peggy had been sent to the University

234

of the West Indies Hospital at Mona in Kingston for more testing, as the doctors suspected cancer in her uterus. She wasn't doing well. He bathed, packed some clothes for his sons and himself, then left, saying he wasn't sure when he would return. He seemed preoccupied, but not overly worried, someone remarked. A man who was one of the conductors on Trevor's bus, and who had been sitting around all morning on Miss Cotton's shop steps, reading the paper, said as Trevor sped out of Kristoff Village, 'Ah guess Bossman Trevor gwane look fah him baby-mother and him new daughter. Is a real young ting him have.' The man flipped a page of the paper. All eyes turned to him; several eyebrows shot up.

Ainsworth had not returned, having gone directly to Marva's parents' village to inform them in person, and to make arrangements for Marva's funeral there. A market woman returning to the village scratched her throat, uttering in a sad tone, 'Poor Ainsworth age overnight. Me heart go out to him, although me neva did like him wife one bit.'

Beryl carried the baby in her arms, showing her off to all around. Her face was aglow, and just as it could be said that Ainsworth had aged overnight, it could be said that Beryl had shed skin and was young again.

'All things made right indeed; all things made right,' Miss Cotton whispered, taking the baby from Beryl. She kissed the baby on both cheeks before passing her to Arnella to suckle. As she opened her freezer to hand out free soft drinks to all present, Miss Cotton danced around and sang, 'Ah have anoda goddaughter to love all over again, ah have another goddaughter to love.'

Beryl looked tenderly at the baby that was now her daughter; her daughter, all six pounds, eight ounces of her, the colour of coffee with just a smidgen of milk, and with a full head of hair. Beryl was certain no voice would any longer call out to her at nights; not when she snuggled up with her daughter, whom she decided to name Joy.

'Thanks Marva,' Beryl whispered, caressing the baby's hand. 'Walk good now, and don't come lookin fah nutten.'

Epilogue:
There's nothing like a good dance

The last crumb had been nibbled, the last drink had been drunk and the last guest had departed. She-Devil kicked off her shoes and let out a satisfied sigh of relief. The smile on her face spread. Devil found one last song and set it revolving on the record player. All the lights were turned off, except a lamp with a green bulb. Devil bowed to She-Devil, kissed the hand that she extended to him and pulled her to her feet and held her closely. The music energised them, and they were pressed so close that not even air could get between them. They rocked, feet glued to the floor, drinking in the fragrance of each other. She-Devil smiled and kissed Devil's neck. She couldn't imagine loving anyone else. Devil had put on their song, the first song they had danced to at their wedding night too many years ago; neither of them remembered the exact year. As the horn, piano and cymbal blended with the duet voices singing, 'You're the only one/You're my true divine', Devil's and She-Devil's arms sought each other, and Devil nestled She-Devil's head close to his chest and kissed her forehead and hair.

The music ended, but their rhythm played on, taking them out on to the veranda. The moon was full and the sky clear, filled with a million stars. Devil and She-Devil held on to the banister, their heads tilted, dreaming on the stars.

She-Devil turned to Devil. 'De only other day I can remember as perfect as dis one, is de day ah made you my husband.'

Devil kissed She-Devil and tasted her honeyed breath.

'Devil, it such a perfect night; let we sleep in you hammock.'

'Good idea,' Devil agreed, disengaging himself. 'But hold on; ah soon come.' So saying he disappeared into the house. She-Devil began reliving all the details of the wedding, but Devil's quick return didn't afford her the time, beyond remembering the absolute beauty that was Tallawah when she stepped out in her royal-blue and lavender gown, her son Anansi at her side, and her other two children behind.

'Come,' Devil said, placing his arms around She-Devil, interrupting her reverie. Barefoot, they walked to the hammock and clambered in. Once secure, Devil poured them tall glasses of rum-punch. They lay back in each other's arms, simply enjoying each other's company, the cool night air, and the joyous sounds of the crickets and other night creatures. The wedding had been a stupendous occasion, without flaws. She-Devil's waterfall wedding cake produced cries of 'ah', as did Devil's artistic arrangements of bougainvillaeas, orchids and anthuriums that circled the stage upon which the wedding vows were exchanged. Tegreg was radiant, eyes onyx, skin smooth crushed nutmeg, an image of the power of motherhood, in her red, silver and gold-thread caftan, belly already pointed – indicating a boy, Devil was certain.

'Didn't Teg-Teg look absolutely lovely?' he asked his wife now.

'Oh, she wears pregnancy like a crown. Her skin is all aglow. And ah neva see Man-Stick more attentive.'

'Nothing like fada-hood to mek a man straighten him back.'

'You telling me,' She-Devil smiled, remembering how her first pregnancy matured Devil almost overnight. Reading one another's minds they both burst out laughing.

'You was a real nervous first-time fada.'

'And you a really awkward first-time moda.'

They kissed, calling an end to that memory.

'Anansi is a really ginnalish little fellow,' Devil beamed.

'But sweet. What him said as him stepped aside for Brimstone to stand by his moda brought tear to me eyes,' She-Devil added.

'Yes,' Devil agreed, nodding his head. 'Dat Anansi is really-really smart. Him gwane mek much dat is wrong right. Mark me word.'

Anansi, his sister and brother had presented Tallawah to the guests, as well as to their step-father. Without coaching or rehearsing, when Anansi stepped aside for Brimstone to stand by his mother, he had looked Brimstone in the eyes and said, 'Mamma is not a ting to be given away. We not giving her to you, but we willing to mek space for you to join our family if you love all a we and continue to mek Mamma laugh.'

Then Anansi's sister had chimed, 'And you promise to continue to give me piggy-back rides and tell us story at dinner time.'

And the other child had added, 'And you build us de tree-house like you promise and tek we bird shooting.'

'If you promise all a dat in front of all dese people,' Anansi had concluded, taking charge again, 'den you can marry we mamma.'

Brimstone crossed his heart and swore to live and then the three children swarmed him, while the guests applauded. When everyone had quieted, Tallawah beamed. 'Well ah guess everything is settled, and ah didn't need to be here.' At which point Brimstone extricated himself from his clan, embraced his bride, and the ceremony proceeded: a play within a play, with musicians, poets, singers, acrobats and mime acts all professing love. No pastor was present to authorise what Tallawah and Brimstone themselves had sanctioned.

'Tallawah is something else,' She-Devil said with meaning. 'She feisty, bright and she passionate. Ah don't think dere ever was a more gorgeous bride. Tegreg not included.' And She-Devil relaxed in the cradle of Devil's arm.

'Tallawah is fine, but me have seen a bride far more beautiful dan she.'

'Oh. Who?' She-Devil asked.

Devil raised himself on one elbow, looked down on She-Devil's face, and in the most matter-of-fact-tone he could muster offered, 'Dere neva has been nor will dere ever be a more exquisite bride or woman dan you, She-Devil, de eros of me life.'

She-Devil's eyes sparkled and she pulled Devil's mouth to join hers.

The stars twinkled. The moon glowed. And all the night creatures were quiet.

THE CARIBBEAN WRITERS SERIES

The book you have been reading is part of Heinemann's long-established Caribbean Writers Series. Details of some of the other new titles available in this series are listed below, but for a catalogue giving information on all the titles and the African Writers Series write to:

Heinemann Educational Publishers,
Halley Court, Jordan Hill, Oxford, OX2 8EJ
OR
Heinemann, 361 Hanover Street,
Portsmouth, NH 03801–3912, USA.

ZEE EDGELL
The Festival of San Joaquín

Luz Marina, cleared of murdering her brutal husband, is released from prison on a three-year probation. Determined to rebuild her life and gain custody of her children, she walks on proudly, sustained by mother love and her faith in God as she fights against the poverty, guilt, vanity and vengeance which threaten to overwhelm her.

MICHAEL ANTHONY
All That Glitters

Based around the mystery of who has stolen a precious gold chain, *All That Glitters* upturns the traditional detective story as the young boy of the novel makes a totally different discovery – that the adults around him are not at all what they seem.

FRANK COLLYMORE
The Man Who Loved Attending Funerals and Other Stories
Introduction by Harold Barratt

An engaging collection of shorter fiction by this multi-talented Barbadian. The title story depicts a man who revels in ritual at the burials of acquaintances, and becomes convinced of his own immortality.

CHRISTINE CRAIG
Mint Tea and Other Stories

A powerful series of Jamaican short stories reflecting upon aspects of women's lives and the choices they make. Enhanced by Craig's natural and evocative use of Creole.

KEVIN BALDEOSINGH
The Autobiography of Paras P.

Paras P.'s whole life has been geared to being 'proper', from early days learning the Queen's English to life as the most upright of politicians. Pity that Paras has never noticed the laughter and ridicule that permeate all the tapes he has kept of his experiences.

Virgin's Triangle

Giselle Karan is twenty-six, attractive, has a blossoming career – and is still a virgin. When she meets Vishnu and Robert, men at opposite ends of the social spectrum, she begins to wonder if this condition is only temporary. But, as the Trinidad Carnival approaches, Giselle becomes increasingly confused by the choice between the journalist and the construction worker. Only the sharp wit of the calypso offers a way out of this virgin's triangle. Juxtaposing references to Freud and eye-liner, Icarus and super-glue, *Virgin's Triangle* gives a humorous commentary on contemporary relationships and Caribbean journalism.

CLEM MAHARAJ
The Dispossessed

The history of Highlands, a Trinidadian sugar estate, is bound up with the lives of the poor people who live and labour on it. Clem Maharaj brings a delicate clarity to his heartfelt description of these workers.

PAMELA MORDECAI AND BETTY WILSON
Her True-True Name: An Anthology of Caribbean Women's Writing

Like the scattered islands themselves, these fragments from 31 women writers display the range and variety of Caribbean cultures and traditions. From memories of turn-of-the-century Dominica to contemporary USA, Africa and Britain, writers from Haiti to Cuba and Jamaica express the longing, pride and passion of the Caribbean identity.

PATRICIA POWELL
A Small Gathering of Bones

Powell explores the complexities of homosexual love in her powerful story of Dale and Nevin and their relationship within the gay community of late-1970s Jamaica.

LAWRENCE SCOTT
Witchbroom

Lavren Monagas de los Macajuelos pours forth epic and intimate tales of conquest, crime and passion in Trinidad and Tobago. As this extraordinary hermaphrodite character both observes and acts in the unfolding drama, we are drawn into his/her account of the quest for El Dorado. Told in the traditional Caribbean style of irony – *mamaguy*.

VANESSA SPENCE
The Roads Are Down

A Commonwealth Writers' Prize Winner
The beauty of the Blue Mountains and the lives of the rural poor in Jamaica provide the backdrop for the story of Katherine's evocative and bittersweet romance.